PEABODY

JOURNAL

OF EDUCATION

James W. Pellegrino, Editor
Susan A. McDowell, Managing Editor

T0346554

SUBSCRIBER INFORMATION

First published by Lawrence Erlbaum Associates, Inc., Publishers
10 Industrial Avenue
Mahwah, New Jersey 07430

Reprinted 2009 by Routledge

Routledge

270 Madison Avenue
New York, NY 10016

2 Park Square, Milton Park
Abingdon, Oxon OX14 4RN, UK

Senior Production Editor: Victoria Reed, Lawrence Erlbaum Associates, Inc.

PEABODY
JOURNAL
OF EDUCATION

Volume 75, Number 4, 2000

Educational Accountability Effects:
An International Perspective

(Continued)

PEABODY JOURNAL OF EDUCATION, 75(4), 1–18

Educational Accountability Effects: An International Perspective

Kenneth Leithwood and Lorna Earl

A significant majority of educational reform initiatives over the past dozen years have aimed to hold schools more accountable. But this desire actually began to surface in most developed countries in the 1960s, acquiring significant new energy during the mid to late 1980s. The reasons for these calls for greater accountability can be traced to the wider economic, political, and social contexts of which schools are a part. Although these contexts have not been uniform across all countries, a core of developed countries (including, e.g., Australia, New Zealand, the United Kingdom, and Canada) have been similarly influenced by "New Right" ideologies (Peters, 1992).

From these ideological perspectives, greater accountability is assumed to have two consequences: (a) better alignment between public aspirations and the purposes schools strive to achieve and (b) improved performance on the part of schools, typically defined by traditional achievement criteria. But how do these two assumptions play themselves out in practice?

KENNETH LEITHWOOD *is Professor and Director of the Centre for Leadership Development at the Ontario Institute for Studies in Education, University of Toronto, Ontario, Canada.*

LORNA EARL *is Associate Professor and Codirector of the International Centre for the Study of Educational Change at the Ontario Institute for Studies in Education, University of Toronto, Ontario, Canada.*

Requests for reprints should be sent to Kenneth Leithwood, Centre for Leadership Development, OISE/University of Toronto, 252 Bloor Street West, Toronto, Ontario M5S 1V6, Canada. E- mail: kleithwood@oise.utoronto.ca

That is the question the articles in this special issue of the *Peabody Journal of Education* address.

In this introductory article, we outline the framework that was used to both select and order the remaining articles in the issue. This framework clarifies our conception of accountability and identifies the assumptions and tools associated with four different approaches to accountability. Subsequent articles focus on one or more tools or mechanisms associated with each of the four approaches, offering insights and explanations about their consequences in practice.

The Meaning of "Accountability"

Rothman (1995) defined *educational accountability* as "the process[es] by which school districts and states attempt to ensure that schools and school systems meet their goals" (p. 189). As a point of departure for us, the focus of this definition on both "processes" and "goals" is central. A focus on processes raises questions about stimulants to such processes and the accountability tools or mechanisms about which the articles in the issue are primarily concerned. A focus on goals indicates that the intention of accountability processes is to influence schools and districts toward the accomplishment of their goals, and that their success in doing that is the most important criterion on which to judge their value.

With Rothman's definition as a starting point, the concept of accountability used in this article is further developed using insights from Wagner's (1987) *Accountability in Education: A Philosophical Inquiry.* Liberally adapted for our purposes, this conception is framed as a response to five questions: What level of accountability is to be provided? Who is expected to provide the account? To whom is the account owed? What is to be accounted for? And what are the consequences of providing an account?

The last four of these questions are substantially the same as the four "attributes" that Adams and Kirst (1999) used to distinguish among different types of accountability in their classification scheme.

What Level of Accountability Is to Be Provided?

Webster's 7th New Collegiate Dictionary (1971), for example, claims that the quality of being accountable means being subject to giving an account, being answerable, and capable of being accounted for (p. 6). The term *account* entails giving a report on; furnishing a justifying analysis or explanation; providing a statement of explanation of one's conduct; offering a statement or exposition of reasons, causes, grounds, or motives; or simply providing a statement of facts or events.

These meanings of "providing an account" point to a fundamental conception of level of accountability, from the relatively simple description of events to justification. A school that distributes a calendar outlining its program options for students—along with other events, policies, and the like that it considers noteworthy for students and parents—is "providing an account" in the descriptive meaning of the term.

Also referred to as part of the meaning of "account," however, is the more difficult offering an explanation for events. The typical school calendar would not suffice as an account, given this meaning of the term, unless added to the calendar was further information about the sources of programs, the reasons for other events, and the like. Even this more elaborate calendar, however, would still fall short of "providing an account" when the term is defined to include justification for events. This meaning of "providing an account" would require the calendar to contain not only descriptions and explanations. It also would require arguments of some sort for why these programs and events were the most appropriate ones for the school to be offering its students.

Based on this understanding of the different levels of accountability, different approaches to accountability can be distinguished in part by asking whether the level of accountability they require is description, explanation, or justification.

Who Is Expected to Provide an Account?

This is a question about the "agent" in Adams and Kirst's (1999) formulation. "Responsibility" is one of two minimum conditions for validating the assignment of any accountability obligation and whatever interpersonal relationships it may entail, according to Wagner's (1987) moral–ethical analysis. The assignment of any responsibility or obligation to provide an account is usually contingent on identifying the person or parties responsible for the act creating it. This depends on the act itself and the institution within which the act is carried out. So, one becomes obliged or responsible to provide an account as a result of either an act that one undertakes or the role that one occupies within an organization.

A person, group, or agency can be causally responsible for an act that is self-evident and ultimately personally obliging. This may be an act actually committed by the person or group, as in the obligation a teacher assumes for the welfare of her students on a field trip. Obligations also arise when the person or group exercises influence on others to perform an act.

3

This type of obligation is acquired by a state department of education, for example, in relation to the quality of instruction in teachers' classrooms and its effects on students when state policies encourage the teacher to implement innovative instructional practices, as in the case of California's adoption of "constructivist" approaches to teaching mathematics, for example (Cohen, McLaughlin, & Talbert, 1993).

Persons or groups may be responsible, as well, for the omission of acts—acts in which the person or group's engagement is considered inappropriate. The teacher taking students on a field trip to the zoo is expected not to detour through the local shopping plaza en route to the zoo. Such persons or groups also may be causally responsible for an act that is initially but not ultimately obligating because of mitigating circumstances. Although the teacher is initially responsible for the safety of his students on a field trip, various natural disasters (e.g., lightening or other "acts of God," as the insurance industry calls them) would be considered beyond the teacher's control, thus absolving the teacher from responsibility providing that he took appropriate precautions on behalf of his students.

And joint responsibility may be acquired for an act incurring a shared obligation among those responsible. The statutes and laws governing elementary and secondary education in most developed countries, for example, hold teachers and principals jointly responsible for students' educational experiences. Individual or joint responsibility may be acquired for an act obligating others, as well. In some jurisdictions (e.g., the Canadian province of Ontario), principals and superintendents are jointly responsible for the quality of instruction that teachers provide their students.

One acquires obligations not only through the acts one carries out oneself (creating causal obligations), but also through the roles or positions one holds in life: For example, educators historically have been expected to behave in both their personal and professional lives in ways that are consistent with the norms of morality held by the communities in which they work. Such roles create noncausal or "expectational" obligations of either a specific (e.g., what we do as teachers) or general (what we are expected to do as good neighbors or citizens) nature. Expectational obligations are in reference to potential acts or performances that are possible to fulfill, consistent with the role from which they are said to derive, and reasonable to expect in light of other considerations that are equally relevant. Most people have acquired both causal and expectational types of obligations, and these types become very difficult to distinguish in real-life circumstances.

It is highly questionable, according to Wagner (1987), whether a person should be held accountable for acts that, causally, he has neither omitted, committed, nor influenced. It is equally questionable whether a person should be held accountable for expected performances (a) that are impossible to satisfy (e.g., ensuring that all students learn to high standards), (b) that are inconsistent with the role from which they are said to derive (e.g., teachers being held responsible for students' use of illegal substances), or (c) whose assignment and satisfaction may be quite unjustified by other factors (e.g., principals being held responsible for improving the average reading scores of students in schools with highly transient student populations). In each of these three examples, it would be legitimate to hold the teacher or principal accountable for making the most productive uses of the resources available to them in an effort to move toward the goal. But this is very different from holding them accountable for actually achieving the goal.

Also, it is questionable whether a person or an organization should be held solely accountable for matters involving a shared, causal responsibility. The success of students in school, for example, is a function of many factors. Although the quality of teachers' instruction is important, it is significantly influenced by such factors over which the community or the government—not the teacher or the school—has control, such as the physical condition of the school building, the size of classes, the time available for teachers to prepare for classes, and the like. In an article making the case for a concept of "community accountability," Henry (1996) described a relevant example of an attempt to hold schools accountable for actions that clearly entail a shared responsibility at minimum: "In Virginia legislation was proposed to combat hunting-related accidents by requiring all students to participate in the 'hunter education curriculum.' This legislation came as a camouflaged alternative to mandating that hunters wear highly visible, orange attire" (p. 87). As he claimed more generally, "Society deposits its drugs, violence, intolerance, and other problems at the school's doorstep" (p. 87), and holding schools solely or largely accountable for solving such problems violates any reasonable assignment of legitimate responsibility.

Nor is it legitimate to hold a person solely accountable for expected performances requiring a shared influence, unless it is specifically understood that the person is answerable for the actions of others, as would seem to be true of parents' responsibility for the actions of their children or executives' responsibility for the work of subordinates. When we know, for example, that family educational culture accounts for at least 50% of the variation in student achievement (e.g., Leithwood & Jantzi, 1999), how is it possible to claim that schools alone should be held accountable for such achievement?

Based on this argument about who legitimately can be held accountable, approaches to accountability can be distinguished, in part, by the nature of the obligation a person or group is assumed to have and the extent to which that obligation is legitimate.

To Whom Is an Account Owed?

This question concerns the "principal" attribute in Adams and Kirst's (1999) formulation. "Entitlement" of the person or group requesting an account is the second minimum condition for justifying such a request. Entitlement is a function of whether a legitimate interest can be shown by those expecting an account. Such an interest must be demonstrated to validate an obligation to satisfy an accountability demand.

There are different degrees of entitlement to an account, and one's entitlement increases with the degree of valid interest one has in the act for which the account is requested. This is sometimes quite difficult to determine. For example, when a teacher is required to provide an account of his or her classroom instruction through participation in a performance appraisal process, it seems clear that the appraisee and the appraiser are entitled to the account. But who else might have a legitimate entitlement to the account? Typically, very few others have access to the results of the appraisal (perhaps a senior school system official through the personnel files kept in the school system's office). But what is the entitlement of the parents of the teacher's students and the students themselves? It does not seem difficult to justify the pre-eminence of their entitlement, although many reasons unrelated to entitlement have been developed to keep formal accounts of teacher performance out of reach of those whose entitlements may be greatest.

Instead, the closest parents and students typically get to a formal account of teacher performance is a report of student achievement, and such reports usually are considered to be more relevant to student than teacher accountability. Indeed, this is clearly a flawed basis for teacher accountability because teachers, parents, students, peers, and a variety of physical and social conditions combine in their contribution to student achievement. Responsibility for student achievement is jointly shared, whereas responsibility for teacher performance is much more unambiguously teachers' responsibility.

This discussion suggests that approaches to accountability also can be distinguished by answers to such questions as: To whom is the account to be given? Do those requesting an account have a legitimate interest or stake in the act being accounted for? Does that stake or interest compete with the interests of others? If so, whose interests ought to take precedence?

What Is to Be Accounted For?

Also among the attributes Adams and Kirst (1999) used to distinguish among approaches to accountability is what is to be accounted in an educational system. It is, most fundamentally, the welfare of individual students. And within the range of possible meanings of "welfare," most agree on the preeminence of academic achievement (Mohrman, Mohrman, & Odden, 1996). Such achievement is a necessary if not sufficient part of the meaning of student welfare in the context of schooling.

In current policy and practice, educators are often held accountable, as well, for features of the organization and the practices of those within it believed to contribute more or less directly to students' welfare. One prominent example is characteristics of the school organization identified by research as accounting for variation in its effectiveness, such as collaborative professional cultures, high expectations for student achievement, and clear goals (Creemers & Reetzig, 1996). These organizational characteristics figure among the criteria government inspectors use in evaluating schools in Scotland and the United Kingdom (Wilson, 1996). Another example of what is to be accounted for, other than student welfare directly, are standards of professional teaching practice. In the U.S. context, such standards for advanced teaching have been developed by several agencies, among them the National Board for Professional Teaching Standards (1998). Parallel standards for beginning teaching have been developed by the Interstate New Teacher Assessment and Support Consortium (INTASC; 1992). The Center for Research on Educational Accountability and Teacher Evaluation has developed a taxonomy of teaching "duties" (Scriven, 1994), something else for which educators may be held accountable.

As these illustrations begin to suggest, then, in addition to being held accountable for student welfare directly, educators in some contexts are held accountable for:

- Ensuring that specific organizational qualities considered to be critical to effectiveness are reflected in their schools or districts.
- Organizational efficiency.
- Meeting standards of professional knowledge and skill.
- Meeting standards of moral behavior.
- Performance of best professional practices or specified duties.
- Skillfully using organizational processes believed to contribute to the successful introduction of change (e.g., strategic planning, school improvement planning, and the carrying out of quality reviews).

Different approaches to accountability may be distinguished by these or other objects for which accountability is expected.

What Are the Consequences of Providing an Account?

Providing an account may trigger three responses on the part of the receiving person or group. The first and least consequential of these responses occurs when accounting is voluntary, as in the Canadian province of Ontario, for example, where a school district can voluntarily participate in the province's pilot indicator program. In a case such as this, the voluntary nature of the account reduces the likelihood of any response at all that could have connotations of accountability.

A second type of consequence is most likely to occur when an account is obligatory but no consequences have been formally specified. In such cases, it seems likely that some response will occur, but this response often will be muted and almost by definition unpredictable. The requirement in the Canadian province of Alberta that school districts annually publish district profiles is an example of an obligatory account unlikely to provoke a predictable response, because the form of the response is unspecified. In this case the obligation is a legal one—an obligation spelled out in policy.

But an account also may be considered obligatory on moral grounds. That is, the person or group providing the account may feel that the actions for which they are responsible carry with them an obligation to account by virtue of the special nature of the responsibility. It might well be the case, for example, that a teacher's newsletter to parents is stimulated by a sense of moral obligation, which results in the teacher voluntarily reporting to parents about the upcoming experiences of the students that these parents have entrusted to his or her care.

Finally, there are increasingly common circumstances where an account is required, and rewards and punishments for the person(s) providing the account are specified. Circumstances such as this prevail in many U.S. states that require the collection of school-level student performance data. In these states, schools have achievement targets that must be met (Rothman, 1995). When these targets are missed, the school may be placed under review, principals and teachers may be required to implement specific improvement measures, or they may be reassigned to other schools.

Wagner (1987) argued that in cases where there is no requirement or obligation that an account be given, there is no accountability. But even when only very simple types of reports are expected (descriptions), if there is a requirement or obligation, then this becomes accountability. So some form of obligation or requirement is an essential part of accountability from his perspective. This position rules out, as a form of accountability, the teacher's nonobligatory monthly newsletter but includes the provincially required district profile, even though both are only descriptive in form.

In distinguishing among different approaches to accountability, it will be useful to ask: Is the person providing the account obligated to do so? What is the nature of that obligation? What are the consequences of providing the account? Adams and Kirst (1999) characterized what we have referred to in this section as consequences as "incentives to compel agents' actions" (p. 477).

Alternative Approaches to Accountability

In this section of the article we examine four different approaches to accountability—market competition, decentralization, professionalization, and management approaches. Each approach responds somewhat differently to the questions that define our meaning of accountability. In addition, each approach makes different assumptions about the amount of change required in schools, the nature of the change, and how best to enact it.

This classification system focuses initial attention on the mechanisms for accountability; this is in contrast to Adams and Kirst (1999), who focused initial attention on sources of authority and control (e.g., legal, bureaucratic, moral). Furthermore, Wagner's (1987) influence on our conception of accountability has led us to give preeminence in our scheme to moral sources of authority and control, believing them to be the most basic and, we speculate, most likely to explain variation in both internal accountability practices and local responses to external accountability initiatives. Both systems, however, address a largely overlapping set of issues. This focus on moral sources of authority is most evident in the earlier discussion of who is expected to provide an account and to whom the account is owed.

Market Competition Approaches

This approach to accountability, increasing the competition for students faced by schools, is especially prominent right now. For example, versions of it are evident in several European countries, Canada, the United States, New Zealand, Australia, and parts of Asia. Specific tools for increasing competition among schools for student-clients include allowing school choice by opening boundaries within and across school systems; school privatization plans; and the creation of charter schools, magnet schools, academies, and other specialized educational facilities. Competition is also increased by altering the basis for school funding so that money follows students (e.g., vouchers, tuition tax credits) and by publicly ranking schools based on aggregated student achievement scores. These tools are often used in combination.

The common thread binding together these different tools for increasing competition "is a deep disillusionment with the unresponsive and bureaucratic public school monopoly" (Lee, 1993, p. 133). Monopolistic, bureaucratic school systems are believed, by advocates of this approach, to have little need to be responsive to pressure from their clients because they are not likely to lose them. Without natural market forces pressing for and shaping product–client exchanges, the organization tends to develop "product and production orientations" (Hanson, 1992, p. 28). In relation to schools, this means that they will come to view their major task as offering programs that they believe are good for their clients: Such organizations seek efficiency on their own terms and are prone to view clients as objects to be treated rather than customers to be served.

The goal of this approach to accountability, then, is to transform schools from "domestic" to "wild" organizations, to use Carlson's (1965) terms; from organizations that do not have to "forage for their fodder," receiving almost all of their funding through average daily attendance of students, to organizations that must struggle and compete for resources to survive. A wild organization—one with a customer orientation—aims to service the needs and wants of target markets through communication, product design, proper pricing, and the timely delivery of services (Kotler & Andreasen, 1987).

In reference to school choice, in particular, advocates of this approach to educational accountability (e.g., Chubb & Moe, 1990) hold a series of assumptions about how such competition is likely to result in greater student achievement. First, increased competition allows parents and students to select schools with which they are more satisfied and which better meet their educational needs. Second, parents who are more satisfied with their child's school provide greater support to that school and to their child's learning. Third, students are likely to be more engaged when their own learning styles are matched to a particular school. Fourth, when teachers have chosen their work settings and have been active in designing their own schools' programs, they will be more committed to implementing those programs effectively. Finally, all of these outcomes will combine to increase student achievement, attendance, and educational attainment (Raywid, 1992).

How does this approach to accountability address the five issues framing the conception of accountability in this article? In terms of the level of accountability to be provided, market approaches clearly require accounts to offer not only description and explanation, but justification as well. For the most part, it is the direct deliverer of service who is held to account, and the immediate receiver of the service to whom the account is most directly owed, although others such as governments or local districts may also demand an account. "Customer satisfaction" is what is owed. Although the information required for such satisfaction may take forms similar to the information required by other approaches to accountability, the central point is that the customer determines what that information should be. And, finally, the consequences of failing to provide an account considered satisfactory by the customer may be fatal to the survival of the school organization under some manifestations of this approach to accountability.

The consequences of market approaches to accountability in this issue are explored in O'Reilly and Bosetti's (2000/this issue) analysis of charter schools in the Canadian province of Alberta.

Decentralization of Decision-Making Approaches

Underlying most of the tools for increasing schools' competition for students is the assumption that clients' power to shape the educational services they receive depends on their ability to chose those services that they prefer. This is one of two options that Hirschman (1970) argued is available for improving the services of monopolies, an option he referred to as "exit." His other option was "voice"—remaining with the school to which your children are assigned, even though you may be dissatisfied with it, and working toward its improvement.

When decentralization or devolution of decision making is used for purposes of increasing accountability, one of its central aims often is to increase the voice of those who are not heard (or at least not sufficiently listened to) in the context of typical school governance structures. When this is the goal, a community-control form of site-based management (e.g., Bryk, Easton, Kerbow, Rollow, & Sebring, 1993; Malen, Ogawa, & Kranz, 1990; Wohlstetter & Mohrman, 1993) typically is the instrument used for its achievement. The basic assumption giving rise to this form of site-based management is that the curriculum of the school ought to directly reflect the values and preferences of parents and the local community (Ornstein, 1983; Wohlstetter & Odden, 1992). School professionals, it is claimed, typically are not as responsive to such local values and preferences as they ought to be. Their responsiveness is greatly increased, however, when the power to make decisions about curriculum, budget, and personnel is in the hands of the parent/community constituents of the school. School councils in which parent/community constituents have a majority of the membership are the primary vehicle through which to exercise such power.

In the context of community-control site-based management, the responsibility for providing an account is shared between school professionals and representatives of the parent and the wider community constituency. It also is the parent and wider community constituency to whom the account primarily is owed. What is to be accounted for is the range of decisions allocated to the school council (budget decisions, personnel decisions, etc.). The level of accountability is likely to be justification, and the consequences are potentially varied: Dissatisfaction with the account could lead to the replacement of the elected parent-members of council. In contexts where councils have extensive decision-making powers, newly elected members might replace the school administration and substantially alter decisions made by previous council members.

Devolution of decision making, however, is sometimes rooted in a broader reform strategy for public institutions, generally, which Peters (1992) referred to as "new managerialism." According to Peters, new managerialism "emphasizes decentralization, deregulation and delegation" (p. 269). Although there are variants on this approach to accountability among countries, Hood suggests that they share in common a shift in emphasis from (a) policy formulation to management and institutional design, (b) process to output controls, (c) organizational integration to differentiation, and (d) statism to subsidiarity (as cited in Peters, 1992).

In countries such as New Zealand and Australia, where school reform has been substantially influenced by the philosophy of new managerialism, creating more efficient and cost effective school administrative structures is a second central goal for devolution. Typically, this goal is pursued through the implementation of an administrative-control form of site-based management that increases school-site administrators' accountability to the central district or board office for the efficient expenditure of resources. These efficiencies are to be realized by giving local school administrators authority over such key decision areas as budget, physical plant, personnel, and curriculum. Advocates of this form of site-based management reason that such authority, in combination with the incentive to make the best use of resources, ought to get more of the resources of the school into the direct service of students. To assist in accomplishing that objective, the principal may consult informally with teachers, parents, students, or community representatives. Site councils are typically established to advise the principal, with membership at the discretion of the principal.

The school administrator is clearly the accountable party with administrative-control approaches to site-based management, the account being owed to the central administration of the school board or district. Achieving or surpassing agreed-on goals within allocated budgets, along with community satisfaction, are what is to be accounted for, typically. This can often be done with descriptive levels of accounting.

In this special issue, the consequences of decentralization approaches to accountability are addressed in reports of (a) Canadian research dealing with school councils (Parker & Leithwood, 2000/this issue) and (b) New

Zealand research focusing on teachers reporting to parents (Robinson & Timperly, 2000/this issue).

Professional Approaches

There are two radically different accountability strategies that have a professional orientation. One of these approaches manifests itself most obviously in the implementation of professional-control models of site-based management. The other approach encompasses the standards movement as it applies to the practices of teachers and administrators. What both strategies hold in common is a belief in the central contribution of professional practice in schools to their outcomes. The strategies differ most obviously on which practices they chose for their direct focus: In the case of professional-control site-based management, the focus is on school-level decision making, whereas individual professional practices (e.g., teachers' classroom instructional and curricular practices) are the focus of the standards movement.

Professional-control site-based management increases the power of teachers in school decision making while also holding teachers more directly accountable for the school's effects on students. The goal of this form of site-based management is to make better use of teachers' knowledge in such key decision areas as budget, curriculum, and, occasionally, personnel. Basic to this form of site-based management is the assumption that professionals closest to the student have the most relevant knowledge for making such decisions (Hess, 1991) and that full participation in the decision-making process will increase their commitment to implementing whatever decisions are made. Participatory democracy, allowing employees greater decision-making power, is also presumed to lead to greater efficiency, effectiveness, and better outcomes (Clune & Witte, 1988; David, 1989; Mojkowski & Fleming, 1988). Site councils associated with this form of site-based management typically have decision-making power, and, although many groups (e.g., parents, students, administration) are often represented, teachers have the largest proportion of members.

This approach to accountability holds teachers, as a group, accountable to parents, students, and the district office for the overall effectiveness and efficiency of the school. Such accountability is likely to be at the level of justification, but the consequences are not clear. Coupled with a choice system, the consequences could include the survival of the school. Absent such a context, parental and district oversight, pressure, and the like seem the most plausible consequences.

Traditional approaches to accountability in the professions emphasizes heavy control of entry to the profession by government, with responsibility for subsequent monitoring of accountability turned over to members of the profession itself (e.g., colleges of physicians, lawyers' bar associations). Such an approach requires clear standards of professional knowledge, skill, and performance, something the professional standards movement in education set out to define, beginning in the United States, for example, in the early 1980s. Different products of the standards movement in education are available by now as the basis for the licensure of entry-level teachers (e.g., INTASC's 1992 Model Standards for Beginning Teacher Licensing, Assessment and Development) and school administrators (Leithwood & Duke, 1993) as well as for recognizing advanced levels of teaching (e.g., The National Board for Professional Teaching Standards, 1998) and school administrator performance (e.g., Education Queensland's, *Standards Framework for Leaders*, 1997).

By themselves, standards hold the individual professional accountable to his or her client for delivering services that meet or exceed what is specified by the standards. As part of a licensure system, the professional is held accountable to the government and, beyond the license, one's professional association of colleagues. Standards require professionals to justify failure to practice in ways consistent with the standards. In the context of licensure and postentry professional associations, failure to comply with standards carries the potential of being barred from entry to the profession, being censured, being limited in one's professional activities, and being removed from the profession.

Consequences of professional approaches to accountability are examined by Blum (2000/this issue) and Earl and Torrence (2000/this issue). Blum reports evidence from a study of the implementation of student standards in a U.S. school district, and Earl and Torrence report the effects of the Ontario government's implementation of province-wide, standards-driven student testing.

Management Approaches

Not to be confused with "new managerialism," this approach includes systematic efforts to create more goal-oriented, efficient, and effective schools by introducing more rational administrative procedures. The main assumption underlying this approach is that there is nothing fundamentally wrong with current school structures. Nevertheless, their effectiveness and efficiency are improved to the extent that they become more strategic in their choices of goals and more "planful" and data-driven about the means used to accomplish those goals. This approach encompasses a variety of procedures for "strategic planning," especially at the district level, as well as multiple procedures for school improvement planning (see, e.g., the states of Illinois, Florida, and Missouri), school development planning (in the United Kingdom see Giles, 1997), and monitoring progress (e.g., the accountability reviews managed by New Zealand's Education Review Office).

When this approach is used, typically it is the organization as a whole that is held accountable, but with more responsibility for such accountability on the shoulders of the senior administrator (e.g., the principal of the school). The school and its senior administrator are most directly accountable to the next level in the organizational hierarchy, such as the district office supervisor to whom the principal reports. Justification is likely the level of accountability required, with the effectiveness of the school in reaching specified goals being that for which the school is held accountable. The consequences of a management approach to accountability are well established and include such responses as administrative promotions, demotions, managerial interventions, and employee transfers. In nonschool organizations, and increasingly in schools, financial incentives and rewards are common (Heneman & Ledford, 1998).

Three articles illustrate some of the consequences of managerial approaches to accountability: Ogawa and Collom (2000/this issue) explore the high-stakes use of educational indicators in California; Raham (2000/this issue) reviews evidence concerning the effects of group-based incentive plans for teachers; and Kelly, Conley, and Kimball (2000/this issue) report original evidence about the outcomes of Kentucky and Maryland group-based, performance-award programs.

Conclusion

In the space of a single journal issue, clearly it is not possible to address the consequences of different approaches to accountability in a comprehensive or exhaustive manner. Indeed, other articles in this issue are focused on selected mechanisms for accountability without any attempt to fully explore all mechanisms within any of the four approaches. We believe, however, that the combined articles in this issue begin to raise a number of questions that deserve much greater attention by both accountability advocates and researchers alike. These include questions concerning:

- The relation between intentions and actual consequences (see, e.g., the case of charter schools in O'Reilly & Bosetti, 2000/this issue; large-scale assessment in Earl and Torrence, 2000/this issue; and educational indicators in Ogawa and Collom, 2000/this issue).

• The challenges faced by those given the responsibility for attempting to realize those values in real schools (e.g., see the case of standards in articles by Blum, 2000/this issue; and by Earl and Torrence, 2000/this issue).

• The factors associated with successful implementation of external accountability initiatives (see, e.g., Raham, 2000/this issue, on group-based pay for performance, and Parker and Leithwood, 2000/this issue, on school councils).

• The power of local history and context to explain differences in the implementation and impact of the same general accountability mechanisms (see, e.g., the case of group-based pay for performance reported by Kelly, Conley, & Kimball, 2000/this issue).

Much of what passes for accountability-oriented school reform is driven more by ideology or philosophy than evidence: In this respect, it is no different than the long list of failed reforms from the past. But we ought (collectively) to know better. Thirty years of research on school change has produced some quite important insights, especially about what not to do. But, with notable exceptions, this knowledge is accessed by very few of those outside the education profession who are actually driving the change inside schools. Furthermore, the current impatience with the normally slow pace of chance seems to have ruled out much learning as we go (Hanushek & Meyer, 1996). Perhaps more attention to actual outcomes will cool off the romance with ideology and increase tolerance for proceeding with evidence.

References

Adams, J. E., & Kirst, M. W. (1999). New demands and concepts for educational accountability: Striving for results in an era of excellence. In J. Murphy & K. S. Louis (Eds.), *Handbook of research on educational administration* (2nd ed., pp. 463–489). San Francisco: Jossey-Bass.

Blum, R. E. (2000/this issue). Standards-based reform: Can it make a difference for students? *Peabody Journal of Education, 75*(4), 90–113.

Bryk, A. S., Easton, J. Q., Kerbow, D., Rollow, S. G., & Sebring, P. A. (1993). *A view from the elementary schools: The state of reform in Chicago.* Chicago: Consortium on Chicago School Research.

Carlson, R. (1965). Barriers to change in public schools. In R. Carlson, A. Gallaher, Jr., M. B. Miles, R. J. Pellegrin, & E. M. Rogers (Eds.), *Change processes in the public schools* (pp. 3–8). Eugene: University of Oregon, Center for the Advanced Study of Educational Administration.

Chubb, J., & Moe, T. (1990). *Politics, markets, and America's schools.* Washington, DC: Brookings Institute.

Clune, W. H., & Witte, P. A. (1988). *School-based management: Institutional variation, implementation, and issues for further research.* New Brunswick, NJ: Eagleton Institute of Politics, Center for Policy Research in Education.

Cohen, D., McLaughlin, M. W., & Talbert, J. (Eds.). (1993). *Teaching for understanding: Challenges for policy and practice.* San Francisco: Jossey-Bass.

Creemers, B. P. M., & Reetzig, G. J. (1996). School level conditions affecting the effectiveness of instruction. *School Effectiveness and School Improvement, 7,* 197–228.

David, J. L. (1989). Synthesis of research on school-based management. *Educational Leadership, 46*(8), 45–53.

Earl, L., & Torrance, N. (2000/this issue). Embedding accountability and improvement into large-scale assessment: What difference does it make? *Peabody Journal of Education, 75*(4), 114–141.

Education Queensland. (1997). *Standards framework for leaders.* Brisbane, Australia: Author.

Giles, C. (1997). *School development planning.* Plymouth, England: Northcote House.

Hanson, E. M. (1992). Educational marketing and the public schools: Policies, practices, and problems. *Educational Policy, 6,* 19–34.

Hanushek, E. A., & Meyer, R. H. (1996). Comments on chapters two, three, and four. In H. F. Ladd (Ed.), *Holding schools accountable* (pp. 128–145). Washington, DC: Brookings Institute.

Heneman, R., & Ledford, G. (1998). Competency pay for professionals and managers in business: A review and implications for teachers. *Journal of Personnel Evaluation in Education, 12,* 103–121.

Henry, G. (1996, September). Community accountability: A theory of information, accountability and school improvement. *Phi Delta Kappan,* 85–91.

Hess, G. A., Jr. (1991). *School restructuring Chicago style.* Newbury Park, CA: Corwin.

Hirschman, A. (1970). *Exit, voice, and loyalty.* Cambridge, MA: Harvard University Press.

Interstate New Teacher Assessment and Support Consortium. (1992). *Model standards for beginning teacher licensing, assessment, and development: A resource for state dialogue.* Washington, DC: Author.

Kelley, C., Conley, S., & Kimball, S. (2000/this issue). Payment for results: The effects of the Kentucky and Maryland group-based performance awards programs. *Peabody Journal of Education, 75*(4), 159–199.

Kotler, P., & Andreasen, A. (1987). *Strategic marketing for nonprofit organizations* (3rd ed.). Englewood Cliffs, NJ: Prentice Hall.

Lee, V. (1993). Educational choice: The stratifying effects of selecting schools and courses. *Educational Policy, 7,* 125–148.

Leithwood, K., & Duke, D. (1993). Defining effective leadership for Connecticut's future schools. *Journal of Personnel Evaluation in Education, 68,* 85–109.

Leithwood, K., & Jantzi, D. (1999). The relative effects of principal and teacher sources of leadership on student engagement with school. *Educational Administration Quarterly, 35,* 679–706.

Malen, B., Ogawa, R. T., & Kranz, J. (1990). What do we know about school-based management? A case study of the literature—a call for research. In W. H. Clune & J. F. Witte (Eds.), *Choice and control in American education, Volume 2: The practice of choice, decentralization, and school restructuring* (pp. 289–342). London: Falmer.

Mohrman, A. M., Mohrman, S. A., & Odden, A. (1996). Aligning teacher compensation with systemic school reform: Skill-based pay and group-based performance rewards. *Educational Evaluation and Policy Analysis, 18*(1), 51–71.

Mojkowski, C., & Fleming, D. (1988). *School-site management: Concepts and approaches.* Andover, MA: Regional Laboratory for the Educational Improvement of the Northeast and Islands.

National Board for Professional Teaching Standards. (1998). What teachers should know and be able to do. [On-line, September 1999]. Retrieved June 30, 1998 from the World Wide Web: nbpts.org

Ogawa, R. T., & Collom, E. (2000/this issue). Using performance indicators to hold schools accountable: Implicit assumptions and inherent tensions. *Peabody Journal of Education, 75*(4), 200–215.

O'Reilly, R. R., & Bosetti, L. (2000/this issue). Charter schools: The search for community. *Peabody Journal of Education, 75*(4), 19–36.

Ornstein, A. C. (1983). Administrative decentralization and community policy: Review and outlook. *Urban Review, 15*(1), 3–10.

Parker, K., & Leithwood, K. (2000/this issue). School councils' influence on school and classroom practice. *Peabody Journal of Education, 75*(4), 37–65.

Peters, M. (1992). Performance indicators in New Zealand higher education: Accountability or control? *Journal of Education Policy, 7*(3), 267–283.

Raham, H. (2000/this issue). Cooperative performance incentive plans. *Peabody Journal of Education, 75*(4), 142–158.

Raywid, M. (1992). Choice orientations, discussions, and prospects. *Educational Policy, 6*, 105–122.

Robinson, V., & Timperley, H. (2000/this issue). The link between accountability and improvement: The case of reporting to parents. *Peabody Journal of Education, 75*(4), 66–89.

Rothman, R. (1995). *Measuring up: Standards, assessment, and school reform.* San Francisco: Jossey-Bass.

Scriven, M. (1994). Duties of the teacher. *Journal of Personnel Evaluation in Education, 8*, 151–184.

Wagner, R. (1987). *Accountability in education: A philosophical inquiry.* New York: Routledge.

Webster's 7th New Collegiate Dictionary. (1971). Springfield, MA: Merriam.

Wilson, T. A. (1996). *Reaching for a better standard.* New York: Teachers College Press.

Wohlstetter, P., & Mohrman, S. A. (1993). *School-based management: Strategies for success.* New Brunswick, NJ: Rutgers University.

Wohlstetter, P., & Odden, A. (1992). Rethinking school-based management policy and research. *Educational Administration Quarterly, 28*, 529–549.

PEABODY JOURNAL OF EDUCATION, 75(4), 19–36
Copyright © 2000, Lawrence Erlbaum Associates, Inc.

Charter Schools: The Search for Community

Robert R. O'Reilly and Lynn Bosetti

Charter schools have been introduced as a means of revitalizing and improving the effectiveness of public schools. The need for change attained national attention after the publication of reports such as *A Nation at Risk* (National Commission on Excellence in Education, 1983), which alleged that the American public school system was in a state of crisis. The Commission's report, and others that noted the failings of the public school systems, provided the impetus for (a) the school effectiveness movement (Barth, 1991; Cuban, 1990); (b) structural changes in the management and financing of public schools (Odden, 1995); (c) attempts to provide greater choice within public education, such as open school boundaries within school districts and even beyond school district lines (Weiss, 1998); and (d) the creation of magnet schools (Smrekar, 1996).

The more dramatic attempts to restructure schools are based on the belief that market mechanisms such as various school choice plans will (a) improve the effectiveness of schools through competition among schools for

ROBERT R. O'REILLY *is Professor in the Graduate Division of Educational Research, University of Calgary, Alberta, Canada.*

LYNN BOSETTI *is Professor in the Graduate Division of Educational Research, and Special Assistant to the Academic Vice-President, University of Calgary, Alberta, Canada.*

Requests for reprints should be sent to Robert O'Reilly, Professor of Educational Management and Policy Studies, Dean's Office, University of Calgary, Faculty of Education, 2500 University Drive, Calgary, Alberta, Canada T2N 1N4. E-mail: roreilly@ucalgary.ca students, (b) reduce inefficiencies in the administration and delivery of education, and (c) have the effect of improved educational outcomes (Chubb & Moe, 1990; Goldhaber, 1999). From these beliefs emerge plans for tuition vouchers (Friedman & Friedman, 1990), greater support for private schools, a growth in home schooling, and the establishment of charter schools.

School choice also arises out of the conditions of postmodern life, characterized by cultural pluralism and a population that is increasingly mobile and unrooted and where there is a lack of common vision or identity. These conditions result in a lack of consensus regarding the goals and purposes of education (Bosetti, 1999). Parents are drawn to schools that reject a value-neutral, "one-size-fits-all" approach to public schooling. Instead, they are seeking schools that resonate with their particular values and beliefs regarding the goals of education and what constitutes good teaching and learning. They are seeking schools that are safe and caring, that are free of drugs and violence, and that provide a sense of community where their children are accepted and feel they belong.

Charter schools are hybrid institutions. They are public institutions that have some of the characteristics of a private agency. For example, they are public schools, effectively financed and controlled by public educational agencies. Typically, they must (a) provide a curriculum mandated by a central governing authority, (b) submit to accountability systems, and (c) be open to all students who may apply without discrimination. At the same time, they exhibit certain private sector characteristics. Each school is autonomous and has a unique charter that states the aims, objectives, and mandate of the school. Each school, beyond its public mandate, is primarily accountable to the parents of the children of the school. Parents are influential members of the governing board of the school, which has the power to set objectives, control finances, and hire and replace employees. Levavic (1995) identified organizations with these characteristics as operating in "quasi-markets." She defined organizations in quasi-markets as public sector organizations that have separate providers and purchasers and an element of user choice. Quasi-markets remain highly regulated. Governments control (a) who may enter the market as providers, (b) levels of investment, (c) the quality of services to be provided, and (d) the price to be paid for the services. Frequently there is no cost to the consumer (i.e., tuition fees; Levavic, 1995, p. 167).

In the United States, as of the Fall of 1999, there are nearly 1,700 charter schools operating in 31 states and the District of Columbia, serving approximately 350,000 students. In 22 states and the District of Columbia, there are 10 or more charter schools. The largest numbers of charter schools are in the states of Arizona, California, Massachusetts, Texas, and Florida (in that order; Center for Education Reform, 1999). This represents a rapid growth of a movement that began with enabling legislation in Minnesota in 1991, followed by similar legislation in California 1 year later. Charter schools became part of the federal policy when President Clinton authorized the *Charter Schools Expansion Act* of 1998 ("Clinton Announces," 1998). Federal support for charter schools amounted to $91 million in 1999; President Clinton has requested $130 million for the program for the Fiscal Year 2000 and has set a goal of 3,000 charter schools by the year 2002. As of Fall 1999, charter school students constituted slightly above 0.66%[1] of all students in American public and private schools, and in only three states does the charter school population make up more than 1% of students in the state (National Center for Educational Statistics, 1999).

The most comprehensive descriptive study of charter schools in the United States is the RPP International study conducted for the U.S. Department of Education (1999). The Third-Year Report of the ongoing study states that charter schools are growing, are gaining support, and are in demand. It also reports that charter schools remain small, with an average enrollment of 132 students, and recruit students with demographic characteristics that are similar to the population in their surrounding area in terms of socioeconomic status and race. In six states, the proportion of students of color is higher in the charter schools than in the surrounding public schools. In 1997, the RPP International group reported that most new charter schools were designed for a student population that was primarily White; however, the majority of "conversion" schools (public schools that became charter schools) served mainly minority students. Charter schools tend to enroll fewer students with special education needs. Most charter schools were created to implement alternative visions of schooling, and 20% of schools targeted particular populations of students. Almost 90% of schools used student achievement tests, augmented by other measures of student performance and school success, as indicators of improved educational outcomes. These indicators were used as accountability measures in reports to parents and chartering agencies (U.S. Department of Education, 1999).

Most major reports of charter schools (Little Hoover Commission, 1996; Manno, Finn, Bierlein, & Vanourek, 1998) are enthusiastic about the prospect that charter schools can revitalize public education. The Little Hoover Commission of schools in California refers to charter schools as "wedges," which spur public schools to change and insert new ideas and innovations

---

[1]Many commentators state that there are 1% of children in charter schools. In September 1999, it is estimated that there are 350,000 in charter schools, and the National Center for Educational Statistics reports that there are approximately 53 million children enrolled in private and public elementary and secondary schools in the United States (http://nces.ed.gov/pubs99/digest98.html). Based on these figures, the total charter school enrollment is about 2/3 of 1%.

into the school system. The Hudson Institute study (Finn, Manno, & Bierlein, 1996) is supportive of charter schools as a vehicle to improve student achievement, manage resources more efficiently, and bring new ideas to public education. In contrast, the UCLA study on charter schools (of 39 representative charter schools in 10 school districts in California) reports that these schools were not achieving the goals and results claimed by charter school advocates (UCLA Research Associates, 1998). In particular, they found that, although charter schools were fiscally accountable, they were not held accountable for academic achievement; private resources were usually required for charter schools to survive, and they were dependent on strong, well- connected leaders. They report that the racial socioeconomic mix of charter schools is similar to nearby public schools and that teachers in charter schools were enthusiastic about their schools; however, they also reported very heavy workloads. Goldhaber (1999), in his review of the empirical evidence of the impact of school choice, claimed that "early evidence on charter schools tends to confirm neither the greatest hopes of choice proponents nor the greatest fears of choice opponents" (p. 19). He concluded that (a) they are not the elite organizations that many feared they would be, (b) they offer few dramatic educational strategies, and (c) their proportions of low-income students and racial composition reflects statewide averages.

Alberta Study

The remainder of this article will describe some of the findings of a 3-year study of charter schools in the Province of Alberta, Canada (Bosetti, 1998). Alberta[2] is the only Canadian jurisdiction that has legislation for charter schools, which was proclaimed in 1994. To date, 12 schools have obtained charters, but only 10 are currently operating. The Alberta case is an interesting addition to the charter school literature. Alberta legislation permits private schools to obtain charters and provides for Roman Catholic charter schools. The legislation in Alberta would be termed *weak* in that government regulations are quite intrusive—only the Minister of Education or school boards may sponsor charters, only certified teachers may be hired, and the government inspects charter schools quite closely. The government's approach over the first several years has changed from a laissez-faire stance to a more centralized, yet supportive, one. Although no one in government openly advocates for charter school organizations, the

---

[2]In Canada, education is a provincial responsibility; there is no federal department of education. Alberta is the fourth province in terms of population (population 2.9 million) and is economically quite strong.

government has recently addressed the needs for start-up funds and for assistance to obtain suitable facilities. There is now an officer of the Ministry of Learning who is directly responsible for the supervision of charter schools (O'Reilly, 1999).

Schools

Of the 12 schools that have received charters to date, one has had its charter revoked for alleged financial mismanagement, and another surrendered its charter to become an alternative school within the public education system. The last school to receive a charter began operation in September 1999 and was not included in this study; another charter school was not included because they were engaged in labor disputes with their teachers. The following 9 charter schools were the focus of the study.

ABC Charter Public School. The ABC Charter Public School was founded by the Action for Bright Children Society (ABC) in 1995 and began operation in the Fall of 1996. The school originally catered to students in Grades 1 to 3 who are gifted or who wish to challenge a program designed for gifted students. In 1998, the ABC Society successfully appealed to the Minister of Education to have their charter extended to include Grades 1 to 9. They are adding one grade per year to their clientele.

The educational philosophy of the school draws on Howard Gardner's theory of multiple intelligences (Gardner, 1993) to provide an educational setting that nurtures the talents and abilities of students. The teachers practice curriculum compacting and encourage children to progress at a rate commensurate with their potential. As a consequence, children are grouped according to their ability rather than grade levels. ABC Charter Public School is filled to capacity, with 152 students and a lengthy waiting list. The school has a well-qualified and experienced teaching staff and principal who are paid at levels comparable to those in the larger public education system.

Almadina Charter School. Almadina Charter School caters to students from a variety of minority groups, many of whom are recent immigrant families who require special assistance with English as a second language. Serving Grades 1 to 9, it is one of the larger charter schools. However, in the past 3 years its enrollment has dropped from 360 to 280. Many of the sponsors of the Almadina Charter School are members of the Islamic commu-

23

nity who noted with dismay the large number of dropouts among children whose first language was not English. Over 60% of the students belong to either one of the Arab or Islamic communities in Calgary. The curriculum is fairly traditional, with optional classes in Arabic.

Given its student population, Almadina has not yet achieved its goal of raising the average pupil achievement to the level of the provincial average. The school has also had some problems of an administrative nature. There has been considerable discord at the board level, with major changes in membership at each annual election. The school has had five principals in the 4 years of its existence. Due to governance issues and the poor academic results of students, the Minister has issued a letter of warning to the school that it must improve immediately.

Boyle Street Cooperative Education Centre. The Boyle Street Cooperative Education Centre is located in the heart of inner-city Edmonton, wedged between the downtown core and "skid row." The charter school evolved from an outreach and educational counseling program for inner-city street-involved youth and is sponsored by Alberta Department of Social Services and Boyle Street Community Services Co-op. The program targets youth aged 12 to 19 who view the inner city as their community and who often deal with poverty, racism, physical and sexual abuse, addictions, criminal involvement, and frequent stays in institutional care.

The educational program is designed to provide a safe environment where students may acquire a basic education that is focused on life skills and job readiness. Students attracted to the school have little chance of being successful in the regular school system. The majority of the 85 students currently enrolled are at an upper elementary to junior high school level of learning. Students in the program receive credits for work experience. The school is operated on a year- round basis, with discipline and attendance policies that respect the students' life styles and needs as learners.

Centre for Academic and Personal Excellence (CAPE). The principal and founder of a private school decided to apply for charter status in the Fall of 1994 so that more students would have the ability to attend the school without the prohibitive private school tuition fees. With considerable community support—including the support of prominent businessmen and the families of students who had previously attended the private school—CAPE was able to create one of the first charter schools in Alberta in the Fall of 1995.

The philosophy of the school is to foster a desire to learn, grow, explore, excel, and achieve. The charter states that the school is aimed at students who are intellectually capable but are underachieving or at risk of underachieving for broad social, emotional, or cognitive reasons. The school promotes a family-like, highly disciplined environment. One of its greatest strengths is its small classrooms with a ratio of 1 teacher to every 16 students.

New Horizons Charter School. New Horizons Charter School was the first fully operating charter school in Canada. It was established through the efforts of 40 parents of children who had been identified as gifted (IQ above 125). Most students reside in a middle-class suburban community. In 1998, the school had approximately 150 students from kindergarten to Grade 9. The focus of the school's educational program is academic mastery and excellence, complimented by a focus on the fine arts. Students are grouped into pods covering two to six grades based on the levels of achievement in specific scholastic areas, rather than on chronological age (Bosetti, O'Reilly, Sande, & Foulkes, 2000).

Suzuki Charter School. Suzuki Charter School is located in a Catholic school board building in southeast Edmonton. The school currently offers the Alberta Program of Studies and Suzuki music methodology from kindergarten to Grade 6, with the ability to expand to Grade 9 if numbers and facilities warrant the expansion. The educational approach based on the Suzuki approach to music education utilizes the "mother tongue method," capitalizing on natural learning processes divided into three phases of task-specific skill development. The first phase emphasizes the learner understanding what he or she is supposed to do. The second phase involves meaningful practice with appropriate feedback, and the third phase involves review that develops and reinforces the automatic execution of skill. Presently, the school is operating at capacity, with just under 100 students enrolled.

Foundations for the Future Charter Academy. Foundations for the Future Charter Academy is based on the notions of discipline, respect, and rigor. The educational program emphasizes a highly structured teaching and learning environment with teacher-directed instruction and mastery learning of concepts. The curriculum focuses on the fundamental basics of core education subjects and incorporates phonics, grammar, regimented mathematics, and a daily homework plan designed to challenge students. There is also a mandatory school uniform. It is operating at capacity with an enrollment of 225 students, but is expected to grow. The school is located in the city of Calgary.

Moberly Hall Charter School.   Located in an isolated oil town in northern Alberta, Moberly Hall Charter School is the only charter school hosted by a Roman Catholic school board. It was converted from a private school to a charter school in 1997. A key characteristic of the school is its use of differentiated teaching directed toward addressing the unique learning styles of students. Currently the school is operating at full capacity with approximately 75 students in Grades 1 to 9.

Mundare Community Charter School.   The Mundare Community Charter School was established by parents in response to the closure of the elementary/junior high school in a small rural community. The charter school had 75 students enrolled in Grades 1 to 9 and was committed to differentiated instruction to meet the individual learning styles of students. Due to financial difficulties, the school was closed by the Minister of Education after only 1 year of operation. It was absorbed into the local public education system as a K–6 alternative program, with differentiation as its distinguishing characteristic.

Method

The study was conducted using a multimethod case study approach to document each charter school situation. The study included document analysis, interviews with key actors, and observations of school and classroom practices. Questionnaires were distributed to charter school administrators, teachers, parents, charter school board members, and students.

The parent questionnaire was sent to parents in six of the nine participating schools during the 1997–1998 school year. Initially, questionnaires were not sent to parents of the school catering to English as Second Language Learners because the majority of the parents did not read English. A translated edition of the questionnaire was distributed the next year. At another charter school, the majority of students do not reside with their parents because they are street youth, and as a consequence their parents were not included in the study. Questionnaires from parents at Moberly Hall were also not available at the time of this study. Therefore, the sample included 248 parents, representing 32% of the students enrolled in participating charter schools.

Questionnaires were sent to all regular teachers at eight of the partici-pating schools in the Spring of 1998. Data from Moberly Hall were not available at the time of the study. Questionnaires were returned in a sealed envelope to a member of the research team or to a school secretary, who passed them on to the researchers. There was an 88% return rate.

Results

In the remainder of this article we draw on the results of our question-naires to profile (a) who selects charter schools and why; (b) levels of satis-faction; and (c) perceived success from the point of view of the teachers, parents, and students who participate in them.

Teachers

There were 61 teachers who responded to the questionnaires. All but 2 were women, and two thirds were in their first to third year of teaching. A strong core of teachers (29%) had 12 or more years of teaching. By law all teachers must have certification, and all are so qualified. Fifty three percent have an interim certificate; the remainder have permanent certification. By law all Alberta teachers must possess a university degree. Twenty seven percent of teachers have two or more degrees at the bachelor's level, and three have one or more masters' degrees. Salaries are not high. Of the 51 teachers who responded to this item, the mean salary is approximately $31,000, which is somewhat less than the salary of a qualified first year teacher in a public board. One school began its teachers at a scale of ap-proximately one half of the neighboring public board.

Teachers, with few exceptions, are very satisfied with their teaching po-sitions. Their greatest satisfaction comes from the opportunity to (a) teach small classes, (b) work in a supportive environment with like-minded col-leagues, (c) work with a school philosophy that resonates with their own beliefs about good teaching and learning, and (d) have a voice in shaping a new school. Teachers express dissatisfaction with the school facilities and limited resources, as well as charter schools' relationships with the teach-ers' union and local school boards.

Teachers view the most important successes of their schools (in order of importance) as the following: (a) creating a high-performing staff, (b) rais-ing student achievement, (c) employing suitable means of assessing pupil achievement, (d) providing for child safety, and (e) retaining students. They believe that charter schools are less successful in obtaining adequate

27

resources for the teachers, in allowing sufficient preparation time for teachers, and in integrating technology into the curriculum.

Charter schools are expected to be innovative. In response to an open-ended question, teachers noted that the major innovations in their schools tend to be curricular in nature (i.e., Suzuki method of teaching, the integration of subjects, the project method of teaching, the emphasis on multiple intelligences and differentiated instruction, and the use of direct teaching and phonics). Innovations also include school organization (i.e., working with small groups of students, multiaged grouping, and ability grouping) and the inclusion of parents in their children's learning (i.e., learning contracts, behavioral contracts, homework contracts, and volunteering in the school).

In response to the question, "What is the school's most significant accomplishment?," teachers made 51 comments. The most significant accomplishment reported by teachers was the social-emotional development of students evidenced by increased self-confidence, acceptance by others, and increased self-esteem (12 comments). Teachers also commented on the success of various programs (7 comments), the resilience and survival of the charter school (7 comments), improved student learning (6 comments), the dedication of the staff and their ability to work together (4 comments), the effectiveness of working with small groups of children to address their specific learning needs (3 comments), and the creation of a safe and caring environment (3 comments).

The major challenges for charter schools, as perceived by teachers, relates to limited instructional resources (5 comments), temporary or inadequate school facilities, and operating on a shoestring. Teachers also raised concern about having to adjust the school program to accommodate the learning needs of those children not targeted by the charter. For example, one charter school that offers a highly structured learning environment has been attracting a high percentage of students with behavioral or learning difficulties. The needs of these children put a strain on the already limited school resources. At another school with a program designed for gifted children, accommodations must be made for those students who attend the school but who are not academically gifted.

Teachers at a few charter schools raised concerns regarding the ability of the school to attract and retain experienced, well-trained teachers and with the resistance of the larger educational community to the charter school concept.

Parents

Most parents who responded to the questionnaire had some experience with public schools prior to choosing a charter school for their children. Over two thirds of all children had attended public schools prior to attending their charter school: 9% had attended Catholic public schools, 9% had attended private schools, 4% had received home schooling, 11% had not attended any school, and 7% had some other form of schooling. It is notable that although there is a full system of public Roman Catholic schools in Alberta, and approximately 20% of the province is Roman Catholics (higher in the urban areas where charter schools are found), charter schools attract only 9% of this population.

Most parents of charter school students do not believe that their children have major difficulties with learning, and 5% of parents indicated that their children had behavioral or learning problems. Some parents noted that their children were underachievers in their previous schools, and many parents believed that their children require special/individualized programming. Few parents reported that their children require Individual Program Plans to address their learning needs. This reflects the literature, which reports that children with learning difficulties are underrepresented in charter schools (McKinney, 1996; U.S. Department of Education, 1999). All of the charter schools in this study offer programs targeted to niche populations of students with particular learning needs (i.e., English as a Second Language [ESL], underachievers, gifted, talented, etc.) or preferred approaches to learning.

Parents report that the most important reasons for choosing charter schools are small classes and greater academic challenge. Other important reasons include discipline, use of phonics in teaching methods, and individualized curricula.

Parents of charter school students speak English as their first language in 88% of the cases.[3] They are well educated, with 77% of both mothers and fathers having at least some postsecondary education. Forty five percent of mothers and 52% of fathers have university degrees or some professional certification (again, the average level of education of parents in the Almadina school would be somewhat, but not dramatically, lower). The family income of parents is high. More than half have incomes greater than $60,000, and 20% have incomes greater than $100,000. Only 6% have earnings less than $30,000. The majority of parents from the Almadina school (who were not part of the questionnaire sample) have annual earnings ranging between $30,000 and $40,000. Most of the students at the Boyle Street Cooperative Education Centre, whose parents are not represented in this data set, are eligible for some form of social assistance.

Parents are very satisfied with charter schools. They are most pleased with the teaching of basics, academic standards, the quality of teaching,

---

[3]This proportion would drop if the data for Almadina School were added, as many of the parents of that school speak Arabic or other non-English language as their first language.

class size, the individual attention given to students, and their access to teachers. They also rate very highly the curriculum, the amount of assistance given to students, and school safety.

Parents are very satisfied with the degree of communication between the school and parents, particularly with respect to student achievement. They are also very satisfied with the values that are promoted by the schools and the general management of the schools, including the use of funds, parent voice in decision making, and the work of the charter school boards.

Some parents are dissatisfied with school transportation facilities (some schools do not provide transportation), the lack of extracurricular activities, and the paucity of teaching resource materials. The major area of dissatisfaction is the quality of school facilities and buildings.

Students

A small sample of students from five charter schools was surveyed regarding their level of satisfaction with their experiences at their school. Return rates varied from between 10% to 28% of students at each school representing Grades 3 to 9.

Students were very positive regarding their teachers and fellow students, the curriculum, and the school culture. The majority of students would recommend their school to a friend. In one school, 94% of the students would recommend their school, and between 61% to 79% would do so at other charter schools.

In general, students reported that there were no differences between their current school and their previous schools with respect to relationships with peers and teachers, but students in three schools reported that they had done "a little worse" in school work at their previous school, whereas the students at the remaining two schools reported that they had done "about the same." Students reported that they thought their teachers were better at their charter school—that they treated them fairly and with respect. They viewed their charter school as a safe and caring environment where they felt (a) academically challenged and (b) that they belonged. Their areas of satisfaction and dissatisfaction mirrored those of their parents and teachers; for example, they commented negatively about school facilities and access to resources.

Success of Charter Schools in Alberta

The success of charter schools in Alberta is evidenced by high levels of satisfaction among teachers, parents, and students, as well as steady levels of student enrollment. The charter school movement has been slow in growth, but a number of the schools have been through the renewal process and are moving into the maturation stage. Operationally, this means that these schools can shift their focus and energy from establishing the charter school and putting into place the required policies, procedures, and templates for accountability and can now focus on the professional development of teachers and curriculum development and bringing clarity to their charter mandate. These schools will be in the position to reflect on, measure, and share what makes them effective and unique. All charter schools are renewed for a maximum of 5 years.

There is evidence from our study that the majority of charter schools demonstrate improved student achievement. Performance results on provincial measures of student learning[4] reveal that students at charter schools are generally achieving at least as well as students in other jurisdictions, are in accordance with what would be expected based on their described learner needs, or both. For example, the Provincial Achievement Test results are reported by the government as the proportion of students in each school who attain the acceptable standard for the grade level and the proportion who achieve the standard of excellence. In the two charter schools catering to the learning needs of gifted students, 100% of the students achieved the acceptable standard, and a significant proportion achieved the standard of excellence (i.e., 71% in one school and 50% in the other). Four charter schools have student achievement results that are slightly above the average for their related public school board and the provincial average. The charter school catering to the needs of ESL and immigrant students has results consistently below the provincial average.

In part, these achievement results can be explained by the targeted group of students admitted to charter schools (i.e., gifted, musically talented, at-risk, ESL students) and by socioeconomic factors. The majority of students who attend charter schools come from well-educated[5] families of middle to upper middle income. These parents are actively seeking an alternative education to what is currently being offered by the public education system and are actively involved in their children's education.

Charter schools are only in the beginning stages of developing (a) appropriate "added-value" assessment measures, (b) measures that address

---

[4]Provincial standardized achievement tests are administered annually to all students in Grades 3, 6, and 9. Diploma examinations are required for all Grade 12 students. The achievement results for Grades 3, 6, and 9 for each school are ranked and published in local newspapers.

[5]Seventy seven percent of parents have some postsecondary education, 45% of mothers have a university degree, and 52% of fathers have such a degree. Fifty six percent have an average family income of over $60,000, and 20.6% have an income over $100,000. Parents of students from Almadina and Boyle Street are not included in this sample and would affect these statistics.

the impact of the charter-specific pedagogical strategies, or (c) the dimensions of the expanded curriculum that students are expected to master. For example, characteristic of all charter schools in Alberta are small class sizes and a consequent low teacher–student ratio, yet none of the charter schools have been investigating the impact of this provision on the enhancement of student learning.

The "missionary zeal" demonstrated by charter school pioneers—in (a) overcoming daunting obstacles and (b) persevering despite limited financial, moral, or technical support from the government or broader educational community—is striking. Teachers work long hours with limited resources and often for less salary than they would earn in the regular public education system, yet they remain satisfied and committed to their charter school. Teachers embrace the challenge of working in a supportive school environment with like- minded individuals and in a school where the educational philosophy resonates with their own. In particular, they report that they feel they can make a difference working in such an environment with small groups of children. Many of these teachers are in their first few years of teaching and have developed deep loyalties to their school and the community. Some teachers, however, are uncomfortable with the "temporary" status of charter schools and low salaries. These teachers are waiting for the opportunity to obtain a more secure and better paying position elsewhere.

Parents are very enthusiastic about charter schools and in most cases are the main impetus behind their establishment. Many have contributed substantial volunteer hours to get these schools established and operational; however, this level of involvement diminishes as the schools mature. Eighty three percent of parents volunteer in their children's charter school, and 82% intend to have their children remain in a charter school.

Parents express highest satisfaction with the quality of teaching, the safe and caring environment, and the academic challenge their children receive. Parents uniformly report their charter school as being better than the previous school their children attended and that their children have demonstrated improved academic performance and self-confidence and satisfaction in their learning.

It is apparent that although no new or dramatic educational strategies have emerged as yet from these charter schools—nor any truly innovative programs—parents and teachers would deem them a success. What distinguishes these charter schools in Alberta from other public schools is that the educational strategies and programs are uniformly applied throughout the school and are not found only in a particular teacher's classroom or subject area. The explicit charter—combined with small class sizes, teamwork, collaboration among parents and teachers, and a supportive and caring environment—has culminated in a cohesive community and a deep loyalty to the school. There is no guarantee, however, that these factors will contribute to a significant educational reform in terms of innovations in teaching and learning or that high levels of satisfaction and commitment equates to quality education or a more efficient public education system. The charter school movement in Alberta has not had the momentum to form a critical mass of schools that would create the necessary choice and competition among schools, which would in turn have a significant impact on or leverage change in the public education system. As a movement or educational reform strategy, charter schools are still in their infancy, struggling to define their place in an ever-changing regulatory environment that governs public education.

The charter school movement, despite its slow growth and size, has created some dissonance in the public education system by increasing awareness among parents and the community at large that not all students have similar needs and that not all parents have similar values and beliefs regarding the appropriate goals of education. Charter schools demonstrate that there are alternative avenues to creating diversity in programs and in ways of governing schools. In some instances, local boards have been challenged by proponents of charter schools to be more responsive to parents' requests for more programs of choice and for the provision of programs and services to address the particular needs of groups of students. School districts have become more explicit in their provisions for school choice, particularly in the large urban areas.

The charter school movement has continued to grow despite the hostile environment created by some stakeholder groups. Their survival may be attributed to their ability to garner grass roots support, create a school from the ground up, operate on a shoestring budget, demonstrate acceptable levels of student achievement, and maintain high levels of parental satisfaction (Bosetti et al., 2000). The movement is still too young to determine its full impact on public education.

Conclusion

The dominant themes of charter schools in practice appear to be the new relationships between parents and the school and the redefinition of the role of the state in the administration of public education.

Parents and teachers identify with their schools in ways that they have not done with a public school board or with most public schools. There is a kind of nostalgia surrounding the charter school movement in Alberta, reflected in parents' search for a small school community where their children are safe, known to all, and academically challenged. Goldring and Smrekar (1997), in their study of parental involvement in magnet schools, found that parents who are active choosers view themselves as separate from other public school parents because their choice represents a significant break from the complacency and compromise experienced in their neighborhood schools. There is a mythology of "specialness" that surrounds each charter school community that teachers, students, and parents draw on to derive their identity and meaning, and to build a culture of sentiment, tradition, and practices. In some charter schools this is reinforced through school uniforms. The sense of community, social trust, and social cohesion are some of the positive outcomes of charter schools in Alberta.

Public education in Canada is already highly differentiated because the communities they serve and legislation permit public funding, in most jurisdictions, to Catholic, French, and private schools. In a pluralistic society, the ideal of a common comprehensive school may no longer be feasible. People want to "decide for themselves the kinds of subcommunity they wish to live in, if indeed they wish to live in a community at all" (Holmes, as cited in Gaskell, 1999, p. 3). Individual choice is a condition of postindustrial society.

There is a clear need for educators and policy makers to engage with each other and with the public in debates regarding appropriate goals for schooling, the role and purpose of schooling in society, and, most important, a vision of the good society and the role of the citizen in the creation and maintenance of society. The debate is too important to be resolved simply through market forces (which work well in the economic sphere) and individual choice. Charter schools are an important experiment in the delivery of educational services in North America. In practice, charter schools in Alberta appear to be less about competition, innovation, and educational efficiency and more about the idea of "charter" itself. That is, they are examples of alternative schools in which parents have a direct voice in the governance of the school; they are driven by an explicit mandate that defines the goals of education, and they operate within a clearly articulated value framework. What distinguishes charter schools in Alberta is the strong sense of commitment and loyalty that develops among parents, teachers, and students as they struggle to maintain their charter school. The creation of charter schools provides an opportunity for the community to engage in a dialogue about the community's aspirations for its children and how to assist the children to achieve those goals. Charters are not just about family choice; they are also about democracy in action within a community.

It is to be expected that each community could create an effective and successful charter school. The question still to be answered is, "Under what conditions would the charter school model be able to serve a large proportion of all children?" The state has a responsibility to (a) create policies; (b) target opportunities and resources toward meeting the needs of those children who have the least social, economic, and political resources; (c) ensure conditions of universal access to programs that meet the needs of children; and (d) address the issues of diversity and equity so that a good and viable society is maintained. The viable role of charter schools in meeting those objectives has yet to be determined.

References

Barth, R. S. (1991). *Improving schools from within*. San Francisco: Jossey-Bass.

Bosetti, L. (1998). *Canada's charter schools: Initial report* (SAEE Research Series #3). Kelowna, British Columbia, Canada: Society for the Advancement of Excellence in Education.

Bosetti, L. (1999, June 9). *Alberta charter schools: Paradox and promise*. Paper presented to the annual meeting of the Canadian Society for the Study of Education, Sherbrooke, Quebec, Canada.

Bosetti, L., O'Reilly, R., Sande, D., & Foulkes, E. (2000). *Charter schools at a cross roads: Final report* (SAEE Research Series #4). Kelowna, British Columbia, Canada: Society for the Advancement of Excellence in Education.

Center for Educational Reform. (1999). *CER releases official charter school numbers for 1999–2000 school year*. Retrieved October 7, 1999 from the World Wide Web: http://edreform.com/press/990830bts.htm

Chubb, J., & Moe, T. (1990). *Politics, markets and America's schools*. Washington, DC: Brookings Institute.

Clinton announces $95 million in support for charter schools. (1999, August 28). [Press release]. Retrieved September 25, 1999 from the World Wide Web: http://www.ed.gov/PressReleases/08–1999/support.html

Cuban, L. (1990). Reforming again, again and again. *Educational Leadership, 19*, 1–13.

Finn, C., Jr., Manno, B., & Bierlein, L. (1996). *Charter schools in action: What have we learned?* Indianapolis, IN: Hudson Institute.

Friedman, M., & Friedman, R. (1990). *Free to choose: A personal statement* (Rev. ed.). San Diego, CA: Harcourt Brace.

Gardner, H. (1993). *Multiple intelligences: The theory in practice*. New York: Basic.

Gaskell, J. (1999, April). *The politics of school choice in British Columbia: Citizenship, equity and diversity*. Paper presented at the Annual Meeting of the American Educational Research Association, Montreal, Canada.

Goldhaber, D. (1999). School choice: An examination of the empirical evidence on achievement, parental decision making and equity. *Educational Researcher, 28*(9), 16–25.

Goldring, E., & Smrekar, C. (1997, April). *Community or anonymity? Patterns of parental involvement and family–school interactions in magnet schools*. Paper presented at the Annual Meeting of the American Educational Research Association, Chicago.

Levavic, R. (1995). *Local management of schools: Analysis and practice*. Milton Keynes, England: Open University Press.

Little Hoover Commission. (1996). *The charter movement: Education reform school by school* [Rep. No. 138 to the Governor and Members of the Legislature]. Los Angeles: Author.

Manno, B., Finn, C., Bierlein, L., & Vanourek, G. (1998). How charter schools are different: Lessons and implications for a national study. *Phi Delta Kappan, 79*, 488–498.

McKinney, J. (1996). Charter schools: A new barrier for children with disabilities. *Educational Leadership, 54*(2), 22–25.

National Commission on Excellence in Education. (1983). *A nation at risk.* Washington, DC: U.S. Department of Education.

Odden, A. R. (1995). *Educational leadership for America's schools.* New York: McGraw-Hill.

O'Reilly, R. R. (1999, June 9). *Assessing Alberta's charter school policy.* Paper presented to the Canadian Society for Studies in Education, Sherbrooke, Quebec.

Smrekar, C. (1996). *The impact of school choice and community: In the interest of families and schools.* Albany: State University of New York Press.

UCLA Charter School Research Associates. (1998). *Beyond the rhetoric of charter school reform.* Los Angeles: Author.

U.S. Department of Education. (1999). *National study of charter schools—The state of charter schools: Third-Year report.* Washington, DC: Author.

Weiss, J. (1998). Policy theories of school choice. *Social Science Quarterly, 79,* 523–531.

PEABODY JOURNAL OF EDUCATION, 75(4), 37–65
Copyright © 2000, Lawrence Erlbaum Associates, Inc.

School Councils' Influence on School and Classroom Practice

Kirsten Parker
Kenneth Leithwood

School councils are a prominent feature of most school restructuring initiatives, despite surprisingly little evidence about their contribution to school improvement. This study examined the influence, on both school and classroom practices, of an advisory form of school councils implemented in the province of Ontario in June 1996. Data from interviews with 50 people from 5 schools, selected for the range of council's influence, were used to address questions concerning the extent of council effects and the characteristics of relatively influential councils.

Results indicated that councils had weak positive to negative influences on both schools and classrooms. More influential councils were characterized by their collaborative team approach with the school staff and their involvement in initiatives related to school improvement objectives. These councils were usually found in schools with a history of relatively extensive parental involvement in many forms. More influential councils had facilitative principals who supported and endorsed the councils; provided information, knowledge, and skills to council members; worked closely with the council chair; and assisted the council to build connections with the school staff.

KIRSTEN PARKER *is Superintendent of Schools, Simcoe County District School Board, Ontario, Canada.*

KENNETH LEITHWOOD *is Professor and Director of the Centre for Leadership Development at the Ontario Institute for Studies in Education, University of Toronto, Ontario, Canada.*

Requests for reprints should be sent to Kirsten Parker, Simcoe County District School Board, 1170 Highway 26, Midhurst, Ontario L0L 1X0, Canada. E-mail: kparker@edctr.scdsb.on.ca

School Councils and related forms of shared decision making are a prominent part of most restructuring initiatives in Canada, the United States, New Zealand, Australia, and the United Kingdom (Malen & Ogawa, 1992; Mohrman, Wohlstetter, & Associates, 1994; Murphy & Beck, 1995). In fact, decentralization has been viewed as the "cornerstone in the current reform edifice [although] it is generally embedded within a larger improvement agenda" (Murphy & Beck, 1995, p. 6). Advocates of decentralization base their reforms on the premise that to ensure improvement in schools, those closest to the students should be given the authority to make important decisions (Chavkin & Williams, 1987).

As a mechanism for accountability, Leithwood and Earl (2000/this issue) classify school councils as a "decentralized approach." Mechanisms within this approach assume that schools will become more client oriented as the distance is reduced between who is being held accountable and who is owed the account. These mechanisms, as a category, represent Hirschman's (1970) "voice option"—an orientation to greater accountability and improvement based on giving more decision-making power to legitimate but previously unheard (or not listened to) stakeholders.

With the introduction of parent-control forms of school councils, as in this study, school professionals are placed in a more direct accountability relationship with the parents of their students. Surprisingly little evidence is available in support of claims that advocates make for the benefits of decentralized decision making using school council mechanisms, however. For example, from their review of 83 empirical studies of the effects of site-based management and school councils, Leithwood and Menzies (1998) concluded that

> there is virtually no firm, research-based knowledge about the direct or indirect effects of [Site Based Management, or SBM, and school councils] on students … . Furthermore, the little research-based evidence that does exist suggests that the effects are just as likely to be negative as positive. (p. 340)

The intent of this study was to inquire about the conditions accounting for variation in the influence of councils on school and classroom practices. More specifically, we asked:

- To what extent have school councils influenced school and classroom practices, and what is the nature of that influence?
- What conditions both inside and outside of the school mediate the influence of councils on school and classroom practices?
- What teacher behaviors are associated with councils' influence on classroom practice?

- What characteristics are associated with councils that do have a positive influence on school and classroom practices?

Ontario schools implementation of the Ministry of Education and Training's *Policy/Program Memorandum No. 122* (Ontario Ministry of Education and Training, 1995) was the context for this study. This policy directed school boards to have policies and procedures in place to ensure the founding of school councils in every school by June of 1996. The purpose of this addition to the existing governance structures of schools was to make recommendations to the principal and school board. No standard version or model was specified for each school council, although membership was to be dominated by parents.

Framework

The framework for this study was developed from empirical research about the nature and effects of school councils, in particular those councils associated with what Murphy and Beck (1995) classified as a "parent control" form of SBM. This research suggests that the influence of councils (in which parents are majority members) on school and classroom practices is mediated by conditions both external and internal to the school. Council influence also depends on the characteristics and behaviors of principals and teachers, as well as on characteristics of councils themselves and their processes for decision making.

Relations among variables in this framework are conceptualized as interactive rather than linear, as suggested by advocates of backward mapping (e.g., Elmore et al., 1990), for example, who seek to identify the "chain" of variables linking altered school structures to changes in classroom practices and their subsequent effects on students.

Conditions Accounting for School Councils' Influence

School conditions. Two overlapping sets of school-level factors that appear to influence the effectiveness of councils can be found in the recent literature. One set of factors has emerged from and is supported by the results of empirical study. Another more speculative set has arisen through efforts to bring conceptual coherence to these results.

In the empirical literature, the most frequently cited obstacles to the development of an effective school council are power struggles and political conflict (Flinspach & Ryan, 1994), lack of council role definition

(Furtwengler, Furtwengler, Holcomb, Hurst, & Owens, 1995), difficulty in recruiting parent members, and lack of training for members (Vasquez, 1991). Commonly identified strategies for addressing these obstacles include provision of training (Ovando, 1994) and creation of a committee structure—principally teacher teams to assist the council (Odden, 1995). Clarification of council roles and tasks (Jenni, 1991), provision of substantial power to the council (Odden & Odden, 1996), and provision of greater sources of information (Odden & Odden, 1996) also have been identified as strategies for implementing school councils. Some evidence suggests that an "instructional guidance" system serves to focus the council on teaching and learning (Wohlstetter, Smyer, & Mohrman, 1994).

Although the empirical evidence about obstacles and strategies is relatively extensive in quantity, the research designs used in its production do not establish robust causal links between the strategies that foster the implementation of effective councils and the subsequent contributions of these councils to teaching and learning. Some promising theoretical work on this problem has been reported by Wohlstetter and her colleagues (e.g., Mohrman et al., 1994; Wohlstetter et al., 1994), who themselves rely heavily on Lawler's (1986) conception of the "high-involvement" or high-performance organization. According to this perspective, the promise of SBM and school councils is to be found in the stimulation of more participative forms of management and greatly increased involvement of those lower in the organizational hierarchy. Lawler's work adds up to a persuasive case that these changes have a significant effect on such key determinants of organizational effectiveness as employee motivation, satisfaction, acceptance of change, problem-solving expertise, and quality of communication.

Of particular interest to Wohlstetter and her colleagues has been what Lawler identified as the four central requirements for legitimate participation—knowledge and skill, power, information, and rewards. These are what must be moved down to the lowest possible level in the hierarchy if organizations are to become more effective. Furthermore, for this to happen many or most aspects of an organization's design may need to be altered over time so as to provide a coherent and supportive context for the distribution of such knowledge, power, information, and rewards.

External conditions. In addition to the school-level factors just discussed, evidence from prior research has begun to identify features—in the wider context in which councils work—that both inhibit and foster their effectiveness. Most of this evidence concerns parents and the school system.

A number of factors associated with parents mitigate against the effective development of councils. Some of these factors are parents' attitudes and beliefs, including (a) adherence to traditional roles (David, 1994; Jewell & Rosen, 1993), (b) lack of interest in educational issues beyond the needs of their own children (David, 1994; Jenni, 1991), (c) low expectations for children (Davies, 1993), (d) negative attitudes concerning the role of schools in responding to social inequities (Davies, 1993), and (e) lack of respect for and trust in teachers (Easton et al., 1991). Also depressing the development of council effectiveness are excessive demands on parents' time (Hallinger, Murphy, & Hausman, 1992) and lack of meaningful contact by parents with schools (Davies, 1993).

School councils develop well when parents are clear about their roles and the goals of the council (Collins, Cooper, & Whitmore, 1995), when there is encouragement for parents to become involved (Sebring et al., 1995), and when they have access to professional development for their participation (Grant, 1994). Also reported to be helpful to council development is expert knowledge among parents about some of the issues facing councils or about effective group processes and oral fluency (Chapman & Boyd, 1986).

Administrators and other staff working at the system level sometimes behave in ways that seriously hinder the work of school councils. Among the more often noted are (a) failure to make available to councils the training, resources, and other support they require (Stevenson & Pellicier, 1992; Vasquez, 1991) and (b) insufficient delegation of power (Collins et al., 1995; Stevenson & Pellicier, 1992). Lack of willingness on the administrator's part to become less bureaucratic (Fine, 1993; Hess, 1994) and resistance to changes proposed by councils (Hess, 1995; Jenni, 1991) inhibit councils' work, as do unresolved tensions between the school system and teacher unions (David, 1994; Lopez, 1992).

School system staff promote council effectiveness by providing adequate training and other resources, establishing clear guidelines for council work, and ensuring clear communication with schools and councils about issues of mutual concern and responsibility (Lopez, 1992; Odden & Wohlstetter, 1995; Vasquez, 1991).

Principals and Councils

Almost all of the existing evidence concerning forms of leadership helpful in fostering the work of school councils is about the leadership provided by school principals. Indeed, principals have demonstrated a remarkable capacity to either derail community-dominated councils to retain decision-making control for themselves (e.g., Malen & Ogawa, 1992) or ensure council effectiveness (Furtwengler et al., 1995; Hess, 1995; Yanguas & Rollow, 1994).

Leadership practices reported to be helpful in fostering the work of community control school councils include creating participatory decision-making structures (Odden, 1995; Odden & Wohlstetter, 1995) and fostering collaborative work among council members (Odden & Wohlstetter, 1995; Yanguas & Rollow, 1994). Clearly defining goals and roles for parents and for the council as a whole (Odden, 1995) seems to be a helpful leadership practice, as does acting as information provider, motivator, and friend of the council (Odden, 1995; Odden & Odden, 1996). Leaders help when they encourage councils to maintain a focus on students and their learning (Odden & Wohlstetter, 1995) and when they focus their efforts on monitoring progress (Flinspach & Ryan, 1994).

Teachers and Councils

Professional commitment and involvement of teachers have been identified as essential to the change process and the establishment of school councils in Chicago (e.g., Flinspach & Ryan, 1994; Hess, 1994). Interaction among teachers around issues of curriculum and teaching appear to be a critical intervening variable in a decentralized system (Hannaway & Carnoy, 1993). Wohlstetter et al. (1994) observed that in active versus struggling SBM schools, teachers had more control over instructional direction, more opportunities to meet and discuss educational issues, and places available for such discussion. Chapman and Boyd (1986) reported that politically active and young staff have an increased interest in and commitment to school success, more involvement in professional development, and confidence in their ability to exercise influence.

School Council Decision-Making Processes and
Other Conditions

The extensive literature on effective team learning (e.g., Janis, 1982; Ketchum & Trist, 1992) and group decision making (e.g., Brightman, 1988; Worchel, Wood, & Simpson, 1992) go some distance toward identifying the individual and collective skills members of effective school councils will need to possess or acquire and apply. But some of the literature already reviewed begins to suggest that councils—because they bring together professional, client, and nonprofessional potentially powerful members—may have unique dynamics as well. In a more exaggerated form than a corporate team, council members have very different backgrounds and potentially disparate and conflicting agendas. This helps explain why power struggles and political conflict are the most frequently cited obstacles to council effectiveness (e.g., Hallinger et al., 1992; Jewell & Rosen, 1993).

Other factors associated with councils' effectiveness include: (a) the make-up of the council (Wohlstetter et al., 1994); (b) the type and quality of the in-service provided to council members (Chapman & Boyd, 1986; Chavkin & Williams, 1987; Daresh, 1992; Davies, 1987; Epstein, 1995; Flinspach & Ryan, 1994; Ford & Bennett, 1994; Hess & Easton, 1991; Malen & Ogawa, 1988; Wohlstetter et al., 1994); (c) parents' educational knowledge and cultural resources (Fine, 1993); (d) council members' genuine involvement in topics salient to the school instructional program (Daresh, 1992; Jenni, 1991; Malen, Ogawa, & Kranz, 1990); (e) the establishment of clear goals, objectives, and purpose for the council (Daresh, 1992; Jenni, 1991); and (f) the governance style of the council itself (Easton & Storey, 1994).

Method

Data were collected in two stages in one large school district 1 year after the implementation of advisory school councils. This district had identified school council implementation as a board priority, developed its own policy on school councils, and provided in-service to administrators and school council teams. Each stage of data collection served different purposes and featured different data collection and analysis techniques to realize the strengths associated with multimethod research (Brewer & Hunter, 1989).

Stage 1

The primary purpose of this stage was to identify a sample of schools suitable for more detailed qualitative study in Stage 2. After field testing, a 16-item survey was distributed to all teachers in each of the 46 elementary and 5 secondary schools in the district. This instrument, requiring about 15 min to complete, asked teachers to estimate the influence of their school's council on their school and classroom practices. It asked, as well, about their knowledge of their council's functioning, characteristics of the council, and the nature of school–parent relationships. Returns were received from a total of 631 teachers in all schools, approximately 50% of the district's total population of teachers.

Stage 2

Results of the survey data were used to select five schools for the study's second stage. These were the two schools with the highest mean influence ratings, two schools with the lowest mean influence ratings, and one school in which teachers reported neutral council influence. The purpose of this stage was to collect interview evidence about conditions mediating councils' influence, principal and teacher practices, and council characteristics and processes.

Interviews were conducted with approximately 9 to 11 people in each school, a total of 50 open-ended interviews with parent council members ($n = 15$), student council members ($n = 3$), teacher council members ($n = 7$), principals ($n = 5$), and noncouncil teachers ($n = 20$). Each interview lasted about 60 min and was transcribed, coded, and analyzed using a modified grounded theory approach (Strauss & Corbin, 1990). This analysis was guided by the original research questions and framework of variables, but was sufficiently fluid to permit deviations as data were grouped and regrouped during analysis. Individual interview responses were aggregated first to the school level, and then cross-school comparisons of patterns in the data were completed.

Results and Discussion

Extent and Nature of Council Influence

Extent of influence. Table 1 summarizes teacher survey ratings of council's influence on their work, aggregated across all schools. Elementary and secondary teacher ratings are also reported separately. Teachers rated council influence as minimal, just above *no influence* but less than *moderately positive*, with elementary teachers rating influence higher both inside and outside the classroom than secondary teachers. The overall mean rating for school council influence on a 5-point scale ranging from −2 (*stipulated in the survey as significant negative*) to +2 (*stipulated as significant positive*) in the classroom was 0.31, with a standard deviation of 0.66. For council influence outside the classroom the mean rating was 0.41, with a standard deviation of 0.69.

Table 1
School Council Influence on Teacher Practices Outside and Inside the Classroom

| | Total Sample | | | | Elementary | | | | Secondary | | | |
| | Outside | | Inside | | Outside | | Inside | | Outside | | Inside | |
Influence	%	n	%	n	%	n	%	n	%	n	%	n
Significant positive	5	30	4	24	6	27	5	23	2	3	1	1
Moderate positive	38	232	27	165	42	195	31	146	25	37	13	19
None	52	318	67	413	46	214	60	282	71	104	87	131
Moderate negative	5	31	2	14	6	28	3	14	2	3	0	
Significant negative	1	4	0	3	1	4	1	3	0		0	
M	0.41		0.31		0.46		0.37		0.27		0.14	
SD	0.69		0.66		0.73		0.66		0.53		0.37	
Total surveyed	615		619		468		468		147		151	

The mean rating for influence of school councils on teachers' work outside the classroom was 0.46 by elementary teachers and 0.27 by secondary teachers. This difference is statistically significant ($t = 3.31$, $df = 335$, $p < .01$). Although both groups rated influence inside the classroom lower, the difference between the groups was somewhat greater with an elementary teacher mean rating of 0.37 and a secondary teacher rating of 0.14 ($t = 5.38$, $df = 462$, $p < .01$).

Data from the survey were aggregated at the individual school level to identify five school sites for further case study analysis according to the extent that teachers reported school council influence on their work. Teachers in schools subsequently referred to as C and D reported that their school's council had a positive influence on classroom practices. Teachers in Schools A and B reported a negative influence, and School E teachers reported little to no influence on classroom practices. These data are summarized in Table 2 (see columns labeled Stage 1: Survey). Teacher ratings of council influence inside the classroom were significantly higher in Schools C and D than in A, B, or E. Influence on classroom practice was significantly higher in School E than B ($F = 10.01$, $df = 473$, $p < .01$). Influence at the school level was significantly higher in School D than either B or A, and higher in Schools C and E than School B ($F = 5.29$, $df = 473$, $p < .01$). In all schools, with the exception of D, teachers reported influence at the school level to be greater or equal to influence in the classroom.

Interview data collected as part of Stage 2 also asked about perceived council influence. Table 2 compares the relative influence reported in the interviews with the influence reported in the surveys. School rank is indicated for both sets of data and the mean rank is reported, with lowest influence ranked 1 and highest ranked 5. Survey and interview results were

Table 2

Comparison of Survey and Interview Data for School Council Influence Across the School and on the Classroom

| | Stage 1: Survey | | | | Stage 2: Interview | | | | | |
| | School | | Classroom | | School | | | Classroom | | |
School	M	Rank	M	Rank	%	n/total	Rank	%	n/total	Rank
A	0.19	2	−0.06	2	20	1/5	2	0	0/5	2.5
B	−0.27	1	−0.36	1	0	0/5	1	−20	−1/5	1
C	1.00	4	1.00	4	100	6/6	4.5	66	4/6	4
D	1.17	5	1.40	5	100	5/5	4.5	100	6/6	5
E	0.43	3	0.22	3	60	3/5	3	0	0/6	2.5

Note. n = number who responded yes; total = total teachers interviewed who answered question on influence; rank 1 = lowest.

consistent in identifying School C and D councils as having more influence on classroom practice than those of School A, B, or E councils. Teacher interview data also indicated differences in teachers' views as to whether their school's council should influence the classroom and their expectations for it to do so. In those schools (C and D) where the councils had greater influence, teachers expected that to be the case.

Nature of influence.   At Schools C and D, councils were involved in discussions regarding school direction or the school's management plan. These initiatives were compatible with the direction of the school and were endorsed, supported, and assisted by the staff and parent community. Teachers at both C and D schools commented on high levels and diverse types of parental involvement in their classrooms and schools, as well as feelings of parental support:

> If you have a parent group who is really backing, maybe not just you but backing education and school and everything else, you tend to work really hard to keep that going because it's important. ... They support our initiatives. (Teacher)

Parents were perceived by staff to be involved in their children's learning, and teachers believed their councils had influenced the school:

> That's why they are setting them up with all these different parameters, and certainly I think our people do make decisions that affect the school and shape it. (Teacher)

These councils distinguished themselves from councils in other schools by their high involvement in initiatives designed to foster school partnerships in the community and to enhance student learning opportunities. The addition of advisory school councils supported and strengthened existing school programs, initiated others, and enabled these councils to have influence in the relatively brief 10-month period of their existence. Other evidence has indicated that structural changes in schools (e.g., site-based management) are typically unsuccessful unless they are embedded within other conditions (Epstein, 1995; Lawler, 1986; Mohrman et al., 1994; Robertson, Wohlstetter, & Mohrman, 1995) and considered as more than instruments for the redistribution of power (Daresh, 1992; Tyack, 1993). The results of this study support these claims. In those schools where councils' initiatives were part of the overall goals of the school, councils had a positive, school-level influence.

Conditions Accounting for School Councils' Influence

School conditions. Three conditions in the school separated more from less influential school councils. First, staff involvement in professional development differed considerably across the five schools with more involvement and positive comments about opportunities from such involvement by staff of Schools C, D, and E. In these schools, teachers cited involvement in school staff presentations, leadership training, action research teams, staff in-services, mentoring opportunities, board level involvement, new initiatives taking place at the school, and involvement in school decision making. For example:

> Our administrators have done everything they can to make it easy for people to develop professionally. Money is available for each and every teacher to go to in-services. … They have brought in supply teachers and we were able to learn how to write outcome-based units and we have consultants there at our disposal. (Teacher)

Secondly, more and less influential councils were distinguished by the extent to which there was a sense of partnership or "teamness." This was the most striking condition of the three. At Schools C and D, interviewees identified the strong partnership or collaborative relationship that existed between the school staff and the council and between the parents, staff, and principal.

> I think the whole idea of support, that parents are here as part of a team. We are not here to fight with each other certainly but we are here to really support one another. (Principal)

> I'm just glad that our school council is the way it is, we get along, and it's a team effort, and there is not a power struggle. (Teacher representative on school council)

This seems to be accounted for by the good communication, enthusiasm, staff appreciation, and knowledge of school council efforts frequently mentioned by School C and D staff, in contrast with doubts about council and lack of knowledge of council efforts, which are evident in comments by several interviewees from Schools B, A, and E.

Third, the history, extent, and nature of parental involvement in the school prior to the establishment of councils differed across the five schools. Interviewees at four schools cited the existence of a previous parents' group (29 mentions) with respondents at Schools C, D, and E commenting on the relatively smooth transition from this group to the school council:

I don't think things have changed a great deal from when it was a parents' council to a school council. The procedures are pretty well the same, the goals are still the same. Like when we get together we discuss the finances and where money can be spent. (Teacher representative on school council)

Twenty-one interviewees commented on high parental involvement. Of these, nine were from School C and eight were from School D, where principals described parental involvement as having both breadth and depth. Areas of involvement included: lunch programs, yard supervision, fund raising, drivers, special events, library, graduation, integrated learning center, Peace Program, and initiatives designed to build school pride and student motivation. This contrasts with data from Schools A and B, where involvement in the classroom and school was low. Some parents commented that parental involvement was not encouraged.

Eight interviewees from School C, and three from School D, felt that parent input was welcomed and recognized:

[Parents] know how the school works, they help out and do what they can. (Teacher)

...We are talking true volunteers, like moms who have kids in grade 3 and 4 and volunteer to help in the cooking program in Junior Kindergarten so that their child doesn't receive the direct benefit. (Teacher)

Only one such comment was made about School B. Three interviewees from School A did not believe parent input was welcomed, and four from School B perceived some parents as political. Eight interviewees from School E said that parents did not want to be involved at the high school level, and four noted the school's history of low parental involvement. School E did have a roster of about 40 volunteer parents, however, who did not choose to be members of the school council, but who were available for parent input when contacted.

In summation, schools with more influential councils had greater staff involvement in professional development, a greater sense of partnership with the council, and considerably more parent involvement in the school prior to the introduction of school councils. Our results are consistent with those of Flinspach and Ryan (1994). They observed that "a school community's approach to improvement is affected by the condition of the school at the start of reform, the leadership of its principal [discussed later], and the professional commitment of its staff" (p. 303).

External conditions. Five district conditions and one concerning the school community were associated, in our results, with councils' influence. District conditions included board involvement with and subsequent support of school councils, school council in-service, provision of materials for councils, and board support of the school.

Six interviewees from School A did not believe the board was involved with school councils, and one did not believe the board supported teachers. At School E, only one interviewee believed the board supported councils, five felt it was ambivalent, and two did not believe the board supported teachers. One, five, and four interviewees from B, C, and D schools, respectively, were not aware of the board's role. Four interviewees at School E believed the board was nonconsultative; others commented on the board's bureaucratic stance, lack of partnership with the school, and limited information provided to school councils.

Interviewees at C and D schools commented positively on improved school facilities, resources and professional development opportunities for teachers, and new curriculum initiatives from the board:

> A lot of things that we do are on our own time. This conflict resolution course was during school time but we take a lot of in-services, our board offers a lot of in-services at night, like after school, 4:00–6:00. Our school is very good at participating at these things. (Teacher)

Opinions and attendance at board-provided in-services on school councils varied. Attendance from the School D council was the highest, with attendees commenting that in-services were beneficial. Attendees from Schools B and E expressed dissatisfaction with the in-services. Six interviewees from School A were aware of the in-services, but only two attended. Several School E and B interviewees commented positively on the Board-designed Handbook for School Councils, stating they refer to it for role clarity and council responsibilities:

> Well this year, we went through that book, we decided on the two issues and that's where we went from and that's what we worked on, we were very clear on our focus this year for that very reason. (Parent)

Relationships between the school and the district, distinguishing more from less influential councils in this study, also have been identified in other studies as influencing the ability of SBM, more generally, to affect school practices. Murphy and Beck (1995, p. 165) cited examples of boards and districts that actively or passively resisted the implementation of councils as threats to their authority. Clune and White (as cited in Murphy & Beck, 1995) concluded "that the effectiveness of SBM is limited by superintendents and central administrators who are reluctant to share authority" (p. 165).

School enrollment in the four elementary schools (A, B, C, and D) ranged between 200 and 350 students. In addition to their small size, Schools C and D were situated in small, rural, stable communities. Interviewees at both A and B schools commented on a more transient school population and the diverse socioeconomic and cultural background of their communities:

> This is an old school, it's a community where you don't normally get a lot of parent involvement. You know it is a lot of second language and people are not comfortable, but we are seeing more people. (Teacher)

These data suggest a relation between school size, community stability, and council's influence on school and classroom practices. The cohesiveness of the small community, coupled with council member's involvement in the community and school and the ease with which the principal could become involved and known in the community, may enhance council's ability to influence the school. Respondents at Schools C and D cited new partnerships with local businesses, school articles in the local press, community pride in their school, principal meetings with neighboring schools, community-supported fund raising, and parent- and community-supported programs offered by the school on parenting.

The challenge for larger schools, suggested by these results, is to create at least some of those conditions that require less effort to develop in smaller schools: It is the conditions, not the smallness, that is fundamentally important. That this is not entirely impossible is illustrated by the relatively large secondary school in our study (E) that did a better job of providing these conditions than two of the much smaller elementary schools (A and B).

Principals and Councils

Evidence concerning principal leadership and council function is reported in this section, as well as the section on council processes. This section is limited to the practices of principals that provided either a supportive or nonsupportive context for council influence in the school. The section on council processes reports what it is that principals did directly with councils that either facilitated or hampered their work.

Earlier research cites principal leadership style on council as an important factor in council's ability to influence policies. Malen and Ogawa (1988) speculated that councils were limited in their ability to influence when they were principal-controlled. Flinspach and Ryan (1994) observed that teachers and parents experimented with new programs in those Chicago schools where principals knew "how to build consensus and encourage collaboration" (p. 304). Our evidence supports these earlier results. More specifically, our evidence suggests that principals' contribution to councils' influence is a product of the personal support they demonstrate for their councils, their own involvement on the councils, their ability to involve others, and their tenure in the school.

Interviewees in the schools of more influential councils more frequently mentioned a general attitude of receptivity and support for the council, and of the staff more broadly, on the part of principals (14 interviewees at Schools C and D but only 6 respondents at Schools A and E). They noted, as well, the principals' availability and receptivity to professional development initiatives and his interest in introducing and supporting new programs in the school:

> [Parents] support us, and they will come in as volunteers also and help with some of the groupings when we have [principal organized common planning time] days. (Teacher)

Interviewees perceived the School C principal, who was council co-chair, to be very involved with the council. He shared with the council the school management plan, board policies, and ministry initiatives; facilitated council in-service on curriculum issues with board consultants; implemented a parent section in the library; and actively involved council members in curriculum issues.

Interviewees at Schools C and D noted their principal's willingness to share decision making with them. For example:

> I think the council is as good as the principal is and I think that we probably will be able to have some impact in the classroom because our principal is so amenable and he is quite receptive to what we have to say. (Parent)

Principals at C, D, and E schools shared their vision of the school with staff and parents, encouraged parent input, provided opportunity for professional development, and facilitated collaboration among staff and between staff and parents. They openly acknowledged the importance and value of the school council and were committed to finding an effective way to work with parents. School D principal arranged council in-service by board consultants on curriculum changes and had encouraged members to discuss boundary changes with the board. This mirrored the action of the School E principal who encouraged council members to attend board meetings.

Meaningful involvement among the key players has been cited by others as a variable affecting councils' influence (Mohrman et al., 1994; Robertson et al., 1995; Wohlstetter et al., 1994).

Interviewees (16) at three schools commented on principal turnover. Five of these comments were from School D, where interviewees were anticipating a new principal next year. Seven interviewees noted the difficult transition between principals at School B, and three mentioned a favorable transition at School E. The lack of evidence concerning principal support—notably trust, receptivity, or sharing—at School B may be explained by a difficult transition: Three interviewees at School B believed the principal influenced their negative response to councils. This principal stated that his mid-year appointment as a new principal was difficult for both the council and himself. Little time was available for the council and principal to gain some common understanding of each other. This had forced him to become more "political" and cautious, which in turn influenced staff's response to their school council. On the other hand, a harmonious principal succession had occurred at School E at the beginning of the school year.

Principal tenure has been noted by Robertson et al. (1995) as a possible mediating variable in facilitating the implementation of school reforms. Length of principal tenure was seen as a possible mediating variable in the introduction of curriculum and instructional changes in SBM schools.

Teachers and Councils

Teachers' descriptions of a new practice that they had introduced into their classroom, how they learned the change, and staff behavior that helped or hindered them were used to compare individual teacher behavior and staff professional behavior across the five schools. Many individual teacher practices for learning and introducing a change were common across all schools including self-teaching, trial and error learning, individual university courses, reading, modification of a board unit, and personal exploration. A minimum of one teacher from each school had attended board in-service to support learning a new practice. Teachers at Schools C, D, and E, where there appeared to be a greater focus on professional development, described specific opportunities for the sharing and dissemination of this information:

Our board offers a lot of in-services at night. ... Our staff is very good at participating at these. ... When they go to a course, and something is really good they present it to us. We have staff meetings twice a month after school. One staff meeting is a business staff meeting and the second staff meeting is a professional development staff meeting. (Teacher)

School E had a leadership team responsible for in-servicing teams of teachers, and School D had monthly staff meetings devoted to professional development in which teachers, with or without the principal, provided in-service to their colleagues. One teacher at School C had partnered with a second teacher on a Team Teaching Track. With the exception of School B, teachers cited discussion with and support of their principal as important in learning how to make a change:

> Our principal is wonderful. He would take our classes for half a day so that we can plan. Or somehow he will get a supply teacher, maybe once a year and we can have a supply teacher for half a day. And he is very good at organizing that. But he doesn't hesitate at all in taking our classes for half a day also so that we can do that. (Teacher)

At Schools C, D, and E, "collaborative" was a frequent staff descriptor. Staff at School D commented that council members had assisted the principal to supervise classes to enable teachers to participate in school-based professional development activities, conferences, and planning. Several teachers at Schools C, D, and E described their principal as a facilitator and supporter of professional development. Comments about professional development opportunities from staff at School A varied: Some did not believe there was a focus on, or money available for, professional development, while others did; one referenced support received from the principal. One teacher at School B commented on a change in the school's professional development priorities that coincided with the arrival of the new principal. Teachers in Schools C, D, and E schools noted staff involvement in school decision making.

Staff differed across the schools in their levels of apprehension about, and comfort with, school councils. Teachers at Schools A, B, and E were the most outspoken about their concerns: School B teachers feared the subtle indications from council members that they would be in a position of hiring and firing; several teachers from School A expressed concern about council involvement in curriculum; and one teacher at School B believed councils were in conflict with the expressed intention of the *Royal Commission's Report on Learning*. School E staff appeared more concerned about overall changes in education and the direction of the government, whereas School C teachers made little reference to ongoing educational changes. Staff morale at School C appeared to be relatively high.

Teachers in the five schools differed in terms of their sharing of information, their sense of belonging to a team, and their perception of their principal's involvement. When these characteristics were evident, and where there was collaboration among the staff and between the staff and the councils, the councils tended to be have greater influence on school and classroom practices.

In sum, in schools where principals encouraged and facilitated professional development, where structures were in place for the sharing of information, where teachers were initiators, and where staff were engaged in learning, councils had the greater positive influence. Such conditions have been identified by others as fundamental to the change process and to the establishment of local school councils in Chicago (Flinspach & Ryan, 1994; Hess, 1994). Wohlstetter et al. (1994) also observed that in actively restructuring schools where there was a push for curriculum and instruction reform, teachers had more opportunities to meet and discuss educational issues. There was a greater interest in professional development (individually and collectively), continuous improvement, and training beyond district offerings. In these schools, staff generally had "more mechanisms for participation in the governance of the school, and a greater percentage of the faculty were involved" (Wohlstetter et al., p. 283). The involvement of teachers in school councils, through either their input or expressed support, also is in agreement with research by Sebring et al. (1995) on Chicago school councils: "Successful improvement efforts are highly unlikely unless teachers seriously engage the reform" (p. 1).

*School Council Decision-Making Processes and
Other Conditions*

Interviewees were asked to comment on council initiatives, central purposes, meeting characteristics, the principal's role on the council, and relationships among council members. Respondents at Schools C and D commented most favorably about these matters. A total of 11 interviewees at these two schools believed that there were no constraints affecting their councils. Frequent comments were made about clarity of roles, knowledge of responsibilities, and members' attempts to be cautious in their approach to the school. In contrast, there were many negative comments at Schools A, B, and E where eight, four, and five interviewees, respectively, commented on the need for greater clarity about the role of the council.

Council initiatives. Members of School C and D councils identified two to three times as many council initiatives as members of School A, B, and E councils, and there was a significant difference in the nature of those initiatives. At Schools A and B, initiatives were directed more toward fund-raising, the physical needs of the school, and the purchase of classroom materials. Councils' focus at Schools C and D was broader. Members were involved in many initiatives, and there were subcommittees aligned directly with the schools' growth plans. Examples of these initiatives included not only fund raising but also curriculum initiatives, parent volunteer programs, and special events. One council member at School D claimed that purchases "were tied very closely to where we are going as a school" and that staff and council members worked together to plan and purchase materials. At School D an improved communication network between the school and the community was identified as a council priority. Initiatives mentioned at School E included board presentations and submissions, an educational forum with local members of parliament, and involvement in financial issues.

Central purposes. The primary, explicit goal of each council was very general, and some interviewees from all schools intimated that their council had not defined its primary purposes. Several councils were in the process of seeking parental and staff input regarding council direction and planned to use the information to establish council priorities and goals for their second year. Council members in each school claimed that they wanted to make a difference, to improve education at the local level, but none were clear about how they should do this. Short-term goals focused on increasing parental involvement (A), improving the school community (B), working with and supporting the school to provide the best for their children (C), enhancing school spirit and pride for the benefit of the school and students (D), and trying to create the best possible learning environment for students while maintaining council membership (E).

Respondents at four schools stated the motivation for their involvement on school council was intrinsic: They believed that they were improving the school. They drew attention to positive comments from teachers, parents, other council members, and the principal that led them to believe their efforts were appreciated. This view was most prevalent in School C (six comments).

Meeting characteristics. All councils reported monthly meetings of between 1.5 and 2 hr, with meetings generally scheduled in the evening. Agendas were set jointly by the principal and chair and, at Schools B, C, D, and E, were forwarded to members in advance of the meeting. Items could be added to the agenda by contacting either the principal or chair. At School

B items could be added to the agenda at the meeting, which the principal described as an open forum design.

Each council, with the exception of School B, anticipated new members for the fall as some positions terminated the first year. Staff representatives at each school had volunteered for the position. All interviewees at Schools C, D, and E agreed that their meetings were well run; this was the case, as well, for most at School B. Only two members interviewed at School A believed this to be the case, citing as reasons ineffective leadership, lengthy agenda without timelines, power struggles, members' frustration, and lack of direction and knowledge.

In contrast, the most frequently mentioned council conditions at School C were consensus decision making, an agenda that was followed, opportunity for input, organized structure, and a comfortable environment. This was similar to School D, where conditions mentioned included complementary roles played by members, clearly specified formal roles, organized agenda, the presence of a facilitator/timekeeper, and effective co-chairs. At School E, frequently mentioned conditions included the opportunity for input, a comfortable environment, an effective chair, and the opportunity for everyone to assume a leadership role.

Principals' role. There was a high level of congruence across all schools with respect to the principal's role as provider of information. This is consistent with evidence, reported by Ford and Bennett (1994), about the role of the principal following the Chicago School Reform Act. Principals had "assumed the responsibility of being the information provider" (p. 241) and had an increased public relations role with the council, staff, and community.

In four schools, interviewees commented on the principal's role as a liaison between the council and the staff and between the council and the community. The principal of School D acknowledged his increased public relation's responsibility as a result of council's initiative to improve communication between the school and the community. The School C principal organized all volunteer involvement in the school, information nights on parenting, and issues relating to children. He was recognized by staff and parents as community oriented. School E interviewees viewed both the current and previous principal as council supporters and characterized them as spokespersons for both the council and school.

The principal at School C believed council leadership should be shared. He endorsed the council; believed that it was a vehicle for parents to share their concerns; and considered it to be a forum for the principal to share, listen, and effectively bring about change: He was strongly supported by staff and parents. The School D principal actively assisted in the evolution of the parents' group to the school council. He was interactive with council members; he mentored the chair; and parents felt he was the impetus for the enthusiasm and pride students, staff, and parents felt about the school. He saw the advantage of a school council as a group of local experts who know the school and the school community. The principal of School E viewed himself as a member of the team with the specific role of advisor or guide. He discussed his own expectations and beliefs with the council and believed with its endorsement it was easier for him to acquire staff approval. The council provided him with a natural liaison between the school and parents who could be easily mobilized for collective discussion. He believed it was important to know parents' perspective on education and learning.

In sum, principals at School C and D, where interviewees reported greatest council influence, articulated their vision of the school with staff and the school council and were receptive, sharing, and supportive of staff. These principals involved staff in decision making, asked for their input, and were involved with and endorsed their school councils. They also encouraged, supported, and facilitated professional development opportunities for staff, and, as a consequence, were trusted and supported by staff and their school councils. Providing information, knowledge, and skills to their school councils was an important set of functions carried out by these principals, who also served as liaison between the school, the council, and the community. They acted as guides and facilitators of their school councils and were considered as part of the school and school council team.

Council members' relationships.   An important set of conditions differentiating positively influential councils from those that were not was the relationship or the dynamics among the people involved. In those schools where councils had the greater influence, the principal, teachers, and members of the councils were described as cohesive, collaborative, sharing, and a team. Although each brought a different perspective, each believed their input was recognized and valued. This parallels research by Easton and Storey (1994) on local school councils in Chicago. They concluded that balanced governance councils exhibited strong democratic tendencies, members shared a common interest in school improvement, members discussed their goals and plans, and the principal offered information to facilitate better council decisions.

In this study, these same factors were noted at C and D schools. Council members were knowledgeable of school direction, and initiatives were effectively designed for school improvement, were supported by the school as a whole, and were facilitated by the principal. Members believed that they were accountable to the school community. Council's focus at both schools clearly centered on children and their local school. Council members of positively influential schools were the clearest about their roles and responsibilities. They had the largest attendance at board-provided in-service and received ongoing in-service from their principals on school, board, and provincial policies.

Conclusion

The conclusion to our previous study of school councils (Leithwood, Jantzi, & Steinbach, 1999) raised serious reservations about the likelihood that SBM and school councils would normally contribute to the accountability, autonomy, efficiency, or equity of schools. These four criteria, to which we added effectiveness as a fifth, were used by Bullock and Thomas (1997) in their analysis of decentralizing initiatives in 11 countries. Evidence from the study reported in this article does little to change our conclusion.

But it is increasingly apparent that, under certain conditions, councils can be useful tools for parent participation and a positive, if moderate, force for school and classroom change. In combination with the legislative requirement that schools establish such councils, this suggests an urgent need to foster the development of these conditions in as many schools as possible. And the likelihood of widespread efforts to make the most of councils directs attention to three issues that we consider here by way of conclusion. These are issues that, one way or another, are concerned with necessary and sufficient conditions for school council and SBM contributions to school improvement.

Key Variable Issue

The first of these issues—Is there one especially critical variable on which everything else depends?—was raised by Beck and Murphy (1998) in their recent attempt to untangle the variables accounting for the effects of SBM. From a case study of one school, they concluded that a commitment to foster student learning might be such a variable. It is a superordinate "imperative" that gives meaning and purpose to three additional and critical commitments, according to the authors: a commitment to capacity building among staff, a commitment to developing a strong sense of community in the school, and a commitment to assume responsibility for honoring these other commitments—a "leadership imperative."

Evidence from both this and our previous study of school councils (Leithwood, Jantzi, & Steinbach, 1999) supports the importance that Beck and Murphy (1998) attributed to all four "imperatives." Significant signs of each imperative were found in those schools in which school councils were relatively influential, whereas the imperatives were much less in evidence in schools with councils that had no, or negative, influence on school and classroom practices. Based on this same evidence, however, we disagree with their nomination of the superordinate imperative—a commitment to student learning. Now the "rightness" of this commitment is hard to argue with. Indeed, virtually everyone in the education business, from scholars concerned with the moral purposes of schools (e.g., Goodlad, 1984), through right wing conservative policy makers downsizing school budgets, to teachers on strike for better working conditions, claim that they are "doing it for the children."

But is this what accounts for variation in the contribution of school councils to the improvement of teaching and learning? Our data do not suggest this, and it is not what our own reading of Beck and Murphy's (1998) data suggests to us either. Most teachers and administrators do not begin with a strong belief that school councils and SBM will have any positive benefits for students (Leithwood & Menzies, 1998), a belief that seems quite rational in light of the modest amount of available empirical evidence (Leithwood & Menzies, 1998). Rather, our interpretation of the evidence suggests that principal leadership is the key to successfully implementing SBM and school councils—a version of Beck and Murphy's leadership imperative. Strong but supportive and facilitative leadership, what we have described elsewhere as "transformational leadership" (Leithwood, 1994), seems to determine the extent to which teachers eventually come to view greater parent participation as a positive force in their schools. It also seems critical to the development of a sense of professional community in schools (Wiley, 1999) and a commitment to capacity building, as well (Leithwood, 1994). It is difficult for us to imagine the presence of those conditions described in Beck and Murphy's case school in the absence of the talented school leader in that school or someone with comparable values and skills.

Principals such as the one studied by Beck and Murphy (1998), the handful included in our studies of school councils, and those found by Mohrman et al. (1994), continue to play an instructional leadership role in their schools. In addition, however, they interact with a larger number of constituents outside their schools, convince staff that parents are legitimate and useful sources of information, and foster a culture that encourages parents and the community to help make decisions to support school improvement. They establish a collaborative, trusting, and working relationship between the parent community and the school staff in order for meaningful initiatives and discussions to occur in a school council environment. Also, they are able to mediate effective relations between the school and the board so that all stakeholders are knowledgeable about each other's roles and responsibilities and genuine support. If SBM and school councils are to be a positive force for change in schools, increasing attention needs to be devoted to these qualities by those selecting new principals and by those responsible for the preparation of aspiring school administrators and the continuing professional development of incumbents. In addition, further research is needed to investigate new staff roles and responsibilities that foster a more collaborative decision-making approach and that empower staff members to become teacher leaders in the context of new structural arrangements such as school councils.

Comprehensiveness Issue

Our second issue is concerned with how broadly one needs to "cast one's net" to be confident that the conditions necessary for successful SBM and school council implementation have been captured. Although Beck and Murphy's (1998) four imperatives clearly seem to be among the necessary conditions for such implementation, for example, both of our studies of school councils found at least two other major categories of variables to be quite important, which we refer to as "conditions external to the school" and "school council conditions and processes."

According to our results, SBM and school councils are much less likely to influence school and classroom practice in the absence of, for example, supportive district conditions and effective group decision-making processes. Restricting the variables used to explain SBM and school council effects to one "level" (the school) seems to fly in the face of institutional theorists (e.g., Meyer & Rowan, 1991), and advocates of systems thinking (e.g., Senge, 1990) who offer compelling arguments for why the broader organizational and social contexts in which schools find themselves need to be considered if we are to arrive at a more adequate understanding of educational change.

Sufficient knowledge is likely available to provide adequate training to school council members for them to conduct their business in an efficient and effective manner. But there remains a considerable need for the training of many councils, based on this knowledge. In addition, research is needed to unpack the more complete set of organizational and social contextual variables influencing the work of councils.

Authentic Participation Issue

Our third and final issue arises from considering the results of research on SBM and school councils in light of Anderson's (1998) deconstruction of

61

the forms of participation found in schools at the present time. Anderson argued that many contemporary reforms are aimed at increasing the participation in schools of parent, teacher, student, business, and other groups. In practice, however, such participation turns out to be "bogus, superficial, or ineffective" (p. 571). This is the case, Anderson claimed, because the real purpose for such participation is often not the empowerment of these groups, as the rhetoric suggests, but the legitimation of existing educational practices or the legitimation of reforms promoted by policy makers or other advocates without initial, widespread public endorsement.

These two purposes for promoting greater participation of parents in schools (empowerment, legitimation) capture the range of motives of the principals and teachers in our studies of school councils quite well. The principals and teachers in schools in which councils had no influence or a negative influence on school and classroom practices at best sought legitimation of their practices through their school councils. In contrast, staffs in schools with influential councils worked hard to empower parents in many different ways, in addition to the role they were encouraged to play on the councils.

In response to the question, Who participates in what areas, under what conditions, and toward what ends?, Anderson (1998) defined as "authentic" or empowering those forms of participation that include relevant stakeholders; create relatively safe, structured spaces for multiple voices to be heard; aim at greater organizational effectiveness in the short run; and aim at "more equal levels of student achievement and improved social and academic outcomes for all students" (p. 575) in the long run.

It seems unrealistic to expect school councils, by themselves, to meet all four of these criteria for authentic participation. Assuming, however, that authentic participation is a desirable goal for schools to work toward, further research ought to inquire about how school councils can contribute to the more comprehensive efforts of schools to foster authentic participation of all relevant stakeholder groups. How can school staffs productively use school councils as an instrument for developing authentic forms of participation? What does such participation look like in more detail, and does such participation differ in form depending on role? These questions add a distinctly political dimension to our understanding of school councils, usefully expanding the scope of the frameworks guiding much of the research on school councils to date.

References

Anderson, G. (1998). Toward authentic participation: Deconstructing the discourse of participatory reforms in education. *American Educational Research Journal, 35,* 571–603.

Beck, L., & Murphy, J. (1998). Site-based management and school success: Untangling the variables. *School Effectiveness and School Improvement, 9*, 358–385.

Brewer, J., & Hunter, A. (1989). *Multimethod research: A synthesis of styles.* Newbury Park, CA: Sage.

Brightman, H. J. (1988). *Group problem solving: An improved managerial approach.* Atlanta: College of Business Administration, Georgia State University.

Bullock, A., & Thomas, H. (1997). *Schools at the centre? A study of decentralization.* London: Routledge.

Chapman, J., & Boyd, W. (1986). Decentralization, devolution and the school principal: Australian lessons on statewide educational reform. *Educational Administration Quarterly, 22*(4), 28–58.

Chavkin, F., & Williams, D. (1987). Enhancing parent involvement. *Education and Urban Society, 19*, 164–184.

Collins, A., Cooper, J. L., & Whitmore, E. (1995). *Total quality leadership for learning project.* Canada–Newfoundland Cooperation Agreement: Human resource development project HRD(E)93–136 Ottawa.

Daresh, J. (1992). Impressions of school-based management: The Cincinnati story. In J. Lane & E. Epps (Eds.), *Restructuring the schools: Problems and prospects* (pp. 109–121). Berkeley, CA: McCutchan.

David, J. L. (1994). *School-based decision making: Linking decisions to learning (Third year report to the Pritchard committee).* Paper prepared for the Pritchard Committee for Academic Excellence, Lexington, Kentucky.

Davies, D. (1987). Parent involvement in the public schools. *Education and Urban Society, 19*, 147–163.

Davies, D. (1993). Benefits and barriers to parent involvement: From Portugal to Boston to Liverpool. In N. F. Chavkin (Ed.), *Families and schools in a pluralistic society* (pp. 205–216). Albany: State University of New York Press.

Easton, J., Bryk, A. S., Driscoll, M. E., Kotsakis, J. G., Sebring, P. A., & van der Ploeg, A. J. (1991). *Charting reform: The teachers' turn.* Chicago: Consortium on Chicago School Research.

Easton, J., & Storey, S. (1994). The development of local school councils. *Education and Urban Society, 26*, 220–237.

Elmore, R. F., and Associates. (1990). *Restructuring schools: The next generation of educational reform.* San Francisco: Jossey-Bass.

Epstein, J. (1995, May). School/family/community partnerships. *Phi Delta Kappan,* pp. 701–712.

Fine, M. (1993). [Ap]parent involvement: Reflections on parents, power, and urban public schools. *Teachers College Record, 94*, 682–729.

Flinspach, S., & Ryan, S. (1994). Diversity of outcomes. *Education and Urban Society, 26*, 292–305.

Ford, D., & Bennett, A. (1994). The changing principalship in Chicago. *Education and Urban Society, 26*, 238–247.

Furtwengler, C. B., Furtwengler, W. J., Holcomb, E., Hurst, D., & Owens, M. (1995, October). *Shared decision making and school site councils.* Paper presented at the annual meeting of the University Council for Educational Administration, Salt Lake City, Utah.

Goodlad, J. (1984). *A place called school: Prospects for the future.* New York: McGraw-Hill.

Grant, L. R. (1994). *Site-based management: A collage in progress.* Unpublished doctoral dissertation, University of Toronto, Canada.

Hallinger, P., Murphy, J., & Hausman, C. (1992). Restructuring schools: Principals' perceptions of fundamental educational reform. *Educational Administration Quarterly, 28*, 330–349.

Hannaway, J., & Carnoy, M. (Eds.). (1993). *Decentralization and school improvement*. San Francisco: Jossey-Bass.

Hess, G. A., Jr. (1994). School-based management as a vehicle for school reform. *Education and Urban Society, 26,* 203–219.

Hess, G. A., Jr. (1995). *School-based management after 5 years in Chicago: The partnership of parents, community and education*. Chicago: Chicago Panel on Public School Policy and Finance.

Hess, G. A., Jr., & Easton, J. (1991). *Who's making what decision: Monitoring authority shifts in Chicago school reform*. Chicago: Chicago Panel on Public School Policy and Finance.

Hirschman, A. (1970). *Exit, voice, and loyalty*. Cambridge, MA: Harvard University Press.

Janis, I. L. (1982). *Groupthink* (2nd ed.). Boston: Houghton Mifflin.

Jenni, R. (1991). Application of the school-based management process development model. *School Effectiveness and School Improvement, 2,* 136–151.

Jewell, K. E., & Rosen, J. L. (1993, April). *School-based management/shared decision making: A study of school reform in New York City*. Paper presented at the annual meeting of the American Educational Research Association, Atlanta.

Ketchum, L. D., & Trist, E. (1992). *All teams are not created equal: How employee empowerment really works*. Newbury Park, CA: Sage.

Lawler, E., III. (1986). *High-involvement management: Participative strategies for improving organizational performance*. San Francisco: Jossey-Bass.

Leithwood, K. (1994). Leadership for school restructuring. *Educational Administration Quarterly, 30,* 498–518.

Leithwood, K., & Earl, L. (2000/this issue). Educational accountability effects: An international perspective. *Peabody Journal of Education, 75*(4), 1–18.

Leithwood, K., Jantzi, D., & Steinbach, R. (1999). Do school councils matter? *Educational Policy, 13,* 467–493.

Leithwood, K., & Menzies, T. (1998). Forms and effects of school-based management: A review. *Educational Policy, 12,* 325–346.

Lopez, R., Jr. (1992). *Study of school-based management in Texas school districts*. Unpublished doctoral dissertation, Baylor University, Waco, Texas.

Malen, B., & Ogawa, R. (1988). Professional-patron influence on site-based governance councils: A confounding case study. *Educational Evaluation and Policy Analysis, 10,* 251–270.

Malen, B., & Ogawa, R. (1992). Site-based management: Disconcerting policy issues, critical policy choices. In J. J. Lane & E. G. Epps (Eds.), *Restructuring the schools: Problems and prospects* (pp. 185–206). Berkeley, CA: McCutchan.

Malen, B., Ogawa, R., & Kranz, J. (1990). What do we know about school-based management? A case study of the literature. In W. Clune & L. Witte (Eds.), *Choice and control in American education Volume 2: The practice of choice, decentralization and school restructuring* (pp. 289–342). New York: Falmer.

Meyer, J. W., & Rowan, B. (1991). Institutionalized organizations: Formal structure as myth and ceremony. In W. W. Powell & P. J. DiMaggio (Eds.), *The new institutionalism in organizational analysis* (pp. 41–62). Chicago: University of Chicago Press.

Mohrman, S., Wohlstetter, P., & Associates. (1994). *School-based management: Organizing for high performance*. San Francisco: Jossey-Bass.

Murphy, J., & Beck, L. (1995). *School-based management as school reform*. Thousand Oaks, CA: Corwin.

Odden, A. (1995). *Decentralized school management in Victoria, Australia*. Washington, DC: The World Bank.

Odden, A., & Odden, E. (1996, September). *The Victoria, Australia approach to school-site management.* [A Report of research sponsored by the Consortium for Policy Research in Education (CPRE) under a grant from the Carnegie Corporation and the Office of Educational Research and Improvement, U.S. Department of Education, University of Wisconsin, Madison, CPRE].

Odden, E. R., & Wohlstetter, P. (1995, February). Making school-based management work. *Educational Leadership,* pp. 32–36.

Ontario Ministry of Education and Training. (1995, April 12). *Policy/Program Memorandum 122.* Ontario, Canada: Author.

Ovando, M. N. (1994). Effects of site-based management on the instructional program. *Journal of School Leadership, 4,* 311–329.

Robertson, P., Wohlstetter, P., & Mohrman, S. (1995). Generating curriculum and instructional innovations through school-based management. *Educational Administration Quarterly, 31,* 375–404.

Sebring, P., Bryk, A., Easton, J., Luppescu, S., Thum, Y., Lopez, W., & Smith, B. (1995, August). *Charting reform: Chicago teachers take stock.* Report sponsored by the Consortium on Chicago School Research.

Senge, P. (1990). *The fifth discipline.* New York: Doubleday.

Stevenson, K. R., & Pellicier, L. O. (1992). School-based management in South Carolina: Balancing state-directed reform with local decision making. In J. J. Lane & E. G. Epps (Eds.), *Restructuring the schools: Problems and prospects* (pp. 123–139). Berkeley, CA: McCutchan.

Strauss, A., & Corbin, J. (1990). *Basics of qualitative research: Grounded theory procedures and techniques.* Newbury Park, CA: Sage.

Tyack, D. B. (1993). School governance in the United States: Historical puzzles and anomalies. In J. Hannaway & M. Carnoy (Eds.), *Decentralization and school improvement* (pp. 1–32). San Francisco: Jossey-Bass.

Vasquez, R. (1991). *A critical analysis of selected intended and unintended consequences of the Chicago school reform act of 1988.* Unpublished doctoral dissertation, Northern Illinois University, DeKalb.

Wiley, S. D. (1999). *Contextual effects on student achievement: School leadership and professional community.* Unpublished academic article.

Wohlstetter, P., Smyer, R., & Mohrman, S. (1994). New boundaries for school-based management: The high involvement model. *Educational Evaluation and Policy Analysis, 16,* 268–286.

Worchel, S., Wood, W., & Simpson, J. A. (Eds.). (1992). *Group process and productivity.* Newbury Park, CA: Sage.

Yanguas, M., & Rollow, S. (1994). *The rise and fall of adversarial politics in the context of Chicago school reform: Parent participation in a Latino school community.* Unpublished manuscript, Center for School Improvement, University of Chicago.

PEABODY JOURNAL OF EDUCATION, 75(4), 66–89

The Link Between Accountability and Improvement: The Case of Reporting to Parents

Viviane Robinson and Helen Timperley

It is sometimes assumed that increased accountability of teachers, schools, and school districts will produce higher student achievement by motivating better performance of the accountable units than would otherwise be the case (Newmann, King, & Rigdon, 1997; Torrance, 1997). Two different types of research evidence tell us that there is a considerable gap between this intention and the reality. First, the research on accountability-driven school reform provides little evidence that test-based accountability of schools and teachers produces better educational achievement (Mehrens, 1998). It seems obvious that regular reporting of information about student achievement may not be sufficient to produce improvement, yet it seems equally obvious that such reporting might trigger attempts to improve. What we need is clarification of the conditions under which accountability might produce improvement and an understanding of how those conditions can be designed into accountability policies and practices.

VIVIANE ROBINSON *is Associate Professor in the School of Education, University of Auckland, New Zealand.*

HELEN TIMPERLEY *is Senior Lecturer in the School of Education, University of Auckland, New Zealand.*

Requests for reprints should be sent to Viviane Robinson, School of Education, University of Auckland, Private Bag 92019, Auckland, New Zealand. E-mail: vmj.robinson@auckland.ac.nz

Insight into some of those conditions can be gleaned from a second type of accountability research—namely, that which is known within social psychology as *accountability theory* (Lerner & Tetlock, 1999; Tetlock, 1998). Although generalizations from this work can be problematic—because much of it was conducted in an ahistorical laboratory or field experiments—Philip Tetlock, the leading researcher within accountability theory, has reported several empirical and conceptual investigations of workplace accountability processes. This work makes clear that accountability is as likely to trigger compliance or cover-up as it is improvement and that fostering the latter requires particular types of accountability processes (Lerner & Tetlock, 1999).

Our overall purpose in this article is to provide an account of the conditions under which educational accountability might prompt improvement in student achievement. In the first section, we define accountability and then build on that definition to identify and critique the logic that purports to link it to improved student achievement. Our critique draws on accountability theory to identify some of the processes that influence the validity of the accountability judgment, the acceptance of the judgment, and the probability that it motivates improvement.

In the second section of the article, we apply this analysis of accountability to the practices employed by a sample of New Zealand primary schools[1] to inform parents of the educational achievement of their children. As the reporting practices of many of these schools do not meet the conditions that link accountability and improvement, we seek to explain the reasons why and to identify the shifts needed to make them more likely to prompt improvement.

Logic of Accountability and Improvement

Lerner and Tetlock (1999) defined *accountability* as "the implicit or explicit expectation that one may be called on to justify one's beliefs, feelings and actions to others" (p. 255). Justification is a social process that implies an actual or imagined dialogue about the adequacy of the relevant cognition or action. Compare this definition with Kogan's (1986) more behavioral version of accountability. For Kogan, *accountability* is "a condition under which a role holder renders an account to another so that a judgment may be made about the adequacy of the performance" (p. 25). Kogan equates accountability with the act of reporting, whereas Tetlock equates it with an expectation that

[1]New Zealand primary schools cater for Years 0 to 6.

one might have not only to report but also justify. According to Kogan's definition, we strengthen accountability by increasing reporting; on Lerner and Tetlock's we do so by increasing the agent's expectation that others require disclosure and justification of aspects of his or her performance.

Given our interest in the link between accountability and improvement, it is worth asking what each of these types of accountability suggests about how improvement is triggered. Kogan's definition suggests a behavioral model of change in which improvement is motivated by the positively or negatively reinforcing power of others' judgments. In Lerner and Tetlock's more cognitive model, accountable agents actively consider the adequacy of their own performance in anticipation of its justification to others. Lerner and Tetlock's approach holds the promise, counterfactual though it may be, that accountability to others acts as a check on, rather than substitute for, internalized evaluative processes. Tetlock's model suggests we understand accountability by understanding how self-justification is influenced by social and institutional norms of adequacy, not just by studying the technical and procedural features of accountability policies and practices.

If accountability involves the expectation that one may have to justify aspects of cognition and behavior to others, how might this expectation improve performance? The answer to this question involves who is accountable (characteristics of the accountable agent), who one is accountable to (characteristics of the audience), what one is accountable for, and with what consequences. Rather than treat each of these components separately, we adopt a more dynamic approach that makes clear their various interrelationships. For example, whether the accountable agent is motivated to improve is as much a function of the characteristics of the audience as it is of the personality of the individual agent.

In the following discussion, we suggest that accountability promotes improvement when the accountable agents accept the validity of the judgment made about their performance, accept appropriate responsibility for improvement, and have the capacity to achieve it. Validity is central to accountability, for it concerns the quality of these judgments (Shephard, 1993). Validity depends, first, on an adequate match between what is reported and the activity it is meant to represent. There may be a mismatch because the agent's report does not capture what is important, because it is inaccurate, or both. The former concern is expressed, for example, in the debate about whether paper and pencil achievement tests measure the most important outcomes of schooling (Torrance, 1997). If they do not, increased accountability for such results could reduce rather than increase educational quality. The complexity of educative purposes and the difficulty of their measurement mean that it is hard to convey valid representations of educational activities.

Validity may also be jeopardized by inaccurate reporting—attributable to technical deficiencies in procedures—or by the fact that accountable agents are motivated more by the desire to please than by accuracy. The desire to please is a more likely motivator when the audience is a powerful constituency whose views are known in advance (Lerner & Tetlock, 1999). Under such conditions, what is improved is the agent's capacity to report what he or she believes others want to hear, rather than the actual work being done. Such compliance effects are especially likely when the audience is seen to lack the expertise needed to make an independent judgment.

Assuming there is an adequate match between the information reported and the work it is meant to represent, validity will then depend on the quality of the interpretation or evaluation of that information. The essence of accountability is not the reporting, but the expectation that the performance will be evaluated. The validity of the evaluation depends on the implicit or explicit criteria employed and the skill with which they are applied to the information reported.

There are extremely complex issues involved in deciding the appropriate standards to employ in different contexts of educational accountability (Bishop, 1996). When it comes to educational achievement, decisions are needed about whether the standard against which the performance is compared is criterion or norm-referenced, and, if the latter, which population unit provides the most relevant norms. For example, if a norm-referenced standard is used, the achievement of students from disadvantaged schools is much more likely to be judged negatively if compared against national norms than against ones derived from students in similar schools. Although setting a national target for such schools may reflect a laudable desire to reduce social disparities, such targets can be counterproductive if judged as unfair by the accountable unit. In other words, too great a gap between what is typical and what is considered desirable may lead to rejection of the evaluation.

Accountability theory (Tetlock, 1998) suggests that people are more likely to strive to meet high standards when they are seen as attainable, when the procedures for setting them are judged to be fair, and when those standards are justifiable in terms of the organization's survival. Gaining such acceptance is more likely if the views of those who are to be held to account have been influential in setting the standard.

Assuming that the standard is known and agreed to, the validity of the evaluation of performance will depend, in addition, on the skill with which the standard is applied in a particular situation. If either the accountable agent or the audience lacks the relevant skill, they may misunderstand each other and disagree about the need for improvement.

We move now from the validity of the evaluative judgment to the probability that it will motivate improvement. If accountability motivates improvement, it means that the unit takes responsibility, not just for giving an account and justification, but also for reducing any shortfall between current and desired performance (Martin, 1994). We know from the organizational literature that such shortfalls do not necessarily motivate improvement, for they can be lived with, or reduced, by lowering the standard rather than improving the performance (Edmondson, 1996; Fiske & Taylor, 1991). For example, in a school culture of low expectations, parents and staff may treat gaps between achievement targets and actual achievement as inevitable, and rather than motivate improved performance, knowledge of such gaps may motivate efforts to change the targets. Furthermore, uncertainty about how to allocate responsibility for performance across multiple contributors may motivate increased blaming of others, rather than increased commitment to improvement.

Is motivation to improve increased by forms of accountability in which there is not only the expectation of justification of performance, but differential consequences for more and less satisfactory justifications? As Lerner and Tetlock (1999) pointed out, such differential consequences are a common feature of many accountability relationships:

> Accountability also usually implies that people who do not provide a satisfactory justification for their actions will suffer negative consequences ranging from disdainful looks to loss of one's livelihood, liberty, or even life. ... Conversely, people who do provide compelling justifications will experience positive consequences ranging from mitigation of punishment to lavish rewards that, for example, take the form of political office or generous stock options. (p. 255)

What do we know about the impact of such consequences? Laboratory studies show that agents are motivated to please their audience even when the encounter is brief and the audience has had little incentive to reprimand or reward the recipients (Tetlock, 1998). Tetlock then speculated that the desire to gain audience approval will be much greater in real organizational contexts where the audience has enduring authority over the accountable unit. Given that the motivation of the accountable unit is shaped by anticipation of the audience's reaction, the normative basis of that reaction is a key to understanding whether or not accountability promotes improvement. If heavy rewards and penalties are tied to outcome levels that the accountable unit perceives as unfair, powerful incentives are created to manage the indicators of success so that they appear as favorable as possible, rather than to improve the actual performance. If outcome targets are set *with* rather than *for* accountability units, the latter are more likely to accept responsibility for reaching them because they will have had an opportunity to influence conceptions of what is possible.

The logic of accountability and improvement outlined earlier assumes that the expectation of describing and justifying one's performance increases motivation and effort, which, in turn, improves performance. There is some evidence that the reverse is the case—that is, that increased motivation and effort are the result, as much as the cause, of improved performance (Barr, Stimpert, & Huff, 1992; Cohen & Levinthal, 1990). The more skilled and knowledgeable the accountable unit, the more likely they are to take responsibility for the detection and resolution of problems. Increased sensitivity to and responsibility for problems is self-defeating in the absence of knowledge of possible solutions or of confidence that one can develop them (Weick, 1995). This suggests that when improvement requires increases in knowledge and skill and not just effort, increased accountability will be insufficient. As Lerner and Tetlock (1999) concluded, "no amount of increased effort can compensate for lack of knowledge about how to solve problems that require special training" (p. 263). The same conclusion was drawn by Newmann et al. (1997) from their study of 24 restructuring schools in the United States: "External accountability alone offers no assurance that a school faculty will have adequate technical knowledge and skill, sufficient authority to deploy resources wisely, or shared commitment to a clear purpose for student learning" (p. 63). So even if the conditions exist under which accountability increases motivation and effort, that may not translate into improved performance.

In summary, when we analyze the conditions needed to forge a link between accountability and improvement, we can see the potential for oversimplifying the relation between the two. If it is assumed that all one has to do to produce reform is to motivate it through the requirement to describe and justify performance, and the allocation of appropriate rewards or sanctions, then disappointment is bound to follow. Whether or not accountability fosters educational improvement depends on the validity of the audience's judgment, whether that judgment—or its anticipation—motivates increased responsibility on the part of the accountable unit, and whether the unit has the capacity to craft more effective practices. Each of these conditions in turn reflects a complex interaction between characteristics of the accountable unit and of its various audiences.

What follows, then, about the appropriate role of accountability in a reform effort? The problem with false expectations is that they trigger overreactions when they are shown to be so. We need to be more thoughtful and modest about the contribution of accountability to improvement, not to dismiss the link altogether. Our position is that although accountability is neither a necessary nor a sufficient condition for improvement, it may contribute to such improvement by increasing the knowledge of educators, parents, politicians, and the public at large about the consequences of current practices and policies. This knowledge may trigger better-informed debate about the meaning and implications of the information. Although educational data are frequently subject to varying interpretations, public data constrain the variety of interpretations and evaluations that would otherwise be acceptable and thus contribute to a public consensus about the performance of the accountable unit. Second, the availability of information about the performance of the accountable unit may prompt debate about what is valued and about how those values should be represented in indicators. Third, the availability of trusted information about what is valued may increase the demand for, and focus on, improvement.

Accountability, Improvement, and Reporting to Parents

The link between accountability and educational improvement has typically been discussed in the context of state or federal school reform efforts in the United States and Canada (Koretz, 1996; Newmann et al., 1997; Torrance, 1997). The overarching question has been whether policies that require schools and school districts to be externally accountable for student achievement have, or indeed can, produce the intended improvements. Our investigation of how a sample of New Zealand primary schools reports to parents on the achievement of their children provides a very different context for this discussion. Although the former studies involve macro-level examination of the impact of policy on school procedures and outcomes, our study examines the microprocesses that might help explain the degree of impact achieved by these more systemic reforms. Micro-level studies can reveal the social psychology of accountability—that is, how accountability demands are understood by those involved and why certain patterns of response are evident.

In the remainder of this article, we describe the ways in which some New Zealand primary schools report to parents, evaluate the extent to which those practices are consistent with the conditions required to promote improvement, and explain why those conditions were seldom met.

School Reports as a Form of Accountability

It is not immediately obvious how school reports to parents are a form of accountability, for "who is accountable?" and "for what?" According to our definition, agents are accountable when they expect to justify aspects of their own performance to others. In the reporting situation, it is clearly teachers who are giving the account to parents, but is it their performance or the student's that is being justified?

Whether teachers see themselves as accountable to parents through the reporting process depends on how much responsibility they believe parents accord them for the achievement of their children. If teachers believe that parents see them as partly or wholly responsible for their child's achievement, they will experience reporting as a form of teacher accountability. On the other hand, if they believe that parents attribute their child's degree of success to the child or to their own parental efforts, they will experience reporting quite differently.

These multiple interpretive possibilities suggest the need for the parties to the accountability relationship to investigate, rather than assume, how each party understands the contribution and responsibilities of the other to the child's current and future performance. In this way, reporting to parents becomes an opportunity to strengthen the home–school partnership by developing a shared understanding of relative responsibilities, supported by mutual accountabilities. We discuss subsequently whether or not our schools viewed the reporting process as such an opportunity.

New Zealand Policy on Reporting to Parents

The governing bodies of New Zealand primary schools are Boards of Trustees, comprising, in the main, elected parent representatives. Boards of Trustees are required, through the principal and staff, to monitor the progress of students against the achievement objectives outlined in the various national curriculum statements (Ministry of Education, 1993). The information gained should contribute to profiles of individual student achievement "which inform teachers about each student's learning and development and [to] provide the basis for feedback to students and parents" (Ministry of Education, 1993, p. 24). Although schools are required to cover all of the broad achievement objectives, they can determine the relative emphasis they are given and, more important for our purposes, which ones they report on (The New Zealand Education Gazette, 1995). The achievement objectives in the National Curriculum are arranged in eight levels that cover the primary, middle, and high school years. These achievement levels provide an indication of a student's development relative to the National Curriculum. The levels are progressive and overlapping, with a student taking 2 years, on average, to master a level in a particular curriculum area. There is no obligation on schools to report against these curriculum levels, though the policy intent is that they provide a coherent framework for teaching, assessing, and reporting.

Schools' reporting practices are likely to reflect their technical resources as well as policy requirements. With the exception of reading and math, age or criterion-referenced standardized assessment tools, suitable for the New Zealand curriculum, are not readily available, and some schools choose not to use those that are (Education Review Office, 1998). The use of standards or targets for the evaluation of student achievement is not a strong part of New Zealand primary school culture because there is a tradition of identifying what children can do, rather than also identifying where they fall short (Timperley, Robinson, & Bullard, 1999).

Most New Zealand primary schools meet their obligations to report to parents through twice yearly written reports and invitations to parents to discuss them with the class teacher during a mid-year parent report evening. Reports typically present information about both academic and social aspects of a child's progress at school. Sometimes a school reports to parents in a booklet that is used repeatedly so that the current report can be compared with that of previous years. Other schools use a new pamphlet or form for each half-yearly report.

Method

This study of reporting to parents is part of a larger evaluation of a national government intervention to strengthen education in two of the economically poorest districts in Auckland, New Zealand's largest city. The 35 schools involved serve predominantly Maori (New Zealand's indigenous population) and Pacific Island families. Many of the latter are recent immigrants for whom English is a second language. One goal of this intervention is to increase the community's involvement in, and influence on, local schools (Annan, 1999).

Achievement levels of students in these schools are well below the national average, and many enter school with low skill levels. For example, assessments of reading achievement conducted in several of our sample schools by an independent research group showed the children to be, on average, 9 months below a nationally normed comparison group, 1 year after school entry (McNaughton, Phillips, & MacDonald, 1998).

Ten primary, one middle, and one high school provided copies of their policies on reporting and a sample of recently completed student reports. These schools are identified by the letters A to L in Table 1. In most cases, the sample included the reports on two high-, two middle-, and two low-achieving students in whichever of Years 4, 6, 7, or 10 were appropri-

Table 1
Descriptors of Achievement Used in 12 School Reports

School	Evaluative Categories	Basis of Evaluative Standard
A	Ratings: Always, usually, sometimes, not yet (against objectives)	Curriculum level. Reading age (stated on report)
B	Ratings: Above average, average, below average	Teacher decides
C	Ratings: Excellent, very good, satisfactory, improving, needs improving	Class referenced
D	Ratings: Achieved high standard, steady progress made, limited achievement	Referenced to each child's perceived potential
E	Descriptive achievement comments. Ratings: Excellent, very good, good, room for improvement	Teacher decides
F	Descriptive achievement comments with some evaluations—no ratings	Not applicable
G	Descriptive achievement comments—no achievement ratings	Referenced to each child's perceived potential
H	Descriptive achievement comments. Progress ratings of A, B, C (intermittently used)	Referenced to each child's perceived potential
I	No achievement comments or ratings (effort only)	Not applicable
J	Ratings: Excellent, very good, average, below average	Teacher decides
K (middle school)	Curriculum level specified	Curriculum levels, reading age (stated on report)
L (secondary school)	Descriptive achievement comments—examination marks intermittently reported	Subject department referenced

ate for the particular school. The principal at the 13th school (Hillside School) was also interviewed because she was unusual in her explicit understanding of reporting as an accountability process. Unfortunately, we could not obtain a sample of completed reports from this school, because their reporting policies and formats were under revision.

The analysis of the written reports themselves focused on how student achievement was described, with particular attention given to the evaluative standards that had been employed. Instructions to teachers on how to report student achievement were identified from schools' policy documents on reporting to parents. We interviewed up to five staff members in six of the schools about the purpose of their reporting process, the nature of the interviews conducted with parents, and the standards used to judge student achievement. In two schools (C and D), we also attended a report evening and asked parents what they had learned from the reports about their child's achievement and about the standards that the teachers had used to judge its adequacy.

The validity of our description and explanation of these schools' reporting practices were checked by inviting feedback on our early findings from meetings of the two local principals' associations. We also asked principals from outside the district and Ministry of Education officials to comment on the extent to which the reporting practices of our sample were typical of those in other New Zealand schools. They reported that the patterns we had described were typical of many New Zealand primary schools.

Our results are organized in three sections. In the first, we take an interpretive perspective by considering whether principals and teachers thought of reporting as an accountability process. In the second section, we describe schools' actual reporting practices in terms of the conditions we outlined as conducive to improvement, focusing in particular on the validity of teachers' and parents' judgments about student achievement. Finally, we provide several explanations of these schools' current practices before discussing their implications for school improvement in the final section.

Teachers' Understanding of Reporting

When we asked the question directly, most teachers we interviewed did not interpret reporting to parents as a process in which they themselves were accountable. The principal of School C, for example, explained it this way:

Researcher: Do the teachers see themselves as being held accountable by parents at report evenings?

Principal: No, I wouldn't think so. You could argue that they just carry on teaching but it is their duty to let the parent know as much as possible.

In this quote, the principal is asserting that her teachers are not accountable to parents at report interviews because they are communicating information to parents, rather than being influenced by them. In Tetlock's terms, however, accountability does not imply influence, for the process of justifying oneself to another is as likely to elicit what he calls defensive bolstering (Tetlock, 1998) as a change in the relevant actions. Despite this principal's direct denial of accountability, other types of verbal response and the actual reporting practices of schools strongly suggested that teachers anticipated that the messages they gave about their students' achievement had implications for the way they themselves would be judged. In other words, reporting practices reflected the dynamics of accountability, even though some teachers did not describe it as such. For example, the principal quoted earlier, who had just rejected the relevance of accountability to parental reporting, went on later to explain how she had instructed one teacher to rewrite her reports because she had rated all children as excellent in every curriculum area.

> Researcher: Why do you think she put everyone as excellent?
> Principal: She thought the report reflected on her. If I got a report with all [comments as] "Needs Improving," I would probably go to the teacher and say "What?"
> Researcher: Do the reports reflect on the teachers?
> Principal: Yes.

Teachers' expectations of being accountable to parents will adapt to their actual experience of the reporting process. If teachers experience parents as willing to ask about the teaching of their child and as having the capacity to judge its quality, their accountability to parents will be much stronger than if they experience them as uninformed and acquiescent to teacher authority. As one principal explained, a big gap between what the teachers know, and what they believe the parents understand and are prepared to ask, limits the extent to which the reporting process can serve accountability purposes:

> Principal: We realize there is a big gap in what parents understand [of] what we do and why we do it, and the reasons why we think we are doing it. Closing that gap is very important, because if we don't we are talking past each other and we're not doing a good job. Some parents are more assertive than others. Some wouldn't dream of questioning the teacher.

One school deliberately set out to strengthen the accountability purposes of school reports by educating parents about its teaching and assessment practices. The principal of this school explained that interviews with parents took 30 min rather than the usual 10 and were attended by both the teacher and the principal. Parents were shown examples of the children's work and profiles that compared their child's achievement with national expectations. As the principal said:

Principal: You have to be able to say, this is where the child is at and compare it with national expectations ... for the younger parents we model accountability and integrity. We tell the parents you must ask us where your child is at and why. *You* must ask those questions. It's about acquiring a relationship of trust ... If the child is not making progress we need them to help at home. We go through the running records [assessment of beginning literacy] and show them what they have to do ... We set expectations for the next time they come and we tell them they must hold us accountable for the child's progress. If they can't speak English they bring the child to translate or use other teachers.

This explicit conceptualization of the reporting process as one of mutual accountability and shared responsibility for improvement was exceptional. It was unfortunate that we could not obtain examples of actual reports from this school. The reason given was that the report format was under revision.

Schools' Reporting Practices

In the remainder of this section, we examine the conditions we have proposed to promote learning through an accountable reporting process, focusing in particular on the validity of teachers' and parents' judgments about student achievement. Parents cannot hold teachers accountable, even if they attribute them some responsibility for their children's achievement, without good quality information. Good quality information describes important features of their children's achievement, evaluates its adequacy, and tells the parents the standard that has been employed to make that judgment.

Important and Accurate Information

The New Zealand curriculum provides broad guidelines to schools about what is important in the form of key objectives in each of seven essential learning areas or subjects. Eleven of our 12 schools reported students' achievement in each of these learning areas. Although the 12th school (School I) also reported against these areas, it reported the children's level of effort in each area and gave no information to parents about achievement.

Many of the 11 schools who did report achievement provided separate information for the various strands that made up a learning area. For example, English (a learning area or subject) was usually separated into listening and speaking, viewing and presenting, writing, and reading, in line with the strands used in the national curriculum documents. Some schools reported more specifically by describing achievement against two or three key objectives, such as "Writes imaginative stories," "Uses adjectives correctly," or "Writes instructions accurately." Because New Zealand curriculum documents encourage teacher-made rather than standardized lesson objectives, these descriptors varied across the schools who chose to report in that manner.

Many schools noted the importance of accurate information in their policy documents. School I—ironically enough the school that did not report achievement at all—stated in its policy document headed "The Objectives of Reporting" that "Reports give clear, honest and accurate accounts of children's progress, achievements and attitudes." Similarly, School F stated in their rationale for reporting to parents, "Reporting to parents is keeping parents informed as to the progress, achievements, strengths and weaknesses of their children."

Both the descriptions and evaluations of student achievement are relevant to a discussion of the accuracy of the written reports. Four of the 12 schools (Schools E–H) provided a description of some aspects of the students' achievement through summary comments such as the following about a child's work in English Writing: "Very good use of descriptive words in her story writing. Stories of good length. Much more careful of proofreading." The limited descriptive information provided on reports needs to be understood in the context of several other opportunities, including in the follow-up report interview, for parents to view the assessments and work samples on which such evaluative comments were based. Although we were unable for ethical reasons to test the accuracy of teachers' descriptive and evaluative comments by matching an identified student's completed reports against his or her teacher's actual classroom assessment records, we argue subsequently that there were far more serious threats to the validity of the reporting process than teachers' ability to describe achievement accurately and parents' opportunities to access such information.

All 11 schools that reported on achievement provided some evaluative comment or rating of either achievement level or progress. The seven schools that provided an evaluative rating frequently combined progress and achievement within the same scale (see School D) and used a variety of scale descriptors. For example, a middle level of achievement was variously described as "Average," "Usually," "Satisfactory," "Steady progress made," and "Good" (see Table 1).

Given the dependence of the parents' evaluation of their child and of their child's teaching on the teachers' own evaluation, it is crucial that we examine the validity and transparency of teachers' judgments. Our first concern about validity was the distribution of the evaluative ratings. Across the whole 12 schools, there was no clear association between each school's evaluative ratings and their nomination of children as low-, medium-, or high-achieving.

Our second concern was a lack of transparency about the standard or benchmark used to judge a child's achievement. Only two schools (A and K) told parents the standard that had been used to judge their children's achievement as "excellent," "average," or whatever was applicable. These schools' reports described, in an easily interpreted form, both the level on the national curriculum at which the child was working and the child's reading age. The remaining schools did not communicate the standard that had been used, so their parents were in no position to judge whether they agreed with the standard the teacher was employing or with the way it was being applied to their child. In the next section, we pursue the validity of teachers' judgments by discussing the implicit standards that teachers had used to evaluate their students.

Use of an Appropriate Standard

In our discussion of the conditions needed to promote learning through accountability, we emphasized the role of evaluative standards so that gaps can be detected between what has and what should have been achieved. Unless parents have considerable knowledge of the New Zealand curriculum, it is hard for them to detect such gaps from descriptions or first-hand observations of their children's work. Because most parents do not have this knowledge base, they are dependent on teachers to communicate the curricular standards that are appropriate for their child.

None of the school policies on reporting discussed the standard against which teachers were to evaluate achievement, so it was not surprising that in some cases (Schools B, E, and J), individual class teachers decided what was appropriate. The Acting Principal of School B frankly admitted his uncertainty about how teachers reported:

Researcher: So when you've got a tick here that says "average," what does that mean compared to whom? How is that determined?

Acting Principle: That's in the teacher's opinion. You know what, I'm not sure whether that means "average" as far as the

> class goes, or "average" as far as the teacher's perception of what the national average is. I don't know.
>
> Researcher: There's quite a big difference.
>
> Acting Principal: Oh, too right there is. There's a huge difference. I have a feeling that it's the teacher's impression of the national average, I would hope it would be. But see, after teachers have been here for a while, your perception ...
>
> Researcher: Changes?
>
> Acting Principal: It does, it does.

A national standard was used, at least for reading, in Schools A and K. Schools C and L used a class or department-based comparison, which meant that "excellent" was awarded for students in the top reading or subject group, even though the whole class or cohort may be achieving at 1 to 2 years behind national levels. Finally, Schools G, D, and H claimed that they evaluated a child's achievement against the teacher's perception of his or her potential. If the teacher judged the child to have low potential, then an "excellent" was awarded if the teacher believed he or she was doing as well as could be expected. The Assistant Principal (AP) of School E explained this self-referenced process as follows:

> Researcher: So if you've got a student who you feel is not achieving at the national average ...
>
> AP: Not achieving to their potential. We don't compare to national, it's their potential. No, we have not been honest with them as compared to the national averages because otherwise we'd be saying to so many of the parents, that your kid's below, below, below. ... We have a lot that we consider average doing well, but they probably are below but we say they are doing well, for us here.

Examples of reports provided by this school showed that some children who were achieving poorly in relation to the national cohort received a majority of "achieved high standard" ratings in their report.

When we asked parents at School C what they thought their child's achievement ratings meant, about half indicated they understood it reflected their child's standing in relation to the rest of the class, whereas the rest believed their child had been compared to all children of their age. Parent interviews at School D established that many believed the standard applied was a national one and, therefore, that the ratings received by their children were far more positive than was the case. The only teacher we asked about this issue was puzzled about these parents' perceptions:

AP: You know, when they say that, do they really think that? I don't—I think they would know—I think they would …

Researcher: If the teacher at the school says they're doing well, then would you disbelieve that?

AP: But they also know they're in Mangere and they are very aware of Mangere, I mean goodness, the newspapers make it quite clear—as opposed to other areas, so I think they do know. When we say "do well" we mean "doing well for here."

The aforementioned quotes suggest, first, that the authority to determine what standard is appropriate is vested in the school and teachers, who have, on the whole, preferred local or class-based standards rather than national ones. The people for whom the reports are intended have had little say over this aspect of schools' reporting policies. Second, because the standard that schools are using to judge achievement is not made explicit on the reports, they are highly likely to be misinterpreted by parents as indicating higher levels of achievement than is in fact the case. Third, the omission of the standard itself from the written report renders it invisible and thus less likely to be the subject of debate between parents and teachers. In short, both teachers' rejection of the more demanding national standard and parents' unawareness of this rejection reduces the likelihood of detection of gaps between the current and desired achievement levels of their children. The teachers' accountability to parents is reduced because the reporting process fails to provide the information that would enable parents to make an independent assessment of the validity of the teacher's evaluation of their child.

Implications for Motivation to Improve

Accountability motivates improvement when responsibility is taken to reduce shortfalls between current and desired performance. Our data suggest that the reporting process was not designed to detect and communicate such shortfalls, because schools had adjusted their evaluative standards to fit their history of achievement, and parents were unaware that this was the case. Although teachers gave parents accounts of their students and, indirectly, of their own performance, parents lacked the resources required to determine whether and where improvement was needed.

We found one exception to this generalization in the school that we earlier described as using school reports to strengthen the mutual accountability of parents and teachers. This school had a strong system of internal accountability in which children's literacy levels were regularly monitored against the national average. The principal of this school could describe instances when children's programs had been changed after discussion at report interviews, and this was confirmed during our observations at this school.

In summary, the parental reporting practices of most schools in Table 1 did not meet the conditions needed to promote improvement through accountability. In some cases, this was because too little information about a child's achievement was given or because that achievement was not evaluated. More often, the achievement was evaluated, but the standard used was not made explicit, and that standard, being child- or class-referenced, produced a much more positive report than would have been the case if a more rigorous national benchmark had been used.

Explanations for Current Practice

We believe it is important to examine the reasons for schools' current reporting practices, for advocacy of alternatives is mere rhetoric if one does not understand and address the forces that sustain the status quo. We suggest the explanation lies in a strong desire of these teachers to be positive, a desire that is deeply rooted in the schools' culture and reinforced by the policy and political context of these particular schools.

A positive focus was evident in many of the policy documents on reporting. Earlier, we quoted from School I's policy statement on the importance of providing accurate information. This statement was followed by a second that read, "Reports are positive and helpful." The desire to be positive inhibits the communication of frank and accurate messages when the accountable agent anticipates the audience will view a more honest message as negative. The principal and deputy principal at School J described the dilemma they experienced between honesty and accuracy as follows:

Researcher: Okay, question to both of you. You know that for most of your students when they arrive, they will not have a whole set of skills that middle class teachers can just take for granted. So you are starting a year or so back, in terms of preschool, in terms of delivering what's needed. Do you tell your parents that?

Deputy Principal: No ...

Researcher: Now why don't you tell them?

Deputy Principal: I suppose it's a self-esteem thing for the children. And I suppose I've always taken the children from where they're at and accepted them where they're at—now let's get on with it and do it from here. So, no, we haven't and that's what I think we have to address ...

Principal: What about the self-esteem, the feeling of security when the parents arrive. I think we have to foster that first before we do.

Researcher: That's the bind isn't it.

Deputy Principal: And the child, if the child feels secure, that mum is on his side, I think learning comes. But when it's out there, it's isolated and that's a little divorced from the norms of the parents and being there. I think this is one aspect that I feel, personally feel, that we foster here before any learning takes place. We foster the being safe, being secure, being happy before kids start the learning process.

Principal: Self-esteem is so important.

For these school leaders, communicating positive messages to parents means not discussing the entry level of their child, so that the confidence of the parent and the self-esteem and security of the child are maintained. Once these dispositions are judged to be at the right level, learning can begin. This well-intentioned, but nevertheless manipulative and patronizing approach is also apparent in the following comments by the deputy principal of School D about report evenings: "It's our job to make the parents feel [like] a million dollars. It's the human face that's important. No one feels threatened—that's what we do well. It's what's not done well at secondary school."

As long as these schools believe that being positive means providing children and parents only with good news, they will be unable to benchmark their report ratings against an explicit standard because there will always be children who do not reach the standard. We suggest that being positive under these circumstances should mean avoiding blame, sharing responsibility for understanding any gap and attempting to close it, and communicating honestly and empathetically.

The economic and social circumstances of the families also contributed to schools' reporting practices. The educational resources in many of these families were limited, so if parents were to hold teachers accountable, schools had to educate them about the curriculum and build bridges between the culture of the school and home. The school in which accountability was a central purpose of reporting overcame this problem by educating parents in how to hold the school accountable and spent long periods of time helping the parents to assist their children reach desired goals. The cost in time for the school personnel was considerable, but they believed it to be worth the effort in terms of the benefits to the students.

Student safety was also a concern in some schools. Several principals and teachers recounted experiences where students had been beaten by parents and caregivers on receipt of a negative school report. However, school leaders who described this risk acknowledged that it applied to only a handful of children and that they had procedures for preventing such treatment, such as inviting parents to discuss the report at school, rather than sending it home. The safety issue did not appear to be as powerful an explanation of the reporting practices as first indicated.

A related concern expressed by many of the schools was the possibility of unreasonable expectations being placed on individual children through making unfair comparisons with others. Nearly all schools included such concerns in their written documentation for teachers, parents, or both. For example, School G wrote in the notes for parents, "Children's natural abilities and levels of attainment vary. This report is specific to your child and it would be unwise to compare the report with that of another." If explicit standards are to be used, the possibility these might lead to unreasonable expectations for individual students is one that schools would have to manage carefully. The quality of the dialogue around what might constitute reasonable expectations for a particular child is crucial in managing this problem. All schools held parent interviews at least once per year. We suggest that this is the appropriate context for reaching shared expectations for individual students.

In summary, the emphasis on reporting positively reduced the risks to parents and children of communicating messages that could evoke negative feelings, whether they be anger or loss of confidence and self-esteem. We now turn to the ways in which these communication strategies also reduced the risks to schools and teachers of negative consequences, ranging from parental criticism to nonenrollment of their children. Understanding these risks requires a brief excursion into the policy and political context of our sample schools.

The two communities in which our schools are located are stressed by poverty and undermined by the negativity of media reports on the quality of schooling in the area. The latest wave of media publicity was triggered by the release of a report in 1996 by the national school audit agency (Education Review Office, 1996) that was highly critical of the quality of the governance, management, and curriculum delivery in approximately 42% of the district's schools. Some professionals and community leaders reacted to the publicity by being determinedly positive about the communities' schools and rich cultural traditions.

The image and reputation of our sample schools are crucial to their survival under a government policy of school choice that has triggered fierce competition for students in some parts of the two districts. Approximately 70% of one of the district's high school students bypass the two state high schools for religious or state schools in neighboring suburbs. There is some evidence that this trend is creeping down the age range to affect primary and middle schools, though in the latter case, roll trends are very variable. It is understandable, therefore, that the leaders of our sample schools are very conscious of the enrollment implications of reporting against rigorous and explicit standards.

In summary, the reporting practices we have described are explained by educators' desire to be positive, which is motivated by both their concern about the esteem of students and families and their desire to build the confidence of the community in themselves and their school. As one principal put it when we presented our draft findings to his local principal's association, "It's quite unprofessional really—but I would be a fool to report against national standards if the neighboring schools used local ones."

Discussion

Our analysis of school reporting policies and practices suggests that in these 12 schools at least, this form of teacher accountability was unlikely to motivate teachers or parents to improve, because it obscured rather than clarified any need for improvement. School reports that compared children to their perceived potential, or to the level of their classmates, did not tell parents how their children were progressing toward the aspirations they held for them. The majority of families in these schools were of either Maori (New Zealand's indigenous people) or Pacific Island descent. Both these ethnic groups have a high regard for education and want their children to enter occupations that require success in national exams and tertiary level study (Nash, 1993; Smith, 1997). Given these aspirations, the state, the wider educational community, parents, and schools need to join together to learn what is involved in reaching them, and that learning is retarded by not evaluating achievement against the standards that are implied by those aspirations. Just as overly punitive accountability processes can be educationally counterproductive, so can those that deflect effort and attention from important problems by substituting reassurance for rigor. In these schools, accountability through reporting to parents was symbolic rather than substantive, serving purposes of reassurance and public relations, rather than of information and learning (Etzioni, 1975).

Although care must be taken in applying the conclusion of experimental research to a situation as complex as the relation of schools and their parents, Tetlock's work is suggestive of what might be required to make the reporting process more likely to trigger improvement. Accountable agents increase effort and thoughtfulness when they do not know the views of their audience, they believe that audience values accuracy, and the audience is reasonably well informed (Tetlock, 1998, p. 259). Our interview data suggest that these conditions were only minimally satisfied in our sample of schools, for school leaders believed they knew parents' views (they wanted to hear good news about their child) and perceived them to be relatively uninformed about the curriculum. Because parents were in no position to judge the accuracy of the teachers' evaluations, and being accurate risked the reputation of the teacher, of the school, and the esteem of the student and family, it is no wonder that many reports were positively biased.

Since reporting our draft results to the Ministry of Education, local principals, and parent representatives, we have been working to increase the accuracy of reporting while reducing the risks of doing so. First, in presenting our findings and the reasons for them, we have both named what is going on, and empathized rather than blamed, by sharing our understanding of the complex dynamics involved. By naming and explaining the processes, we have encouraged teachers to test the various assumptions they have held about what parents know and want to hear and to involve parents in the policy reviews that several schools are now undertaking. Second, we have advocated that schools use and communicate some nationally standardized assessments, so that both teachers and parents can benchmark their own assessment standards. This point of view has been reflected in the recently released national primary school policy on assessment (Ministry of Education, 1999).

The issue of what standards are appropriate for judging the achievement levels of students in low-decile schools is debated among educators (Bishop, 1996), but so far, in New Zealand at least, has not included the very families who are most affected by the debate. In advocating the use of more rigorous benchmarks in evaluating student achievement, we are not suggesting that local benchmarks be abandoned. If individual children's achievement is reported solely against national benchmarks, then there is a high risk that the likely shortfall will be interpreted as a fault of the child or the family. If the national comparison is made available to parents alongside the local one, they can see that the problem is a collective rather than individual one and can join with other parents and educators to debate what is a "realistic" aspiration and what can be done collectively and individually to reduce the gap. The double comparison is essential, because a national comparison that is not contextualized in local circumstances places too much of a burden on individual families and schools. On the other hand, the avoidance of the national comparison absolves the families and local educators from the responsibility of facing the extent of the underachievement in their community and from developing a partnership, based on accurate information, to help students and families reach their goals.

References

Annan, B. (1999). *The evolution of a three-way partnership, schooling and development project* (Annual Report of Strengthening Education in Mangere and Otara, September 1997–June 1999). Wellington, New Zealand: Ministry of Education.

Assessment Issues. (1995, March 29). *The New Zealand Education Gazette, 74*, 1–2.

Barr, P. S., Stimpert, J. L., & Huff, A. S. (1992). Cognitive change, strategic action, and organizational renewal. *Strategic Management Journal, 13*, 15–36.

Bishop, J. M. (1996). Signaling incentives and school organization in France, the Netherlands, Britain and the United States. In E. A. Hanushek & D. W. Jorgensen (Eds.), *Improving America's schools: The role of incentives* (pp. 111–145). Washington, DC: National Academy Press.

Cohen, M. D., & Levinthal, D. (1990). Absorptive capacity: A new perspective on learning and innovation. *Administrative Science Quarterly, 35*, 128–152.

Edmondson, A. C. (1996). Learning from mistakes is easier said than done: Group and organisational influences on the detection and correction of human error. *Journal of Applied Behavioral Science, 32*(1), 5–28.

Education Review Office. (1996). *Improving schooling in Mangere and Otara*. Wellington, New Zealand: Education Review Office.

Education Review Office. (1998). *Assessing children's curriculum achievement* (Education Evaluation Reports). Wellington, New Zealand: Education Review Office.

Etzioni, A. (1975). Alternative conceptions of accountability. *Public Administrative Review, 35*, 279–286.

Fiske, S. T., & Taylor, S. E. (1991). *Social cognition*. New York: McGraw Hill.

Kogan, M. (1986). *Education accountability: An analytic overview*. London: Hutchinson.

Koretz, D. E. (1996). Using student assessments for educational accountability. In E. A. Hanushek & D. W. Jorgenson (Eds.), *Improving America's schools: The role of incentives* (pp. 171–195). Washington, DC: National Academy Press.

Lerner, J. S., & Tetlock, P. E. (1999). Accounting for the effects of accountability. *Psychological Bulletin, 125*, 255–275.

Martin, J. (1994). The role of the state in administration. In A. Sharp (Ed.), *Leap into the dark: The changing role of the state in New Zealand since 1984* (pp. 41–67). Auckland, New Zealand: Auckland University Press.

McNaughton, S., Phillips, G., & MacDonald, S. (1998, December). *Curriculum channels and literacy development over the first year of instruction*. Paper presented at the New Zealand Association for Research in Education 20th Annual Conference, Dunedin.

Mehrens, W. A. (1998). Consequences of assessment: What is the evidence? *Education Policy Analysis Archives, 6*(13) [On-line]. Retrieved January 20, 1999 from the World Wide Web: http://olam.ed.asu.edu/epaa/v6n13.html or http://epaa.asu.edu/epaa/v6n13.html

Ministry of Education. (1993). *The New Zealand curriculum framework*. Wellington, New Zealand: Learning Media, Ministry of Education.

Ministry of Education. (1999). *Information for better learning: National assessment in primary schools: Policies and proposals*. Wellington, New Zealand: Ministry of Education. (Available online at: http://www.minedu.govt.nz/Schools/Assessment/EnglishBooklet.htm)

Nash, R. (1993). *Succeeding generations: Family resources and access to education in New Zealand*. Auckland, New Zealand: Oxford University Press.

Newmann, F. M., King, M. B., & Rigdon, M. (1997). Accountability and school performance: Implications from restructuring schools. *Harvard Educational Review, 67*(1), 41–74.

Shephard, L. A. (1993). Evaluating test validity. *Review of Research in Education, 19*, 405–450.

Smith, G. H. (1997). *The development of kaupapa Maori: Theory and praxis*. Unpublished doctoral thesis, University of Auckland, New Zealand.

Tetlock, P. E. (1998). Losing our religion: On the precariousness of precise normative standards in complex accountability systems. In R. M. Kramer & M. A. Neale (Eds.), *Power and influence in organizations* (pp. 121–144). Thousand Oaks, CA: Sage.

Timperley, H., Robinson, V., & Bullard, T. (1999). *Strengthening education in Mangere and Otara evaluation* (First Evaluation Report). Wellington, New Zealand: Ministry of Education.

Torrance, H. (1997). Assessment, accountability and standards: Using assessment to control the reform of schooling. In A. H. Halsey, H. Lauder, P. Brown, & A. S. Wells (Eds.), *Education, economy and society* (pp. 320–331). Oxford, England: Oxford University Press.

Weick, K. E. (1995). *Sensemaking in organizations*. Thousand Oaks, CA: Sage.

PEABODY JOURNAL OF EDUCATION, 75(4), 90–113

Standards-Based Reform: Can It Make a Difference for Students?

Robert E. Blum

Implementation of standards is among the leading approaches to school reform. With one exception, every state has developed or is developing standards for what students should learn in school. Initially, standards development has focused on communication (reading, writing, speaking, and listening) and mathematics (math knowledge and problem solving). Standards related to other subjects are being developed as well. States are following content standards with development of assessments aligned to the standards. State standards-aligned assessments make it possible to establish performance standards, setting benchmarks for student learning. Becoming clear about standards and targets for learning by all students is essential to successful school reform. And if standards and benchmarks go beyond trivial, easy-to-measure concepts, they deserve a central place in school reform. Clear performance standards and benchmarks set the stage for accountability. When all stakeholders—parents and community members, students, school and district staff, state and local board members, legislators, and others—have a common, clear understanding of what all

ROBERT E. BLUM *is the Director of the School Improvement Program, Northwest Regional Educational Laboratory, Portland, Oregon.*

Requests for reprints should be sent to Robert E. Blum, Director, School Improvement Program, Northwest Regional Educational Laboratory, 101 Southwest Main Street, Portland, OR 97204. E-mail: blumb@nwrel.org students must learn and how well they should learn it, schools and districts can become accountable for learning by all students.

The premise underlying this article is that standards-based reform is insufficient alone. Agreeing on common standards and benchmarks is a good beginning step, but school improvement processes are essential for schools and districts to become accountable for learning by all students. Schools, with strong support from their district, must know how to continuously improve their practice so that increasing numbers of students learn at higher and higher levels. Schools must know how to organize information about student performance and share the information with their constituencies, including the community and local board of education. Strong standards-based reforms and school improvement processes have potential to impact learning to high standards by all students. Schools will become increasingly accountable as they learn to use standards to guide continuous improvement.

Approach

This article examines long-standing school improvement processes in the Reynolds School District and relates school improvement to standards-based reforms. It establishes the Oregon context, describes school improvement processes used in the district, describes standards-based reform and school improvement in the district, explores relations between the two efforts, and shows results to date. The approach used to prepare this article was to (a) review a national study of curriculum/standards-based reform (Carr, 1998; Mid-Continent Research for Education and Learning, 1998), (b) review literature on school reform and improvement in Oregon, (c) conduct interviews with key staff in the Reynolds (Oregon) School District, and (d) draft the article.

An in-depth interview was conducted with the assistant superintendent. During the interview, documents were collected and subsequently reviewed. Key documents were the district strategic plan and Oregon standards-based test data. Review of the documents resulted in follow-up questioning of the assistant superintendent. Interviews with other central office staff were conducted as part of the national study on curriculum-based reform. These notes were also reviewed. Information from the interviews was the primary source for developing the section on school improvement and standards-based reform in Reynolds.

As this article was being drafted, a separate article on improvement was being developed on one elementary school in the Reynolds School District. *Learning by Example: Story 2. Glenfair Elementary School* (Linik, 1999) was reviewed to determine the extent to which various aspects of the formal school improvement process initiated in 1984 were still active in schools in 1999.

The initial draft of this article was reviewed by selected staff in the Oregon Department of Education and the Reynolds School District for accuracy and completeness. The draft was reviewed by selected staff from the Northwest Regional Educational Laboratory (NWREL) for clarity and usefulness, and their reviews resulted in revisions to the article.

School Reform, Part I: Standards-Based Reform in Oregon

People in Oregon have been working consistently toward standards-based reform and an accountability system since the mid-1970s. The initial effort was competency-based education. Oregon was a national leader in the Competency-Based Education (CBE) movement. CBE in Oregon began in 1972 with a decision by the Oregon State Board of Education to adopt a new set of requirements for high school graduation, moving from certification based solely on attendance and courses completed to certification based on competence achieved by students, in addition to the two previous factors. The revised Oregon Minimum Standards for Public Schools adopted by the Board in 1974 incorporated these requirements and extended the concept of CBE to elementary and middle level schools. The Oregon Minimum Standards mandated that all local school districts in the state adopt instructional and management processes essential to the successful design and operation of CBE programs (Butler, 1982).

In 1980, the Oregon State Board of Education modified the Minimum Standards for Public Schools. Timelines for implementation were lengthened, and many of the requirements were adjusted so that less change was mandated. This set the stage for the next phase of reform in Oregon.

Oregon's journey to comprehensive educational reform continued in 1984 with the Oregon Action Plan for Excellence. The Action Plan for Excellence charged the State Board and the Department of Education with the development of common curriculum goals and essential learning skills that would be the basic level of competence expected of students in Oregon schools. This was followed in 1987 by the School Improvement and Professional Development legislation, which provided funds for the development of "lighthouse" schools that would seek out and try innovative strategies to solve educational problems. The 21st Century Schools Program, passed in 1989, invited schools to apply for waivers for statutes, rules, and so forth that might inhibit progress toward school improvement. Although these pieces of legislation facilitated school restructuring, the major impetus for system-wide educational change came in 1991 with the passage of the *Oregon Educational Act for the 21st Century, HB 3565* (Oregon State Legislature, 1991; Roeber, 1996).

The stated purposes of House Bill 3565 were that Oregon would have the best educated citizens in the nation by the year 2000 and a workforce equal to any in the world by the year 2010. The major elements of the plan were high standards for all students; establishment of a Certificate of Initial Mastery (CIM) and a Certificate of Advanced Mastery (CAM); establishment of early childhood programs; development of academic professional technical programs for the CAM; establishment of community, business, and educational partnerships; and development of on-the-job training and apprenticeships with partner sites. The legislation mandated world-class content and performance standards coupled with statewide assessments to measure progress toward those standards (Oregon State Legislature, 1991).

As with earlier legislation and other initiatives, concerns were raised. There was a perception that the legislation was passed without substantial public input. Concerns included low academic standards, overemphasis on school as preparation for work, and inadequate funding for implementation. After an in-depth review of HB 3565, a combined House and Senate committee drafted new legislation that retained major aspects of HB 3565 but modified those elements to respond to the aforementioned stated public criticisms (Oregon State Legislature, 1995). The new legislation (HB 2991) made academic excellence the primary focus of the education system, with content and performance standards to be grounded in academic disciplines. Districts in Oregon are working under this legislation today.

Using the Common Curriculum Goals and Essential Learning Skills documents developed as part of the Action Plan for Excellence, as well as published national and international standards, the Oregon Department of Education drafted content and performance standards that were reviewed by educators, parents, business groups, and a national review team. The Common Curriculum Goals document containing content and performance standards for the CIM was adopted by the State Board of Education in 1996.

The developing assessment system in Oregon plays a significant role in the drive to have students reach high standards of academic excellence. The purposes of assessment are tracking student progress toward standards, providing information for teachers that can inform instructional practice, and making schools accountable for raising student performance levels (School Implementation Team, 1997). State assessments have been developed and are in use in mathematics (including mathematics problem solving), reading and literature, writing, and science. The schedule for other subjects follows (School Implementation Team, 1997):

2000–2001 Social Sciences
2001–2002 Arts (local assessments)
2002–2003 Second Language (local assessment)

The drive toward accountability continues. In 2000 (for the first time ever), the Oregon Department of Education published school report cards. Using performance on state tests, school context factors, and other information, the state rated the performance of each school. Ratings were from exemplary to unacceptable.

In a parallel effort, the state is using funds from the Comprehensive School Reform Demonstration Program and Goals 2000 to provide support for the lowest performing schools in Oregon. Schools below the acceptable level have the opportunity to apply for planning grants and then, assuming planning is productive, larger implementation grants. Oregon Department of Education staff provide planning assistance to low-performing schools and review their plans for quality. The Oregon approach aligns well with the professional control model for accountability described in the framework for this special issue. The state tests and school report cards are pushing schools to become increasingly accountable for results. At the same time, the Oregon Department of Education is providing support and resources to schools as they work to improve.

School Reform, Part II: Performance-Focused
School Improvement

Continuous school improvement is the second aspect of reform. Onward to Excellence (OTE) is a research-based school improvement process aimed at improving the performance of all students. Based on the results of over a decade of effective schooling research, OTE helps schools (a) set goals, performance standards, and targets for improvement; (b) implement quality school practices; and (c) improve student achievement, attitude, and social behavior. OTE assists schools as they learn to be accountable for results. OTE is a strong match with the professional-control model of site-based management. Training and assistance is provided as schools come together as a community, use research as the basis for making productive decisions about which practices to change, implement changes, monitor results, and report progress to their community and the local board of education. Since 1981, over 2,000 schools across the country have been trained in the OTE process to focus the whole school on reaching high levels of learning for all of the students served by the school.

OTE emphasizes five basic principles and beliefs: (a) student performance must be the focus, (b) improvement must be continuous, (c) improvement must be managed, (d) the school is the fundamental unit for improvement, and (e) improvements should be research based. Schools engaged in OTE go through a 10-step improvement process (see Figure 1).

OTE is structured to encourage participation in school improvement from many stakeholders. The change process is managed by a school leadership team composed of the principal, teachers, other staff, and, often, parents. Improvements take place school-wide via teams that lead learning, planning, and implementation of agreed on improvement strategies. The leadership team is trained in seven workshops led by an experienced OTE trainer.

Although OTE was initiated in Alaska as the Alaska Effective Schools Project, pilot testing in Oregon began in the Fall of 1983. Three high schools in the Portland metropolitan area were selected as pilot schools. As the pilot test progressed, other schools and districts became interested, and the first contract for OTE training and technical assistance service was initiated in the Fall of 1984. From this modest beginning, additional districts within and outside Oregon contracted for OTE training service.

Interest and participation in OTE was developing concurrently with the Oregon Action Plan. The two efforts were conceptually aligned, with the Oregon Action Plan, developing statewide goals and standards while OTE was preparing schools to use data from tests and other sources as the basis for improving student learning. In 1984 there were no state tests, so most districts used national standardized tests. OTE focused schools and districts on improving student performance as measured by standardized

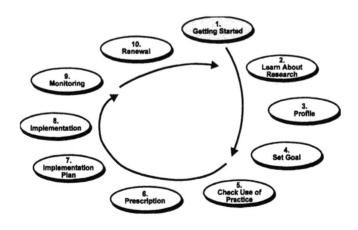

Figure 1. OTE: 10-step improvement process.

tests and other measures such as indicators of student thinking skills and student attitude and social behavior.

In 1987, Oregon legislation focused on professional development and school improvement. Under this legislation, schools applied for funding to improve student learning through strong professional development in school improvement. OTE proved to be central to the actual work of schools and educational service districts as they used resources from the state to focus on school improvement. In addition to grants to schools, the legislation established within-state regional professional development centers. Scaling up OTE became the primary content for services provided by the professional development centers. The NWREL contracted to serve as the Northwest Oregon Professional Development Center and to adapt OTE to fit the Oregon context specifically. NWREL trained trainers from the other two professional development centers to provide OTE training and technical assistance services. Through this training of trainers effort, capacity to provide service was established in six education service districts, and nearly one third of all schools in Oregon were trained to use the OTE school improvement process.

In 1994, NWREL began an effort to redesign OTE. Both national and regional contexts had changed since OTE's inception in 1981, and NWREL had learned from two studies of OTE about its impact on improvement in schools. The transformation of OTE from a linear to a systemic process is nearing completion. The second generation process, called OTE II, moves district/school/community systems toward seven system outcomes, including quality and equity in learning. A full description of OTE II is found in *Comprehensive School Reform: A Program Perspective* (Block, Everson, & Guskey, 1999). OTE II retains the strong focus on improvement of learning for all students, involves all key stakeholders at district and school levels, and connects tightly to state standards.

Bringing Reform Together: The Reynolds Story

The Reynolds School District, formed in 1957, is located 10 miles east of downtown Portland near the confluence of the Sandy and Columbia Rivers. The district covers 27 square miles. Nearby are several colleges, many with graduate programs in education. Facilities for camping, fishing, picnicking, boating, and hiking are located within the district. Several ski areas are within an hour of the district.

The Reynolds community is varied, including Troutdale, Wood Village, Fairview, and portions of Gresham and Portland. The economy ranges from berry farms to corporations such as Viking Industries, U.S. Bank,

EconoMax, and Donnelley Norwest Inc. A general aviation airport is located within the district.

There are 14 schools in the district: 1 high school, 3 middle schools, and 10 elementary schools. Enrollment stands at 8,785 in 1999 and is projected to be 9,500 when the 2000–2001 school year begins. The district offers a wide array of programs to meet the needs of all students.

Characteristics of the student population in Reynolds are changing. Following are key indicators of the nature of the changes:

- In 1995 the percentage of White students was 86.3, whereas in 1999 it was 74.6.
- The percentage of Hispanic students increased from 6.6 in 1995 to 15.4 in 1999.
- In 1997 the percentage of students eligible for free or reduced-price lunch was 44.4, whereas in 1999 it was 47.6.
- The number of ESL students grew from 847 in 1997 to 1,572 in 1999, an 85.5% increase.

According to federal lunch program and census data, 37% of the students are from families who live in poverty. The dropout rate is 6.94%; 20 to 25% indicate they will attend 4-year colleges, and 35 to 40% indicate they will attend 2-year colleges.

School Improvement in Reynolds

Reynolds High School participated in the pilot of OTE beginning in the Fall of 1983. Along with two other high schools, Reynolds High chose a leadership team of over 10 staff members including the principal and assistant principal. The three leadership teams participated in training together. Two 1-day sessions were conducted in each of 2 years, with follow-up tasks being completed by the teams with their full staff.

The Reynolds School District believed the high school experience with the earliest version of OTE was productive and contracted with NWREL to provide training for the remaining schools in the district. OTE training began with one group of elementary schools in Reynolds in April of 1984, continuing until June of 1985. The final group of schools began training in August of 1985 and continued through the 1985–1986 and 1986–1987 school years. Between the first group of schools and the second, the OTE training process was stretched from 1 to 2 years. The common OTE training began a commitment to OTE principles, including (a) focus on student performance with data to support claims of improvement, (b) the school as the center of improvement with autonomy in decision making, (c) team leadership in schools and in the district, (d) use of research-based practices to make decisions about changes intended to improve student learning, and (e) striving for continuous improvement.

As NWREL began disseminating OTE on a broader basis, establishment of an OTE training cadre was initiated. The assistant superintendent in Reynolds was among the first individuals to become an OTE trainer. This individual has continued to train for NWREL on a part-time basis since 1986 and remains in the Reynolds School District as assistant superintendent. Consistency of leadership in Reynolds and continuing training for NWREL has contributed to continuing use of OTE by schools in Reynolds, although their school improvement process is not called OTE today.

In recent interviews with the assistant superintendent, it was discovered that several aspects of OTE are still in use and that those aspects have been strengthened. Remaining elements of OTE are congruent with state requirements and intents.

Focus on student performance. When OTE was started in Reynolds, the district used national standardized tests to determine levels of student performance and set school improvement goals. Today, Reynolds is using the Oregon state tests as the basis for accountability and improvement. State tests are administered at Grades 3, 5, 8, and 10. According to the assistant superintendent, Reynolds needs off-year tests to enhance its improvement efforts. Oregon is in the process of having such off-year tests developed. The two areas in which Oregon tests are in use are literature/reading and math, including math problem solving. A writing performance assessment is also administered at the same grades. Reynolds is very concerned about performance in the areas being tested, particularly reading.

At the central office level, the district is data based. This orientation was developed through OTE. Results of state tests are analyzed and organized to assist schools with their improvement work. Reports provided to schools include reports from the state and locally developed diagnostic information. A list of the reports provided to each school follows:

- Percent of students not meeting, meeting, and exceeding state standards for each grade at which tests are administered, with comparison to district and state results.
- Average scale score for each grade level at which tests are administered, including comparison to district and state results.
- Scale score gains and losses from year to year.
- Number of students not meeting, meeting, and exceeding state standards at each grade by number of years students have been in the district.

- Number of students exceeding, meeting, and not meeting state standards, with the not meeting segment divided by the number of score points below the standard (1–3 points below, 4–6 points below, etc.)
- A listing of names of students not meeting state standards with scale scores for subtests and total test.
- A list with the names of each teacher at each grade level tested with the number of students not meeting, meeting, and exceeding state standards in each test and subtest.

The amount of data showing overall results and diagnostic information is more than adequate. What is not known at this time is how the information is used in the schools.

Another continuing use of OTE processes is gaining focus by setting one or more school improvement goals and targets. The approach and language used in Reynolds remains as learned through OTE training in years past. Goal setting is done in each school biennially. Each principal reports the goal to the assistant superintendent, and they discuss the process used to involve staff and community in the process. The goal setting process was learned through the OTE training provided between 1983 and 1986. Sample goal statements from one school follow:

To increase the percentage of third graders meeting the Standard in reading from 57% in 1996 to 65% in 1999.
To increase the percentage of fifth graders meeting the Standard in reading from 50% in 1996 to 65% in 1999.

In this school, the focus is reading, and the 3-year targets are very specific.

A change from the OTE process is that the district specifies that each school will have an academic goal. They may have social behavior or other student performance goals, but an academic goal is a must. Although this district decision reduces autonomy somewhat, it also brings increased focus to improvement work.

A key OTE concept that is not being used in Reynolds is aggregation to the school level (combining results from Grades 3 and 5 at the elementary level) and aggregating to the district level (combining results from Grades 3, 5, 8, and 10). Aggregation to the organization level allows staff to watch school-wide or district-wide performance. An example of aggregation is shown in the Results section.

The school is the center of improvement.   Reynolds, like most school districts, is struggling with the relation between school autonomy and district direction. There are signs that schools have increasing amounts of control and autonomy. Schools now have major responsibilities for managing funds that relate to their daily operations and instructional practice. This applies both to general funds and Title I funds. Schools set their improvement goals and targets and write specific objectives for each grade level. Schools establish their focus and make decisions about how to meet their improvement goals. Schools can arrange their daily schedules to allow time for staff to work and learn together, and they can arrange for school-level training and technical assistance.

Improvement is led by a team. Each school in Reynolds has a site council. They are in compliance with the Oregon requirements regarding site council member selection and council composition. Leadership teams were established when OTE training was provided. The OTE leadership teams became the basis for site councils. The teams were modified to meet Oregon selection and composition requirements. Between 3 and 4 days of training on team building have been conducted in every school to improve site council and school staff functioning. The site council has responsibility for overseeing improvement work in the school, including goal setting, plan development, provision of professional development, implementation monitoring, and review of results each year. Principal and leadership functioning contributes to success and/or failure of improvement efforts.

Improvement is continuous. Every school is expected to include improvement in its work. This has been ongoing for well over 10 years. Schools review student performance data annually, set improvement goals and performance targets biennially, and prepare improvement plans. Using the plan format learned through the OTE process, each school submits a plan to the assistant superintendent biennially. The initial review is for plan completeness only. No judgments regarding the quality of plan content are made. After 1 year of implementation, the assistant superintendent meets with site councils at each school to review results and speculate on how to improve further. Plans are reviewed in relation to results, and feedback is provided. This review/feedback process is focused on test results and begins to show to whom the schools are accountable. Schools are accountable to the district, and they are accountable for results. The district uses the review/feedback process as one form of support for schools.

Improvements are research based. Use of research as the basis for making decisions about what to change to improve learning for students is differential by school. In some schools, reviewing research, gaining information from other schools, and reflecting on school practice are normal ways of doing business. Staff in these schools trust research and spend the time necessary to learn from research. In these schools, change is a learning process. In other schools, changes come from brainstorming sessions. There is distrust of research. The staff does not take time to learn from external sources.

The elements of OTE that are strongly used seem to be provision of data for decision making and centering improvement at the school level. Improvement planning processes seem to be in place. The focus is on student performance, with data for each school being reviewed annually and reported to the local board of education. Less evidence is available on real implementation of new practices. Function of site councils, effectiveness of principals, focused professional development related to school-specific changes, and follow-through in actually making planned changes are not well understood.

There is some evidence that real, lasting changes have been made. For example, the high school has core teams in place at Grades 9 and 10. A team of four teachers (language arts, social studies, science, and math) and 100 students are grouped together for half the school day. Each team has full flexibility in using the time and grouping students. This change has been ongoing for 5 years and seems to be institutionalized. It has caused shifts in relationships among teachers and between teachers and students. Teaming is an integral aspect of district functioning that grew from the strategic plan. Core teams were first established for 9th grade at Reynolds High School, then moved to 10th grade and to the middle level. Grade level teams are being implemented at the elementary schools.

Standards-Based Reform in Reynolds

Prior to state legislation and the development of content and performance standards, the district had become concerned about the quality of the educational program. There were particular concerns in reading and mathematics. Test scores were lower than expected. Numbers of students whose primary language was not English were enrolling in the district, and this was challenging teachers. High mobility in the district meant that many children were not experiencing consistency in their school experiences. Statewide standards and assessments were seen as ways to help with these concerns.

In the 1993–1994 school year, as Oregon's reform legislation was just underway, the Reynolds School District embarked on a process to develop a plan for continuous improvement district wide. Through an application process, a System Improvement Team (SIT) was appointed to lead the planning effort. In addition to concerns about poor performance in reading and math, the need resulted from rapid changes in technology, economics, society, and society's expectations for education (Reynolds School District, 1995). Although school improvement had been ongoing for several years, there was a perception that schools were not pulling together as a system. A common vision did not exist, and district and school priorities were not always congruent. The charter for the SIT included the following:

Purposes:

- Involve stakeholders to align all core elements with the organization to allow the district to reach its vision.
- Create an environment for all staff that allows them to provide the best possible education for all students.
- Proactively redesign the district to be better prepared to lead changes for increased student learning.
- Determine a means to continuously improve processes throughout the district.
- Search for ways to better manage scarce funds.

Major Premises:

- Education is a systemic process.
- Teachers' ownership for students must be increased.
- Student development is the focus.
- Quality needs to exist throughout the educational process.
- Teams are used to improve quality education and team performance. (Reynolds School District, 1995)

Working throughout the 1994–1995 school year, the SIT drafted a strategic plan that enunciated a vision for the district allowing for autonomy among schools but focusing on strategies that are effective in moving students to achieving high standards. The draft plan recommends wide ranging changes. A proposal was presented to the Board of Education during the summer of 1995, it was adopted, and implementation began in the Fall of the 1995–1996 school year.

Development of the plan was a learning process. The SIT spent a great deal of time collecting, reviewing, and reflecting on information about the Reynolds School District and community. It completed social/cultural analysis via employee questionnaires and interviews; environmental analysis via parent questionnaires and interview/discussions with students, school advisory committees, business leaders, and government leaders; business analysis via interviews with the business manager; and work flow analysis via interviews with department leaders and work flow chart development by departments. A thorough literature review was undertaken by the SIT. Cutting-edge ideas related to team building, total quality management, organizational learning, and learning communities were collected through common reading and discussion. The draft plan was a result of this process of learning and thorough review, analysis, reflection, and discussion.

A vision statement is articulated in the strategic plan:

Reynolds School District Vision Statement

To Empower All Students for Choices and Challenges of the 21st Century

- Respect self, others, and the environment.
- Think critically.
- Communicate effectively.
- Work cooperatively.
- Participate responsibly and productively.

The strategic plan lays out a broad, ambitious agenda to move the district toward the vision. Although the initial timeline has not been updated, work is progressing toward implementation of plan elements. Brief descriptions of key elements of the plan follow:

- *District-wide quality measurements.* This includes student performance measures (state tests and portfolios of student work); business, parent, student and staff satisfaction surveys; and monthly financial and absentee reports. Data are collected and reviewed annually.
- *Expected outcomes.* A living document defines expected outcomes at each grade level in all curriculum areas (reading, writing, speaking, math, science, social studies, health, art, technology, media, social skills, and music).
- *Student service full-range model.* The two aspects of this element are quality loops (interventions to assure that students falling behind are provided with needed support and time to meet expected outcomes) and integration of services (talented and gifted, English as a second language, special education, and counseling).
- *Required syllabus.* All teachers develop and send a letter to parents outlining expectations for their class.
- *Grade level configuration.* The district shifted to a K–3, 4–6, 7–8, and 9–12 grade level configuration to facilitate team development and work.

• *School-to-work-center.* This is a facility for students to work on meeting CAM requirements, connect with the community, and develop talent. This may be a county-wide facility.
• *Star teams.* Cross-district and stakeholder groups assume leadership for development of critical district functions, including training and development, continuous improvement, and budget. There are also project teams for special purposes such as full service development, implementation of the CIM, and student transition (school to school).
• *In-school teams.* Core teams at the secondary level (math, science, social studies, and language arts) are multi-age and multi-grade (7–8 or 9–10), responsible for quality loops, and responsible for all expected outcomes. Elementary teams are formed by grade level. Each school has a site council that is responsible for improvement in the entire school.
• *Parent contract.* This agreement signed by parents and teachers spells out parent, student, and school responsibilities to assure student success.
• *Prekindergarten packet.* This packet outlines how parents can prepare their children for success in school.
• *Training and development strategy.* There is a wide range of opportunities for all employees to develop skills necessary to perform their work with quality. One critical aspect of this element is a growth-oriented teacher evaluation plan. Teacher evaluation has a focus on identifying and developing skills teachers need to implement standards-based reform.
• *Substitute folders.* A packet of materials for substitute teachers helps them be successful in their role. (Strategic Plan for System Improvement, 1995)

The district is moving systemically to implement elements on an agreed-on timeline. Resources are being allocated to key elements as needed. Priority is given to elements that have high potential to achieve the purposes established for the strategic planning process.

According to the assistant superintendent, the operational and conceptual leader of the improvement effort, standards-based reform has three key components:

• There are content and performance standards. The CIM makes the standards explicit. The standards drive instruction. Students know they must master the standards to graduate. (District policy states that students must earn a state CIM to graduate. Students who have not earned a state CIM by the time they are seniors have the option of presenting a portfolio of work samples in all required areas. If the portfolio is deemed to meet the state standards, the student may graduate with a Reynolds CIM.)
• Curriculum and instruction are aligned with assessments throughout the district. The state tests and portfolio assessments are providing the targets to

which curriculum and instruction are aligned. Portfolio assessments are developed from the same standards and rubrics as state tests and include assessments related to Reynolds standards that go beyond what the state is currently measuring. All stakeholders are gaining a common focus for their work.

• All students have opportunities to learn so they can meet standards. Standards-based reform is high stakes for students, and they must have multiple opportunities to learn and practice until they are successful in meeting standards. (interview with Assistant Superintendent)

Assuring that all students have multiple opportunities to learn is moving on two fronts. The district is providing resources to schools for quality loop interventions. Quality loop interventions are based on strong research supporting the need of some students for additional time and support to learn successfully. Since implementation began in 1995, after-school help has been available in all three middle schools and some elementary schools. This is from 2:00 to 4:30 p.m. each day with additional bus service provided to get students home. Library hours have been extended through 8:30 p.m. 2 days each week for student and community use. The district is funding summer school for all students. Students at all levels not meeting standards are invited to participate in the summer program to increase their skills. Only the credit recovery program for high school students who fail a course during the year requires payment of tuition. There are within-school and district-wide alternative learning settings for students who are not successful in the regular program. Self-contained classrooms in the middle schools, special basic skills courses in secondary schools, and the Reynolds Learning Center are examples of alternative learning settings.

At the same time that the quality loop interventions are being implemented, each school is planning and improving its own program so that increasing numbers of students meet standards. Improvement efforts in schools and those developed at the district level work together to provide all students the opportunities needed to successfully meet standards. District interventions and school interventions are integrated at each school. They are not duplicative. Although the district provides specific interventions and resources to support them, each school must make the district interventions work in its setting. The strategic plan is the basis for pulling school and district efforts together.

Progress in Implementation

The Reynolds School District has been working to improve student learning formally since 1983. The work and progress has been continuous since that time. In regard to structuring for success, substantial progress has been made.

• *Standards and measures are known.* The Reynolds School District worked from state standards to establish district standards. Standards for what students should know and do are written, published, and publicized. Specific activities have been undertaken to assure that all stakeholders, including students, know the standards and believe they must meet them to graduate from high school. Measurement of student performance has been brought into alignment with standards. The district stopped administering norm-referenced standardized tests and now uses state tests as the basis for judging student performance. Portfolio assessments are underway and are aligned with local and state standards. The standards are clear to everyone.

• *Expectations are set.* As noted earlier, to graduate from high school, students must master the standards for the state CIM or the Reynolds CIM. They must also complete 27 credits, up from 22 in 1990. Reynolds is the only school district in Oregon that has retained the CIM as a graduation requirement even though the state made the CIM optional.

• *Use of student performance data for decision making is established.* Data from state tests are the primary driver of decision making in the district at this time. This information is organized in several ways to help schools diagnose needs and focus their planning and programs. Data analysis and use is a well-established way of doing business in Reynolds.

• *Grade configuration is complete.* The reorganization into K–3, 4–6, 7–8, and 9–12 grade level groupings is complete.

• *Teaming is becoming a way of doing business.* Core teams are firm at the high school level and are becoming firm at the middle level. Grade-level teams are being implemented at elementary schools. Schools are scheduling so teams have opportunities to meet and plan together. Oversight teams are in place and active at the district level. Star teams for continuous improvement, professional development, and budget are ongoing. Project teams for quality loops and level-to-level transitions (e.g., elementary to middle) are active. All teams include multiple stakeholders and are responsible for development and monitoring progress in their respective areas.

• *Formal school improvement processes are ongoing.* Early OTE training set the stage for school improvement on a school-by-school basis. Although the process has been adapted to meet current conditions, many of the basic elements continue. Schools have control of increasing aspects of budget and make decisions about improvements of day-to-day practice to improve student success in achieving standards. Schools are empowered to make changes and are expected to improve results. This is the exact manifestation of the professional-control model of site-based management described by Leithwood and Earl (2000/this issue) in the introductory article.

• *Some resources to increase time and support for student success are provided.* Quality loop interventions such as after-school help, extension of library hours, summer school, and alternative options are increasing the potential for all students to be successful.

• *Teacher evaluation and professional development are focused on standards-based reform.* A new teacher evaluation process has a focus on professional growth. Schools have time and resources for professional development related to implementation of their school improvement plans. District professional development is offered to build skills across the district related to standards-based reform. All aspects of evaluation and professional development are aligned with implementation of standards-based reform.

• *Parent and community involvement is increasing.* Parents and community members are members of teams, including school site councils, parent advisory committees, and star teams. Teachers communicate expectations to parents every year or at the beginning of each course. Parent–student–teacher conferences are increasing. All parents have the list of the standards their children are expected to master and are asked to contribute to the success of their children. The district is extending below kindergarten to parents of very young children. A packet of materials is distributed widely, helping parents know how to help their children get ready for success in school.

• *Client satisfaction surveys are done annually.* Surveys for parents, business people, current students, former students (graduates and drop-outs), and staff are administered annually, and the information is used to determine client satisfaction.

Results to Date

Organization and analysis of student performance data at the district level is in the early stages. Figures 2 and 3 show reading and math performance district-wide (test results for Grades 3, 5, 8, and 10 aggregated to the district level). The data displays show performance over a 4-year period indicating percentages of students not meeting, meeting, and exceeding state performance standards on the tests.

Some good news is revealed in the data displays. In reading, district-wide, the percentage of students exceeding standards increased from 14 to 22% between 1996 and 1999. The percentage of students not meeting state standards decreased from 50 to 41% over the same 4-year period.

107

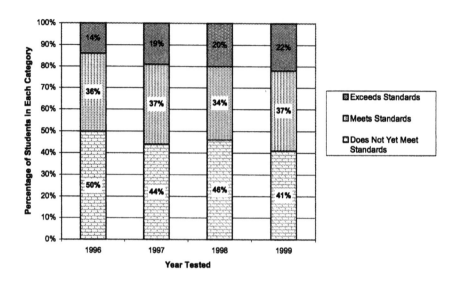

Figure 2. Reynolds School District: Reading.

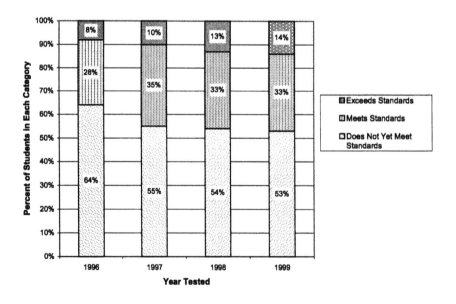

Figure 3. Reynolds School District: Mathematics.

The percentage of students exceeding state standards in math increased from 8 to 14% between 1996 and 1999. The percentage of students not meeting math standards decreased from 64 to 53% over the same 4-year period. There is much more analysis to be completed, including disaggregation of data to discover differences in learning success for various groups of students, analysis of math problem-solving scores, and analysis of writing scores.

Because students graduating from high school in the Spring of 2001 must meet state standards, results at Reynolds High School are of particular interest. Progress is being made, but there is much more to do.

The percentage of 10th grade students meeting or exceeding state standards in reading increased from 36 to 61% between 1996 and 1999, an increase of 25 percentage points (see Figure 4). In writing, the percentage of 10th grade students meeting or exceeding state standards increased from 62 to 82% between 1997 and 1999 (see Figure 5; results for 1996 are not available).

Improvement in mathematics seems to be a substantial challenge. The percentage of 10th grade students meeting state standards increased from 24 to 32% between 1996 and 1999 (see Figure 6). This means that 68% of 10th graders in 1999 did not meet standards. In math problem solving, the news was somewhat better, however. The percentage of 10th grade students meeting or exceeding state standards increased from 21 to 51% between 1997 and 1999 (see Figure 7; results for 1996 are not available).

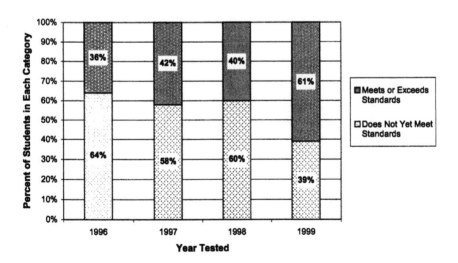

Figure 4. Reynolds High School: Reading.

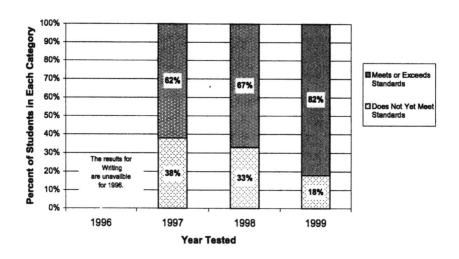

Figure 5. Reynolds High School: Writing.

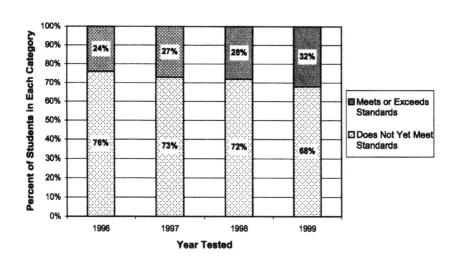

Figure 6. Reynolds High School: Mathematics.

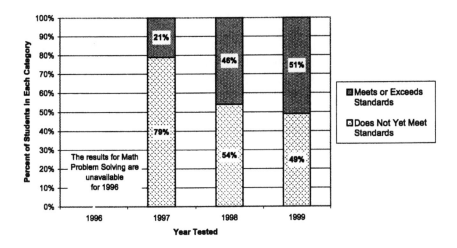

Figure 7. Reynolds High School: Math problem solving.

Based on the results of the state assessment, a listing of students not meeting standards in any or all of the areas tested has been sent to Reynolds High School. This report provides not only the names of students not meeting standards, but also specific areas of weakness for each student. This is powerful diagnostic information, and if used well, will contribute to continuing improvement in student performance as measured by state tests.

To put this analysis into the Reynolds context, the 10th grade students who took the test in 1999 are in the first class (class of 2001) who are required by district policy to pass the state CIM (or the local portfolio option) to graduate from high school. With the information provided, the high school community (students, staff, and parents) know they have 2 years to get all students up to the standards. It will be a challenge.

Summary

The Reynolds case shows congruence of approach to reform between the district and the state, including use of a national reform model, OTE. All efforts are moving the Reynolds system toward a professional control model of site-based management as the basis for increasing accountability of schools for continually improving student performance.

111

- The state provides tools for accountability through standards and tests. Both standards and tests focus on knowledge acquisition and use. Performance-based writing and math problem-solving tests measure application of knowledge and are challenging students statewide. School report cards are published and show the extent to which schools are meeting quality standards related to student performance and other indicators.
- The Oregon Department of Education is providing assistance to low-performing schools as they begin working toward establishing professional control leading to improved student performance. This is the support side of accountability, and two schools in Reynolds are receiving this direct support from the state.
- OTE is a national reform model that provides training and technical assistance to schools as they become professional learning communities, taking control of decisions that affect student learning and becoming increasingly accountable to the district and their constituencies for results.
- The Reynolds School District is using and extending state accountability tools, state support for low-performing schools, and key features of the OTE model to move all schools in the district toward increasing accountability for results.
- The Reynolds School District has established firm direction, is using some mechanisms for accountability (e.g., school review/feedback processes), has decentralized budget control to schools and expects professional control in budget decisions, and supports schools as they work to improve. The district is moving toward a consistent, system-wide approach to standards-based reform and accountability.

The Reynolds School District is an example of how standards can influence student performance. Gains have been modest to date, but there have been gains. This achievement takes on added importance when considering the fact that the percentages of low-income students and limited English speaking students have increased. Ethnic diversity among the student population is increasing, with the percentage of White students decreasing and that of students of other ethnic backgrounds increasing. Improvement in light of these factors is positive.

Through continuous effort since 1983, progress has been made toward a professional control model of site-based management as the approach to accountability. The stage has been set for real progress. Stay tuned. More to come in future years.

References

Block, J. H., Everson, S. T., & Guskey, T. R. (1999). *Comprehensive school reform: A program perspective.* Dubuque, IA: Kendall/Hunt.

Butler, J. A. (1982). *Development of competency-based education in Oregon.* Portland, OR: Northwest Regional Educational Laboratory.

Carr, M. S. (1998). *A regional depiction: Standards-based curriculum reform in the Northwest.* Portland, OR: Northwest Regional Educational Laboratory.

Leithwood, K., & Earl, L. (2000/this issue). Educational accountability effects: An international perspective. *Peabody Journal of Education, 75*(4), 1–18.

Linik, J. (1999). *Learning by example: Story 2. Glenfair Elementary School.* Portland, OR: Northwest Regional Educational Laboratory.

Mid-Continent Research for Education and Learning. (1998). *Taking stock of states' curriculum-based reform efforts: An interim report of the Laboratory Network Program's Curriculum, Learning and Instruction Project.* Aurora, CO: Author.

Oregon State Legislature. (1991). *Oregon education act for the 21st century: HB 3565 ORS.* Salem, OR: Author.

Oregon State Legislature. (1995). *Oregon Education Act for the 21st century: Improvement and reform.* Salem, OR: Author.

Reynolds School District. (1995). *Strategic plan for system improvement.* Troutdale, OR: Author.

Roeber, E. (1996). *Review of the Oregon content and performance standards.* Salem, OR: State Education Improvement Partnership.

School Implementation Team. (1997). *Framework for implementing K–12 school transformation in Oregon* [On-line]. Retrieved January 8, 1998 from the World Wide Web: http://www.ode.state.or.us

PEABODY JOURNAL OF EDUCATION, 75(4), 114–141

Embedding Accountability and Improvement Into Large-Scale Assessment: What Difference Does It Make?

Lorna Earl and Nancy Torrance

Assessment-led reform has become one of the most widely favored strategies to promote more credible forms of public accountability (Black, 1998). Unlike the assessment agenda of the 1960s and1970s, assessment programs in the 1990s and beyond are part of a broader scheme for changing education. Large-scale assessment has become the vehicle of choice for accountability purposes around the world, and testing has become the lever for holding schools accountable for results (Firestone, Mayrowetz, & Fairman, 1998).

Assessment reform, like other educational initiatives, is not singular, nor is it static. Like other reform efforts, it is caught in a maelstrom of rapid change and uncertainty. The knowledge base on assessment is being developed as the assessment procedures are being implemented, and many states, provinces, and countries are on a quest for the "best" approach.

LORNA EARL *is Associate Professor and Codirector of the International Centre for the Study of Educational Change at the Ontario Institute for Studies in Education, University of Toronto, Ontario, Canada.*

NANCY TORRANCE *is a Senior Research Officer at the University of Toronto, Ontario, Canada.*

Requests for reprints should be sent to Lorna Earl, Department of Theory and Policy Studies, OISE/University of Toronto, 252 Bloor Street West, Toronto, Ontario, M5S 1V6, Canada. E-mail: learl@oise.utoronto.ca

There is general agreement that large-scale assessment should have an impact on schools and on changing education. There are, however, at least two prevailing views about how educational changes might occur. As Darling-Hammond (1994) described them,

> One view seeks to induce change through extrinsic rewards and sanctions both to schools and students, on the assumption that the fundamental problem is a lack of will to change on the part of educators. The other view seeks to induce change by building knowledge among school practitioners and parents about alternative methods and by stimulating organizational rethinking through opportunities to work together on the design of teaching and schooling and to experiment with new approaches. This view assumes that the fundamental problem is a lack of knowledge about the possibilities for teaching and learning, combined with lack of organizational capacity for change. (p. 23)

These different philosophies have resulted in the development of very different large-scale assessment systems. In some cases, there has been a preoccupation with assessment results as evidence of accountability and the assessments used to provide incentives or sanctions for performance (Fuhrman, 1999; Guskey, 1994). In others, assessment is viewed as mechanisms for promoting higher standards of teaching and more powerful learning (Gipps, 1994; Murphy & Broadfoot, 1995). Districts, states, provinces, and nations are experimenting with various approaches to assessment, and the knowledge base on large-scale assessment is being developed at the same time as the assessment procedures are being implemented in what amounts to high-stakes field tests (Earl, 1996). Assessment programs are being put into place and evaluated at the same time to discover their impact on educators and on students.

In this article, we describe a large-scale assessment program that was initiated where none had existed before. The agency responsible intentionally tried to embed an improvement orientation into the assessment by focusing on how large-scale assessment can contribute to learning. The study is an investigation of the impact of the assessment on the way that schools were addressing accountability and improvement after the program had been in place for 2 years.

Developing Large-Scale Assessment on a Tabula Rasa

Large-scale assessment is a relatively recent phenomenon in the province of Ontario, Canada that began in this era of centralized reform. With

115

the exception of a few sample assessments of students during the 1970s and 1980s, the province had almost no history of large-scale assessment and none with "high stakes" for students, schools, or districts. During the 1980s, a nervous public was expressing concern about the educational system, and, in the early 1990s, both the provincial auditor and a Royal Commission on Learning mentioned inconsistency in education in the province and made recommendations that the school system should demonstrate how well it was doing. This led, in 1996, to the creation of the Education Quality and Accountability Office (EQAO), an arms-length agency of government charged with collecting, evaluating, and reporting information about educational quality, in particular large-scale student assessment.

EQAO had the opportunity to study the experiences and the research from other jurisdictions with a longer history of large-scale assessment before making decisions about the nature of their assessment program. The challenge that emerged was to develop a large-scale assessment program that was high quality and would also change practices in positive ways in classrooms. EQAO identified the following issues from their analysis of what had occurred elsewhere in the world as important to consider in making early decisions about the provincial assessment system:

• Assessment can be a powerful lever for educational change. Throughout the world, large-scale assessment had become the vehicle of choice for accountability on almost all educational reform agendas. Assessment reform can be based on beliefs that educational change is best realized when some external authority puts pressure on the system for compliance with mandates, or it can be envisioned as internal processes that occur when teachers reflect, question, plan, study, and learn (Darling-Hammond, 1992; Earl & LeMahieu, 1997). The focus can be on exposing and blaming or it can be on learning and capacity building. Both of these views have strong proponents, and the nature of an assessment can be influenced by and influence the direction of reform activities.

• Establishing the purpose of testing programs is paramount. There are many purposes for assessment, and these different purposes require very different approaches (Gipps, 1994). How an assessment can be interpreted and used is directly related to its original purpose. In the 1980s, testing was moving from being primarily an instrument for decision making about individual students to being the measure for holding schools accountable for results (Firestone et al., 1998), with the emphasis shifting to certification, accountability, and meeting standards (Torrance & Pryor, 1998). In recent years, assessment has become increasingly political. In England, for example, the purpose has shifted from influencing school practice to being the currency for accountability (Black, 1994).

• Assessment can be a control mechanism exercised by legislators to reward and punish or it can be a mechanism for focusing learning. In many locations, assessments were serving as the arbiter of decisions about things like performance pay and student intake. The effect was being felt directly in schools, and the assessments were designed to serve as motivation for increased performance. On the other hand, many authors were suggesting (e.g., Popham, 1999) that when large-scale assessment is disconnected from instruction and learning, it can lose its possibility of contributing to improving the caliber of schooling for children.

• Multiple choice tests were being criticized for placing too much emphasis on facts and procedures and failing to elicit a range of higher order thought processes. There was concern that these tests were based on a conception of learning that assumed complex concepts could be broken into discrete components and reassembled at a time when psychologists were proposing a very different learning model that required the integration of complex tasks (Darling-Hammond, 1994). Others were cautioning about the complexity and difficulties that were embedded in using performance tests (Linn, Baker, & Dunbar, 1991).

• Consequential validity was becoming an important issue for discussion in large-scale assessment (Linn et al., 1991; Messick, 1989, 1995; Moss, 1992). If validity were not a property of the assessment but a process of constructing and evaluating arguments for and against proposed test interpretations and uses (Haertel, 2000), then the nature of the assessment could directly influence schooling practices. For example, when "high stakes" were attached to the test, there was evidence that curriculum and instruction were being affected in unintended ways because of "teaching to the test." If the intention of large-scale assessment was to improve schools, narrowing and simplifying the curriculum was counterproductive. If the interpretations, conclusions, and decisions that emerge from the assessment are not valid, an assessment may be more problematic than it is useful (Goldstein, 1993). Many jurisdictions were discovering that, along with anticipated consequences, there were often unanticipated consequences of a large-scale assessment. Very often the unanticipated consequences were more aligned with political and moral issues rather than testing issues. Nevertheless, they have important implications for assessment programs.

• School effectiveness and improvement research was drawing attention to the fact that schools could make a difference in student achievement, but that they were not the only factors that contributed to student learning. Researchers were beginning to collect contextual information about student demographics, prior achievement, classroom practices, teacher experience and training, and so forth, that might have an influence on achievement, in order to get better estimates of the factors that make a difference.

• Educational assessment and accountability had become a central issue in public discourse. Because education is important to everyone, it is always a "lightning rod" for attention. A great deal of energy was being focused on how to communicate about schools with parents and the public. Large-scale assessments were contributing to decision making by students, parents, and the general public. How could assessment procedures and scores be presented in ways that were transparent and understood by a naïve audience? What was the best way to ensure that the results will be interpreted and used appropriately?

Moving From Learning to Doing

Both accountability and improvement were central to the mandate of EQAO. Their task was to develop and implement a large-scale assessment system that provided data for accountability and that contributed to improved teaching and learning. As the CEO, Joan Green expressed the EQAO focus, in the first Provincial Report on Achievement (Education Quality and Accountability Office, 1997):

> EQAO believes that large-scale assessment can contribute to positive educational change when it engages educators, parents and students in thought and discussion about what takes place in the classroom. We are testing what children know and can do. We are measuring against provincial standards to obtain information on what we need to do so that all students can learn more and learn better. (p. 3)

Within this framework, EQAO assessments were intended to ensure both accountability and improvement at the same time. EQAO decided to approach the task within the framework of change theory and attempt to create an assessment system that was designed to balance the pressure and support that underpin successful change in schools (Fullan, 1991). The introduction of the assessment itself constituted a powerful source of pressure for schools. The initial reaction to the focus on accountability was anger and foreboding. Educators felt as if they were being placed under public scrutiny and were both hurt and frightened by the prospect. Because there was no history of assessment for accountability in Ontario, EQAO examined what it might mean in practice to use assessment to "be accountable." They settled on a definition of accountability that focused on engaging the public in the educational debate. Although there is general agreement that accountability is a good thing, there is little agreement about what it is.

Accountability is often framed as gathering information and preparing a report so that interested parties have the information that they believe to be pertinent. EQAO determined that this approach was too narrow and more consistent with "accounting"—using assessments to provide a summary of the state of affairs at a point in time that has already passed. They adopted the broader interpretation of "accountability as conversation"—using assessments, along with other knowledge, as the starting point for a conversation about current performance and next steps. Much more than statistics, accountability was viewed as a deeply human enterprise that depends on openness; sharing of information; and ongoing conversations among and between educators, students, parents, and the community as they explore available information and establish action plans. Accountability engenders trust; relationships; and a willingness to engage in clear, candid, and considerate discussions (Earl & LeMahieu, 1997).

Along with this expanded notion of accountability, EQAO decided that improvement activities based on the assessment could not be left to happenstance. Changes in practices that could affect learning were only likely to happen if teachers and others had the knowledge and the capacity to do something different. EQAO decided to intentionally focus their efforts on how the assessment could influence teaching and learning. If the assessment was to offer support for improvement, not just pressure, the support had to be incorporated into the process and provide images of different ways of behaving, along with the training and practice necessary to actually embed those changes into routine practice.

Getting to Both Accountability and Improvement

This article focuses specifically on the Grade 3 assessments of Reading, Writing, and Mathematics that occurred in 1996–1997 and 1997–1998 (the first 2 years of the assessment program). These were the first assessments undertaken by EQAO using their accountability and improvement framework. The official purposes for the EQAO Grade 3 assessment were as follows:

- Monitor and report on the knowledge and performance of students in Ontario schools.
- Provide recommendations and resources for improving knowledge and performance levels of students.
- Contribute to the improvement of classroom instruction and assessment at the classroom level.

The explicit commitment of EQAO to both accountability and improvement provided them with a foundation for decisions about the nature of the assessment and the approach to reporting and public communication. The focus was intentionally on developing high-quality assessments that contributed to valid and reliable interpretations and on building the capacity of educators to understand and use assessments wisely to promote student learning. EQAO recognized that large-scale assessment was a new phenomenon for most educators and that there would be a steep learning curve. With this in mind, every stage of the assessment process was designed to contribute to building new skills and knowledge for teachers and administrators:

• The assessments were designed as integrated reading, writing, and mathematics units of work that included instructional tasks and assessment tasks and were completed over a number of days. They were intended to give concrete images of good practice that make connections among the subjects and to provide a model for a balanced and integrated mathematics and language arts program. The tasks called for complex thinking and the ability to apply knowledge in novel situations. The tasks were curriculum-based and standards-referenced and included a number of response formats, with most of the questions presented as open-ended extended response. If teachers were going to "teach to the test," the assessment units were designed to be worth emulating. The tasks represented a full range of assessment strategies with most of the assessment tasks being open-ended. They included engaging and novel activities and resources that were appealing to students in the pilot phases. EQAO develops new assessment units each year so that the past assessments can become part of a teacher's classroom repertoire.

• A cadre of teachers, representing every district in the province, were trained as trainers to provide teachers in the province with a full day of training to implement the assessment and to become on-site resources to support teachers and administrators during and after the assessment.

• The EQAO assessments were accompanied by a number of questionnaires designed to gather information from teachers, students, parents, and principals about the nature of the program and instruction, resources, characteristics of the students and their home lives, student attitudes, and so forth, as a basis for investigations of the salient features in student achievement.

• The completed booklets (reading, writing, and mathematics, separately) were scored holistically using a 4-point rubric with anchor papers and detailed descriptions of the evidence that was used in the anchor papers to support the classification. These rubrics emphasize the quality of the thinking and problem solving that are evidenced in the students' responses to the assessment tasks. They were scored in reading and writing on dimensions of reasoning, communication, organization of ideas, and application of language conventions. In mathematics, the scoring included understanding of concepts, application of procedures, problem solving, communications and content related to measurement, spatial sense and geometry, number sense and numeration, patterning and algebra, and data management and probability. Students could demonstrate their understanding in a variety of ways.

• Teachers of Grades 1–3 were paid to do the scoring in the summer in one central location with intensive training and monitoring of their work. In this way, the scoring was not only monitored for reliability but also served as concentrated staff development for practicing teachers. The teachers worked together to enhance one another's understanding of instruction and curriculum, develop agreement about the nature and quality of instruments and approaches for assessing student work, challenge and question their own beliefs about expectations for students, and develop confidence in their decisions and their ability to describe student achievement to the outside community.

• Individual reports were prepared for students that provided a profile of their performance and a strategy for teachers to use the exemplars to talk to parents and their child about how the information fit with the program and other information about the child. Schools and districts were required to prepare their own reports based on the material provided by EQAO and augmented by other material (e.g., demographics, program descriptions) that included their interpretation of the results for the particular school and an action plan based on the interpretation. EQAO provided schools with guidelines to help them discuss the students' reports with parents and to prepare school reports that included more information about the school than just assessment results.

• EQAO released a provincial report and provided support to administrators in talking about it to their communities. Messages about the appropriate and inappropriate interpretations were embedded in all communications and emphasized in all media coverage. At the time of reporting, EQAO refused to release results ranked by school and worked very hard with the media to develop different angles for their stories that focused on interpretations with an improvement focus. EQAO produced a provincial report that identified four general recommendations (creating a culture of assessment, focusing the curriculum, supporting student learning, communicating and interpreting assessment findings) and 21 recommendations specific to primary and junior programs that could be implemented almost immediately. These included classroom activities for teachers, professional activities for teachers, parent activities, and activities for school councils and school administrators.

• The provincial, district, and school reports were intended to be the starting point for the conversations that EQAO associated with account-ability. The focus was on providing simple, accessible, and transparent in-formation to educators, parents, and the community. The intention was that they could use the information to rethink and refocus their priorities and their resources for assisting all children to be successful in developing the foundations of reading, writing, and mathematics in the primary years of schooling.

• EQAO mounted an intensive public relations campaign to familiarize the educators and the public with the nature and uses of the assessment process and results. The public communication strategy emphasized hav-ing a focus on conversations directed toward improvement and learning, with considerable emphasis on understanding the kind of learning that was expected of the students and what "good work" looked like. After the reports have been released, they continue to analyze data and distribute monographs and press releases based on the findings from the research.

What Difference Did the Assessment Process Make?

EQAO believed that, taken together, all of these activities would influ-ence the way that educators and the community viewed assessment and utilized the findings. Assessments that model good practices are con-nected to the curriculum and provide a range of ways to consider how the findings ought to change practices in the schools and help teachers de-velop the necessary capacities to enhance the amount and quality of stu-dent learning.

As EQAO knew from its early review of the literature, the actual be-haviors of stakeholders can be very different than was intended. EQAO tried to design the Grade 3 assessment and their communication strategy to ensure that schools saw the assessment as a valuable part of their ac-countability to the community and of their planning and efforts to adjust and enhance instruction and learning in the schools. They had some early indication from surveys conducted with the teachers who participated in the scoring of the assessments that the staff development had been enor-mously successful and that they were, indeed, changing programs and instruction as a result of their experience (EQAO, 1997). Although there were anecdotal reports that the assessment was having a positive influ-ence on school programs, there were also many rumblings about the neg-ative effects of the assessment on morale and on curriculum focus. It was not at all clear what the impact of the assessment had been on the prov-ince's schools generally.

In the Spring of 1998, the authors undertook a study to investigate the extent to which the EQAO Grade 3 assessments that had taken place in the 2 prior years had influenced accountability and improvement in Ontario schools. An extensive survey was sent to each elementary school in the province ($N \approx 2,400$) asking about their participation in the assessment, use of the reports, changes in the school, implementation of the EQAO recommendations, and the extent to which any changes were attributable to the EQAO assessments. Surveys were returned from 839 schools for about a 35% response rate. Surveys were returned from all districts in the province, but it is not clear how well they represented the demographic makeup of the province, which contains one very large metropolitan city, a number of midsize cities, and many rural areas.

In this article, we have analyzed some of the data from the survey in an attempt to examine the extent to which the EQAO assessments were actually achieving their stated goals. Were the accountability conversations happening in local communities or not? Were the recommendations being implemented? Had anything changed in the schools as a result of the assessment process or the recommendations? Did the assessment influence allocation of resources, staff development, teaching and learning strategies, assessment approaches, and so forth? Were there any unanticipated consequences?

Given the low response rate and the likelihood that the responses came from schools that are engaged in some of the activities that were included on the survey, the results are likely over-estimates of the actual impact and should be considered in that light.

Accountability

EQAO routinely emphasized that accountability was fundamentally related to using the assessment process and results to talk about curriculum, school programs, and student learning. They intended that districts and schools would use the assessment as an opportunity to engage with parents and the community and to share their action plans for enhancing student learning. Several survey questions focused on the extent to which and the ways in which schools had used the Grade 3 Assessment to further conversations among teachers within the schools and with parents and the community by using the Provincial Report and its recommendations, as well as their own school results.

Table 1 gives a summary of the extent to which the Provincial Report was in different forums. The respondents indicated that the Provincial Report was a focus for discussions in schools all over the province of Ontario. The

Table 1
Use of Provincial Assessment Report

Provincial Assessment	% Yes
Recommendations discussed at one or more staff meetings	92
Recommendations discussed at one or more parent meetings	82
Recommendations discussed at one or more community-wide meetings	19
Recommendations circulated to school teaching staff	90
Recommendations circulated to other school staff	43
Recommendations circulated to parents of all students	42

recommendations were discussed at staff meetings and at parent meetings. The form of the discussions with parents is not clear, however, and fewer than half of the schools actually circulated the recommendations beyond the school or even within the school to nonteaching staff. Although educators appeared to be very involved in conversations about the recommendations made by EQAO based on provincial analysis, many of them were keeping the discussion within the school. This is surprising because many of the recommendations were directed specifically at parents and the community.

In addition to the provincial report, each school was expected to produce a school report that included the EQAO results along with other information about the particular school that might contribute to interpretation. The schools received a handbook from EQAO to assist them in producing their school report. The survey results indicated that about 75% of the schools that responded actually prepared a school report, and 91% of those who prepared a report shared it with the school community. This means that over 30% of the schools that responded either did not prepare a report or, if they did, did not share it beyond the school.

When schools shared the school report, they used the dissemination approaches presented in order of frequency in Table 2. These categories were not mutually exclusive; respondents could select as many as applied. This table allows a closer look at the mechanisms that schools used to provide information to the public. It is clear that they relied on print dissemination, most often as part of a routine newsletter. It appears that the schools were incorporating the assessment into business as usual and not drawing undue attention to the assessment process or the results. Very few schools created opportunities for the kind of conversation that EQAO intended. When there was a face-to-face discussion, it was more likely to be with the parents of the children in the assessment, and very few (17%) schools convened a community conversation.

At the same time as the schools were gently introducing the assessment results to their communities, the media was much more aggressive. Most

Table 2
School Report: Dissemination Approaches

Dissemination Approach	% Yes
Report incorporated or summarized in a newsletter	63
Report sent home to parents of Grade 3 students	54
School announcement that report was available on request	49
Report sent home to all parents	45
Board announcement that report was available on request	38
Parent's night for parents of Grade 3 students	27
Parent's night for all school parents	26
Discussion in a community-wide forum	17

newspapers in the province elected to rank the local schools, and many featured stories about the best and the worst schools in the district or the province, based solely on the Grade 3 assessment results.

Improvement

EQAO intended that the Grade 3 Assessments would influence school practices in a number of ways. They were designed to provide teachers and administrators with models of teaching and learning that would be emulated and adopted in their schools. Specifically, EQAO hoped that schools would make changes to their practices and perhaps even begin to develop instructional units based on the same principles as the assessment units. The results for individual students invited a conversation with parents that focused on the nature of the reading, writing, and mathematics programs and how they are different from what parents might remember. Provincial, district, and school reports were presented and discussed in ways that EQAO expected would influence the focus and amount of staff development that was available to and utilized by teachers. The specific recommendations in the Provincial Report provided suggestions about activities that could begin almost immediately, and EQAO anticipated that teachers would incorporate some of them into their routines and suggest others to parents and the community. The more general overall recommendations provided a framework for assessment-led reform in the province over the next few years.

The survey asked for information about how schools were using the information and the recommendations from the Grade 3 assessment. About 80% of the schools indicated that the assessment had led to changes in the reading and in the writing programs, and 90% said they had made changes

125

in the mathematics program. Ninety percent indicated that they made changes to instructional strategies and 80% to assessment strategies. Table 3 shows the kinds of changes that were made in school programs and planning generally.

School administrators took the results seriously and established a distinct focus on reading, writing, and mathematics that, in many schools, translated into more resources. In some cases, they used the results as the impetus for rethinking of their program and timetable for instruction, but very few of them took drastic moves like reworking the program or hiring new staff. However, teachers in over 75% of the schools increased their participation in staff development in reading, writing, and mathematics and took advantage of district staff development programs linked to the assessment.

The survey contained a series of questions that asked about the extent to which the activities mentioned in the specific recommendations for action to support learning in reading, writing, and mathematics were happening in the school, along with the extent to which each one had been influenced by the EQAO assessment process and recommendations. The results from these questions are displayed in Tables 3, 4, and 5, respectively, displayed in rank order based on regular or frequent occurrence.

Recommendations for Improving Reading

The results in Table 4 show that many of the recommendations for improving reading were already standard practice in many schools. However, the assessments had been influential in promoting or sustaining the activities. As might be expected, the influence was particularly obvious for activities that were directly related to the information that was provided as a

Table 3
Changes in School Programs and Planning

	% Yes		
Change	*Reading*	*Writing*	*Math*
More resources put into the program	82	66	89
More time given to instruction	37	41	55
Complete reworking of the program	17	17	31
New hires with expertise in the area	13	10	5
More participation in professional development related to reading, writing, and/or mathematics		74	

result of the assessment (questionnaire results, provincial results, etc.) It was also evident in questions related to the provincial curriculum and to classroom resources. Educators were using the assessments to focus their attention on curriculum, instruction, assessment, and resources and ensure appropriateness and coherence. They were not using the reading assessment to change their interaction with parents or to promote self-evaluation in their students.

Recommendations for Improving Writing

Table 5 shows that, with the exception of working with parents on writing-related activities, encouraging student self-evaluation, and referring to a provincial writing project, many of the activities were already happening in the schools. Where the recommendations were directly related to the assessments or to the curriculum expectations, it was obvious that they had an influence. In other areas, the influence of the assessments was present but more modest, with 30 to 50% of the schools acknowledging that the assessments had influenced their practices.

Recommendations for Improving Mathematics

In mathematics (Table 6), like reading and writing, student self-evaluation and working directly with parents on mathematics-related activities were the least implemented recommendations, although the respondents indicated that the assessments had influenced the self-evaluation that was happening. The other recommendations were happening in most schools, and they had been influenced by the assessments in 50 to 75% of the schools.

Overall Recommendations

The EQAO Provincial Report put forward four overriding recommendations designed to set the stage for implementation and interpretation of large-scale assessment in the province for years to come: creating a culture of assessment, focusing curriculum, supporting student learning and communicating, and interpreting assessment results. Each of the recommendations included a number of specific activities for teachers, parents, and schools.

Survey respondents were asked to indicate the extent to which the activity was happening in the school and the extent to which it had been influ-

Table 4
Schools' Response to Recommendations for Improving Reading

Reading Recommendations	Happening in the School (% Regularly or Frequently)	Influenced by Assessment (% Yes)
Use of a variety of individual and group approaches to teach skills and extend students' understanding.	94	41
Observation of individual students to identify necessary interventions.	93	42
Use of a wide range of reading materials and text forms.	93	12
Ensuring that students pay attention to features of text-like organization or ideas and tables of contents and use them to improve their understanding.	88	46
Encouraging parents to listen to their children read.	83	26
Identifying from questionnaire data the areas of strength and weakness that need to be addressed.	83	79
Reviewing student achievement results in relation to provincial results.	82	77
Reviewing the language expectations defined in the curriculum for each grade level and identifying the progressive and cumulative nature of the skills in these categories.	82	59
Paying attention to the kinds of materials that girls and boys find interesting and using it to motivate both groups to read.	81	32
Reviewing the EQAO materials, including samples of student work at different levels and the scoring scales.	80	78

Reviewing EQAO's scoring scale for reading with particular attention to the specific components identified within each category and to how scale describes achievement across the four levels.	76	77
Determining other resources and in-service support needed to adapt and modify teaching and learning practices and strategies.	76	59
Developing competence in using a range of assessment strategies for evaluating reading.	72	43
Encouraging parents to talk about reading with their children.	71	31
Reviewing reading programs to determine whether the skills associated with each category are incorporated appropriately in all grades.	66	56
Working to increase adult awareness of the value of reading to children.	58	26
Working together to develop ways to describe good work in reading so that students become better self-assessors.	51	46
Collaborating with others to assess their students' work at various stages.	48	47
Using EQAO assessment activities and exemplars to develop classroom assessment tools.	46	69
Encouraging parents to pay attention to the kinds of materials that girls and boys find interesting and using it to motivate them to read.	42	28
Having students interpret EQAO reading scales in their own words and use them to evaluate their own work.	30	50

Note. EQAO = Education Quality and Accountability Office.

Table 5
Schools' Responses to Recommendations for Improving Writing

Writing Recommendations	Happening in the School (% Regularly or Frequently)	Influenced by Assessment (% Yes)
Giving students instruction and practice in correcting and revising both the organization and the conventions of their own writing.	91	38
Encouraging students to do more writing and write frequently in a variety of forms.	90	39
Keeping dated and annotated samples of each student's writing and using them to show the student and the parent(s) the progress that has been made.	89	34
Using regular and precise observation of individual students' writing skills to identify students who require intervention to be successful.	88	42
Providing opportunities for students to work individually and collaboratively through the various stages of the writing process with particular attention to the revision and editing stages.	88	33
Giving students detailed feedback, both orally and in writing, about early stages and drafts of their writing and monitoring improvements in subsequent efforts.	87	38
Ensuring that all writing skills are included in the writing program by using the overall and specific language expectations in the curriculum.	84	50
Identifying from questionnaire data the areas of strength and weakness that need to be addressed.	80	74
Reviewing achievement results for students in the context of provincial writing results.	78	72
Using classroom reading activities as opportunities to model the ways in which published writers organize and develop their ideas and use different organizational patterns and voices to convey information or opinions.	73	33
Reviewing the language expectations defined in the curriculum across all grades to identify the progressive and cumulative nature of the skills and determine which writing skills fit into which categories.	73	57

Activity		
Reviewing EQAO's scoring scale for writing with particular attention to the specific components identified within each of four categories (reasoning, communication, organization of ideas, and application of language conventions) and to descriptions of achievement across the four levels.	72	74
Reviewing the EQAO materials, including samples of student work at different levels and the scoring scales.	72	72
Determining other resources and in-service support needed to adapt and modify teaching and learning practices and strategies.	69	55
Using scoring scales and anchors to assess student work and to improve assessment of student work and provide better feedback.	65	54
Reviewing district and school writing programs to determine the extent to which the skills associated with the categories are incorporated across the grades and in specific programs within the grade.	62	53
Working with other teachers to develop ways to describe good work in writing to help all their students become better self-assessors.	58	47
Checking the frequency and extent to which the skills are integrated through real writing experiences for different purposes and audiences.	55	47
Referring to the material in the provincial Writing Exemplars Project.	39	51
Having teachers and parents work together to engage students in enjoyable and useful writing activities such as lists and notes about everyday activities, poems, letters, neighborhood newsletters, or classroom publications.	32	27
Having students interpret EQAO's writing assessment scale in their own words and encouraging them to use it to evaluate their own and other students' writing.	28	43

Note. EQAO = Education Quality and Accountability Office.

Table 6
Schools' Responses to Recommendations for Improving Mathematics

Mathematics Recommendations	Happening in the School (% Regularly or Frequently)	Influenced by Assessment (% Yes)
Distributing time spent on mathematics across all five strands so that all of the concepts and procedures are taught.	92	52
Using regular and precise observation of individual students' mathematics skills to identify students who require intervention to be successful.	89	39
Ensuring that the mathematics program addresses all strands and components within each category and includes activities that call for higher order thinking; referring to the overall and specific mathematics expectations in the curriculum and the category and strand descriptions in EQAO's scoring scales.	87	54
Identifying from questionnaire data the areas of strength and weakness that need to be addressed.	85	75
Determining what resources and in-service support are needed to improve programs.	81	62
Reviewing achievement results for students in the context of provincial mathematics results.	78	72
Using a range of activities (e.g., practical problem solving, drill, etc.) to extend students' understanding and application of number sense and numeration.	74	45
Ensuring that students have opportunities to communicate using everyday and mathematical language, both orally and through journal writing.	74	57
Reviewing EQAO's scoring scale for mathematics with particular attention to the specific components identified within each of four categories (problem solving, understanding concepts, applying procedures, and communicating in mathematics) and five strands (number sense and numeration, geometry and spatial sense, patterning and algebra, and data management and probability) and to how the scale describes achievement across the four levels.	74	71
Reviewing the specific mathematics expectations defined in the curriculum across the grades and determining the progressive and cumulative nature of the skills in these categories.	74	57

Regularly integrating activities that involve mathematics across all subject areas in the school.	72	40
Reviewing EQAO materials, including samples of student work at different levels, and the scoring scales.	70	72
Communicating with parents, describing home-based and out-of-school activities they can do with their children to develop mathematical skills in number sense, patterning, geometry, graphs, and probability.	64	48
Taking part in staff development in the areas where teachers indicate discomfort or where the students' results clustered in Levels 1 and 2.	60	58
Reviewing school and board programs to identify whether the skills associated with each category are incorporated in specific programs within and across grades and ensuring that skills are integrated through real-life applications of the various mathematics activities within strands.	58	54
Using the EQAO assessment materials as one basis for developing activities and questions that address each strand and category.	54	61
Working with other teachers to develop ways to describe good work in mathematics to help all their students become better self-assessors.	50	50
Having teachers and parents work together to engage students in enjoyable and useful mathematics activities and using mathematics in the home and asking children to explain their thinking.	18	32
Working with school councils to encourage students to apply what they know and can do in mathematics beyond the school environment.	11	27
Having mathematics fairs that involve parents and/or initiate family mathematics programs (in which parents and children work together on mathematical concepts).	4	18
Having students interpret EQAO's mathematics assessment scale in their own words and encouraging them to use it to evaluate their own and other students' work.	31	49

Note. EQAO = Education Quality and Accountability Office.

enced by the EQAO assessment process and recommendations. Their responses are summarized in Tables 7–10.

In a culture of assessment, teachers, students, parents, and the community come to regard assessment as essential feedback to learning. In such a culture, assessments are not frightening, but are taken seriously and used to identify ways to promote and support learning for all students. It appears from Table 7 that they were somewhat successful in their goal, even in these early years of the provincial assessment process. The assessment documents were being used for planning in schools and districts, for identifying and acquiring needed resources, and for decisions about instruction in classrooms. Some schools were using the assessment to make changes to the way teach-

Table 7
Recommendation: Creating a Culture of Assessment

Activities for Teachers, Parents, and School	Happening in the School (% Regularly)	Influenced by Assessment (% Yes)
(S) Reviewing school results in relation to province and district	90	78
(S) Identifying areas of strength and weakness that need to be addressed	89	84
(S) Determining required resources and district and community supports	88	60
(S) Encouraging staff to develop and share their expertise with each other	86	52
(S) Determining key issues to be addressed in the school plan and integrating them into initiatives	82	67
(T) Classroom assessment activities to find out where students are in their learning and what they need to do next	82	50
(S) Reviewing district planning documents to establish their utility in school initiatives	81	58
(P) Teachers and parents encouraged to review the assessment results and share in the development of individual learning plans	81	59
(T) Consulting with parents and community to establish action plans based on the assessment	61	62
(T) Using assessment to create individual learning plans for students	52	58
(T) Adopting team-based assessment approaches	47	43

Note. S = school; T = teachers; P = parents.

Table 8
Recommendation: Focusing the Curriculum

Activities for Teachers, Parents, and School	Happening in the School (% Regularly)	Influenced by Assessment (% Yes)
(T) Reviewing student time-on-task to ensure effective use of instructional time	60	34
(T) Using the expectations in the provincial curriculum to plan instruction	85	41

Note. T = teachers.

Table 9
Recommendation: Supporting Student Learning

Activities for Teachers, Parents, and School	Happening in the School (% Regularly)	Influenced by Assessment (% Yes)
(S) Creating opportunities for students to use computers as learning tools	93	21
(S) Showing students and parents that effort and motivation are key factors in success	91	36
(S) Monitoring the level of involvement and motivation of students	89	24
(S) Monitoring the progress of special needs students toward the standard	87	22
(S) Reviewing programs to identify strategies that foster improved student attitudes	87	33
(S) Involving community members as active participants in the school	85	27
(T) Diagnosis of strengths and weaknesses and focusing instruction for individuals and groups of students	80	40
(T) Using assessment rubric and exemplars to explain expectations to students	75	49
(T) Teaching students how to assess themselves and providing practice	71	43

Note. S = school; T = teachers.

ers were diagnosing and teaching their students. Although there was some encouragement for and some beginning activities designed to engage the parents and the community in using the assessment for planning, not much of this activity appeared to have actually happened.

Although many of the schools reported that they were already focusing the curriculum based on the provincial documents (Table 8), this activity

Table 10
Recommendation: Communicating and Interpreting Assessment Findings

Activities for Teachers, Parents, and School	Happening in the School (% Regularly)	Influenced by Assessment (% Yes)
Continuing the conversations about student achievement and improvement strategies.	85	53
Communicating about the purpose of the assessment, the expectations for students, quality of student work, and how schools and the home provide support for learning.	78	54
Identifying factors that are related to student achievement.	66	43

was strengthened for many of them by their involvement in the provincial assessment. This is not surprising because the assessment is a visible representation of the curriculum in practice. It provided teachers and administrators with some concrete examples of what they might do in their schools and classrooms.

Table 9 shows that teachers and schools were continuing with their past practices of promoting the use of computers, monitoring student involvement in their learning, monitoring students with special needs, reviewing programs, and involving the community in the school. About 20% to 50% of the schools indicated that these activities were influenced by the assessment. The assessment may have provided them with a catalyst or provided the motivation for continuing with activities in which they already engaged.

Assessment-related activities were more directly affected by the provincial assessment. In the cases of using assessment to focus instruction, explain expectations, and develop skills of self-assessment, almost half of the schools felt that the assessment influenced their behavior. Because these are important parts of enhancing learning, they are likely valuable additions to the repertoire of activities that schools are using. Nevertheless, there were still around 25% of the schools that were not engaged in any of these practices.

The final recommendation from EQAO was focused on the ways in which schools were using the provincial assessment process and results to learn more about their students and to share what they knew with the community. The respondents indicated (Table 10) that they were using the assessments as vehicles for communicating outside the school about assessment and curriculum and for investigating the factors that affect learning in their schools. These are seen, in over half the cases, as having been influenced by the assessment process and recommendations. Because so few of the schools indicated being involved in formal interaction with members of the community to talk about the process or the results, this activity is likely done on an informal basis by the administrators and teachers.

Overall, it seems that the assessment process and recommendations had a noticeable effect on improvement planning and practices in Ontario schools. Most of the recommendations were being addressed by a substantial percentage of the respondents, and many of them attributed their activity to the assessment, at least in part.

Conclusions and Implications

Using large-scale assessment as a vehicle for educational reform is a very complex and uncertain undertaking. As Fullan (1999) reminded us, there are many forces at work in educational change, and they operate together in unpredictable ways. It is particularly important for policy researchers to routinely investigate the actual consequences of policies that are enacted. In this case, large-scale assessment was intended to influence beliefs and practices—a very big undertaking.

EQAO, the provincial assessment agency in Ontario, began its work with the intention of not only providing credible information about student achievement, but also of stimulating accountability conversations and facilitating activities that were likely to improve teaching and learning. The findings from this province-wide survey provide a snapshot of the extent to which the schools' responses to the Grade 3 provincial assessments in 1996–1997 and 1997–1998 were consistent with EQAO's intentions.

Accountability

EQAO had a fairly clear notion of what accountability would look like, if their wildest expectations were met. The conversations that the agency identified as fundamental to building the trust, confidence, and community responsibility for education would be rampant in schools, the media, community centers, and places of worship; at sporting event and concerts; and in board rooms and living rooms. Teachers, principals, parents, and the community would be talking and thinking about education, about what students need to learn and how learning happens, about the nature of schooling, and about what role they can each play. In the short term, the provincial assessments were seen as an opportunity for schools to begin the conversations in small ways in their local communities. The assessments could be the "stuff" of conversations about things like the curriculum expectations, changes in instruction and resources, and ways that parents and others can participate in children's learning. The findings from this survey are disappointing in this regard. Most of the schools who responded indicated that they had engaged in many conversations based on the assessment, the provincial recommendations, and their own school results. Unfortunately, most of these conversations were internal—teachers with teachers and principals with teachers. Although most of the schools had complied with the requirement that they produce a school report, they downplayed the assessment in communication with noneducators, even the ones who worked within their school. The results were disseminated in writing as part of a newsletter and/or shared with only a selected segment of the population. There was little evidence that educators showed enthusiasm for the public interface that accountability conversations require.

If accountability is conceived as a public conversation, moving "Out There" is an important part of the educational reform process. Hargreaves and Fullan (1998) dedicated a complete book to an exploration of why teachers and principals should work with others outside the school for better teaching and learning within it. They make a compelling case for changing the educational stance toward the wider world beyond schools and making the boundaries more permeable. Their analysis also identifies many reasons why there is resistance and suspicion about what such bold moves might lead to. Opening the doors is a frightening prospect that may leave schools and educators feeling very vulnerable. Schools have survived over the years by being self-contained and have accumulated all kinds of structural and cultural habits that keep others out.

Perhaps most important, Hargreaves and Fullan (1998) pointed out the difficulties inherent in the transition and offer a number of suggestions about how to proceed. Positive relations with the world outside school are not all straightforward. Educators need to capture the imagination and commitment of individuals and groups with whom they have little experience or connection. To do this, they need to acquire a whole new set of skills and the confidence to use them to make formal and informal connections grounded in a commitment to education, to each other, and to the community.

In addition to "getting out there," educators are often uncomfortable and insecure about their capacity to talk about large-scale assessment. As Stiggins (1995) has often reminded us, our society is increasingly dependent on tests, assessments, indicators, and statistics as the basis for making decisions, but we are so "assessment illiterate" that we are unable to distinguish between sound and unsound assessments or to interpret assessment results accurately for the public. Becoming "assessment literate" can help teachers and principals be more self-assured and at ease in public conversations.

Improvement

Within the context of educational reform, capacity is the ability of the education system to help all students meet more challenging standards (O'Day, Goertz, & Floden, 1995). If the capacity of the educational system is not sufficient to accomplish the intended goals, the obvious strategy for making changes is to increase the knowledge and the skills of the teachers and administrators who work in it. In this view, teachers as learners sit at the center of school change.

The Grade 3 assessments, from development to reporting, were designed with a conscious focus on improving learning by building the capacity of educators and the general public to support learning for students. The rationale was that significant and sustainable change is not likely to happen unless there are changes in classroom practices of instruction, assessment, and student motivation. To do this, teachers were given images of and opportunities to acquire both knowledge and skills and to practice, reflect, and incorporate new ideas and approaches into their daily activities. The Grade 3 assessments were designed to give them opportunities and resources to facilitate their learning.

The survey findings suggest that their intentions were borne out, even in these early years of the assessment program. Schools were focusing their efforts, teachers were participating in staff development, curriculum was being reviewed and connected to instruction, and teachers were working together to refine their programs. All of these activities have the potential to build schools' capacity to improve and sustain student learning (Stoll, 1999).

Making a Difference

This case example provides some insight into the complexity of using a large-scale assessment process as a mechanism for both accountability and school improvement. The efforts to foster capacity building were making an impact that ought to result in improved student learning in future evaluations. The issue of accountability was much more intractable. Educators were reluctant to use the assessment as a starting point to move outside their insular worlds and engage in educational conversations in the community. It is likely that educators do not have the training or experience that they need to fulfil this role. This suggests another domain for capacity

139

building. Educators will need images, opportunities to learn and to practice, and supports to engage in "accountability conversations."

References

Black, P. (1994). Performance assessment and accountability: The experience in England and Wales. *Educational Evaluation and Policy Analysis, 16*, 191–204.

Black, P. (1998). *Testing: Friend or foe? Theory and practice of assessment and testing.* London/Washington, DC: Falmer.

Darling-Hammond, L. (1992, November). Reframing the school reform agenda. *The School Administrator*, pp. 22–27.

Darling-Hammond, L. (1994). Performance-based assessment and educational equity. *Harvard Educational Review, 64*, 23.

Earl, L. (1996). Comprehensive assessment and accountability. In K. Leithwood (Ed.), *The knowledge base for educational reform* (pp. 3–20). Toronto, Canada: Ontario Institute for Studies in Education/University of Toronto.

Earl, L., & LeMahieu, P. (1997). Rethinking assessment and accountability. In A. Hargreaves (Ed.), *Rethinking educational change with heart and mind. 1997 ASCD yearbook.* Alexandria, VA: Association for Supervision and Curriculum Development.

Education Quality and Accountability Office. (1997). *Provincial report on achievement: English language schools.* Toronto, Canada: Queen's Printer for Ontario.

Firestone, W., Mayrowetz, D., & Fairman, J. (1998). Performance-based assessment and instructional change: The effects of testing in Maine and Maryland. *Educational Evaluation and Policy Analysis, 20*(2), 95–113.

Fuhrman, S. (1999). *The new accountability* [Consortium for Policy Research in Education (CPRE)]. Philadelphia: Graduate School of Education, University of Pennsylvania.

Fullan, M. (1991). *The new meaning of educational change.* Toronto, Canada/New York: OISE/Teachers College Press.

Fullan, M. (1999). *Change focus: The sequel.* Philadelphia: Falmer.

Gipps, C. V. (1994). *Beyond testing.* London: Falmer.

Goldstein, H. (1993). *Assessment and accountability* [Parliamentary Brief]. London.

Guskey, T. (Ed.). (1994). *High-stakes performance assessment: Perspectives on Kentucky's educational reform.* Thousand Oaks, CA: Corwin.

Haertel, E. (2000, Winter). Validity arguments in high-stakes testing: In search of evidence. *Educational Measurement: Issues and Practices, 19*(1), 5–9.

Hargreaves, A., & Fullan, M. (1998). *What's worth fighting for out there?* Mississauga, Canada: Public School Teachers' Federation.

Linn, R. L., Baker, E. L., & Dunbar, S. B. (1991). Complex, performance-based assessment. *Educational Researcher, 8*(20), 15–21.

Messick, S. (1989). Validity. In R. L. Linn (Ed.), *Educational measurement.* New York: Macmillan.

Messick, S. (1995). Standards of validity and the validity of standards in performance assessment. *Educational Measurement: Issues and Practices, 14*(4), 5–8.

Moss, P. A. (1992). Shifting conceptions of validity in educational measurement: Implications for performance assessment. *Review of Educational Research, 62*(3), 229–258.

Murphy, R., & Broadfoot, P. (1995). *Effective assessment and the improvement of education: A tribute to Desmond Nuttal.* London/Washington, DC: Falmer.

O'Day, J., Goertz, M., & Floden, R. (1995). *Building capacity for educational reform* [Consortium for Policy Research in Education (CPRE)]. Philadelphia: Graduate School of Education, University of Pennsylvania.

Popham, W. J. (1999). Where large-scale assessment is heading and why it shouldn't. *Educational Measurement: Issues and Practices, 18*(3), 13–17.

Stiggins, R. J. (1995, November). Assessment literacy for the 21st century. *Phi Delta Kappan*, pp. 238–245.

Stoll, L. (1999, January). *Building capacity for school improvement*. Keynote address at the International congress for school effectiveness and school improvement, Dallas, TX.

Torrance, H., & Pryor, J. (1998). *Investigating formative assessment: Teaching learning and assessment in the classroom*. Buckingham, England/Philadelphia: Open University Press.

PEABODY JOURNAL OF EDUCATION, 75(4), 142–158

Cooperative Performance Incentive Plans

Helen Raham

Can school performance awards benefit our schools and students? This article surveys what is known about Cooperative Performance Incentive (CPI) Plans. It describes and compares existing models, analyzes their impacts on student learning and school practices, and suggests the policy lessons learned and areas for further research.

Description

CPI plans may be defined as "award programs which provide teachers and often other school staff with pay bonuses for the achievement of specific school-wide educational objectives" (Kelley, Heneman, & Mianowski, 1999, p. 4). CPI plans differ from individual performance or merit pay in that *all* teachers in the school receive the bonus based on meeting an objective predefined goal. The concept, first piloted in South Carolina in 1984, has been adopted in many U.S. states and is now being introduced in Canada and Britain. Implementation details vary considerably

HELEN RAHAM *is the Executive Director of a Canadian education research agency, the Society for the Advancement of Excellence in Education, Kelowna, British Columbia, Canada.*

Requests for reprints should be sent to Helen Raham, The Society for the Advancement of Excellence in Education, 201 1451–B Ellis Street, Kelowna, British Columbia, V1Y 2A3, Canada. E-mail: hraham@direct.ca

142

between jurisdictions. Most commonly used for school units, CPI plans are also suitable to other educational settings including programs, departments, whole districts, or broader jurisdictions.

Context

The 1990s have been characterized by comprehensive educational reform efforts. One dominant policy thrust has been the creation of systems to measure performance and strengthen accountability. Performance information is not only thought of as the currency of good governance, but as the means to better management of resources. This approach has engendered a range of government measures to create more goal-oriented and effective schools. Strategies to accomplish this objective include annual assessments of student achievement at various levels, increasingly robust data collection and management systems for a broadening array of performance indicators, and public profiles and classification of schools based on annual evidence of measurable progress. Increasingly, states are using this monitoring to identify high- and low-performing schools for targeted rewards and interventions. As a result, schools face a revolutionary new accountability environment.

Rationale for CPI Plans

As governments seek to strengthen performance results and increasingly recognize schools as the unit of improvement, the challenge is: How can we cause schools to focus on goal-setting for improved results? CPI plans are a mechanism to achieve this intended focus.

The premise of CPI plans is that when an entire school community works together to raise student performance over its own previous benchmarks, there are more positive results than with plans that merely reward individual efforts. Their group nature encourages teachers to work together and focus on specific outcomes while avoiding the divisiveness of individual merit pay.

The interest in school award programs parallels the rising use of group performance plans in the private sector. The new economy is altering the organization of the workplace, decentralizing management, and creating multifunctional work teams with the authority to accomplish organization and team goals and with accountability for results. As a result, collective awards for adding value to performance are now becoming common in companies of all sizes, sports teams, and some

143

public agencies. Under this strategy, individuals are not paid on the basis of seniority or a narrow job description. They are encouraged to develop new competencies to support continuous improvement and to work across traditional roles, and a portion of the team member's pay can depend on the collective team effort.

Educational reform trends also require significant changes in the organization of work in schools. The new learning environment is continuously evolving, and increasing collaboration among school teams is required as standards are raised. Today's teachers are expected to acquire the professional expertise to teach a world-class curriculum to a diverse student body; to be accountable for student achievement outcomes; and to take a broader leadership role in school management, organization, and instruction. This suggests a need to realign teacher compensation and rewards to these emerging practices (Kerchner, Koppich, & Weeres, 1997).

Goals, rightly defined and pursued, are the most crucial element in any school system that hopes to get better results (Schmoker, 1997). Although the classroom has proved remarkably well-insulated from most mandated policies, using student scores on prescribed tests to make judgments about the quality of education provided in a particular school or district *has* evoked changes in what happens in the classroom (Murnane & Levy, 1996). Recent national comparisons of standardized achievement results have demonstrated that jurisdictions in both the United States and Canada implementing the strongest assessment and public accountability programs have realized the largest gains in student achievement (Fuhrman, 1999).

The coupling of school assessment with school-based performance awards appears to offer the promise of transforming the school culture to raise student and teacher productivity. Indeed, Kentucky, Texas, and North Carolina, using CPI approaches for 5 or more years, are demonstrating significant gains and shifts in school practices. This evidence and other outcomes available to date will be examined in detail in further sections of this article.

Examples of CPI Plans

Fourteen U.S. states, Britain, Switzerland, and the provinces of Alberta and British Columbia are among those experimenting with plans providing monetary rewards to schools or districts meeting their individual improvement targets on a variety of measures. Six different CPI models are briefly described here.

Kentucky. As part of a court-ordered reform of the education system in 1990, the Kentucky accountability program provided rewards to schools for improving student performance and sanctions for schools with declining performance. Assessment indicators were based on a school's annual scores in seven academic subjects in Grades 4–5, 7–8, and 11–12, as well as attendance, retention, and dropout figures. Academic achievement was assessed through a combination of standardized and nonstandardized instruments such as portfolios. The state target was for each school to increase its scores by 10% over its baseline score in 1991–1992 in a 2-year cycle. Reward schools—those exceeding this goal—received a pool of funds based on the degree to which the school exceeded its goals. The vast majority of schools (98%) used the awards for teacher bonuses. The maximum bonus per teacher in reward schools was about $3,690 in the first cycle, reduced to $2,600 in the second cycle, and $1,100 in 1998. Although government funding for the program actually increased slightly over this period to a maximum of $27,235,000, the number of qualifying reward schools doubled, thus decreasing the size of the bonuses (Kentucky Department of Education, 1999).

The plan also included sanctions for schools dropping below their baseline, as well as assistance and resources to develop an improvement plan. In the second cycle, 177 schools were designated "in decline" and 9 "in crisis." By the end of this cycle, 88% of these schools had improved sufficiently to receive rewards (Kelley et al., 1999, p. 3).

North Carolina. The Charlotte–Mecklenburg School District (CMS) established its Benchmark Goals Program in 1991 to reverse a record of low student achievement and low success with minority students. In 1996 the program was superceded by the introduction of a state-wide accountability program with many of the same elements. The CMS program set out improvement goals for student achievement in four academic areas measured by standardized tests. Other indicators include primary grade readiness, enrollment in higher level courses, attendance, and dropout rates. Following the establishing of initial baseline performance for each school in 1992, annual improvement goals were reset by the district, including distinct goals for particular subgroups of students. Maintenance goals were set where schools were already performing at high levels. Schools received points for each goal achieved, and schools acquiring 75–100 points were designated as "Exemplary." Teachers in Exemplary schools each received $1,000 bonuses, and support staff received $400. Teachers in schools in the "outstanding" category (60–74 points) each received $750, whereas support staff earned $300 bonuses.

There were no formal sanctions associated with the CMS plan, although schools with chronically low achievement were designated as "priority schools" to receive additional guidance, assistance, and resources.

Texas. In 1993, the Texas Education Agency (TEA) began rating schools on test scores and other factors in an accountability system combining deregulation for schools with high expectations for students of all races and income levels. The Texas Successful Schools Awards System has been an integral component of this policy direction, with $2.5 million state funding annually allocated for these cash awards. In 1998, 13.5% of Texas schools earned awards in the Exemplary, Recognized, or Acceptable categories.

The yardstick for the TEA ratings is the Texas Assessment of Academic Skills (TAAS), a series of annual tests in reading and math for Grades 3 to 8 and Grade 10. Unlike the Kentucky system, Texas schools are not rewarded simply for making progress each year, but must reach a set of absolute benchmarks to improve their standing. The percentage of students passing each of the tests, the dropout rate, attendance, an average growth indicator, and a significant gain factor are considered. Since the ranking system was created in 1993, the thresholds have been raised annually for each category. In 1998, to qualify as Exemplary, schools must score in the top quartile of the state on TAAS, have a dropout rate of 1% or less, have an attendance rate of at least 94%, and at least 90% of all students must pass all tests. In 2000, an Acceptable rating will require a school to have 50% (rather than 40% in 1998) of its students pass all TAAS exams. Students with limited English proficiency or special education needs may be exempted from TAAS, but no other allowances are made for a school's socioeconomic or demographic circumstances as part of the state drive to raise standards for all students (Palmaffy, 1998).

The cash awards to qualifying schools are calculated by enrollment, with the average award in 1998 being $2,430. The award must be used primarily for the purposes of the enhancement of academics and cannot be a substitute for any regular funds. Campus committees make the decisions about the manner in which the performance bonuses are used. At the other end of the scale, schools designated as Low Performing receive sanctions, assistance, and close monitoring. If improvements do not occur, these schools may be reconstituted.

Dallas, Texas. The Dallas School District has been rewarding effective schools since the early 1980s. The present CPI model, introduced in 1991–1992, is noteworthy for its complexity. Since this plan was instituted, the annual school award fund has ranged between $1.5 and $3 million. It is possible for schools to receive awards under both the district and the state plan.

The "value-added" methodology used in Dallas is much more complex, and the indexes are richer than the state plan. The Dallas School Improvement Performance Awards system employs multiple standardized assessments, including non-English tests for minority groups. Other measurable school-level indicators used include promotion rate, dropout rate, on-time graduation rate, percentage of students taking accelerated and/or Advanced Placement (AP) courses, and the percentage of students writing and passing SAT and AP exams. Schools compete against their own previous scores and in comparison to the performance of their peers, not against absolute norms. They are clustered more narrowly according to grade level (K–3, 4–6, etc.), size, and alternative programs. There are elaborate and weighted formulae for control of school and student characteristics, such as percentage of minorities, language proficiency, income and poverty indexes, mobility, student and teacher attendance, gender, school crowding, and so forth. Schools are permitted to exempt only 5% of their populations from testing to qualify for performance awards (Gonzalez, 1997).

From this extensive data collection and analysis, the Dallas Research and Evaluation and Information Systems Division provides predictions of student and school outcomes as annual targets for each school. Schools are required to develop annual improvement plans to achieve these. Schools that exceed the predicted targets by half a standard deviation or more receive awards. These are currently set at $1,000 for each professional staff member, $500 for each support staff, and $2,000 for some school activity or project.

Britain. By September 2000, teacher pay and school budgets in England and Wales will be linked to performance. This is the latest feature of a decade of far-reaching policies to reform schooling introduced by the Conservatives and extended by Tony Blair's Labor government. A consultative Green Paper (Department for Education and Employment, 1999) has designated 60 million pounds for a School Performance Award Scheme that provides annual performance-related bonuses for schools showing the most improvement, as well as the best-performing schools. Even failing schools making rapid progress will be eligible. Under-performing schools will not be eligible, even if their test results are good.

The Department for Education expects between 6,000 to 8,000 schools (or about one in four schools) to qualify for the annual bonus. The awards would be allocated (see "Blair's Carrot," 1999) as follows to:

- The top proportion of schools according to the outcomes of national assessments in the previous academic year.
- The top proportion of schools showing the highest level of sustained improvement against the same indicators.
- Schools coming out of special measures (a category for failing schools) faster than planned.

147

- Other types of alternative schools, based on their achievements against individualized targets.

Although the Green Paper suggests "the school governors and head decide how to distribute the funds among staff, based on the criteria set out in the school's performance management policy" (Department for Education and Employment, 1999, Section 93), the government is seeking further input on how best to distribute the bonuses within the schools. In addition, the government is proposing an incentive scheme to reward individual "high-performing" teachers in the classroom, those taking on greater responsibilities in the school, and those taking professional training related to school goals during summer vacations.

Alberta.   The Alberta government introduced a School Performance Incentive Plan in its March 1999 budget (Alberta Education, 1999). The first such program in Canada, it offered $104 million in additional funding in the 1999–2001 school years to school boards who reached provincially set and determined improvement targets for student learning. In rewarding school districts rather than individual schools, it resembles the Mississippi CPI model. Awards were to be determined by a combination of local targets and provincial performance indicators, such as achievement test and diploma examination results and graduation rates. Voluntarily participating districts were to be measured against their own previous 3-year baseline, not ranked against other districts. The cash awards could be used for staff bonuses, technology enhancement, hiring additional staff, or other resources as determined by the local school board and its employees.

In June 1999, this plan was temporarily "placed on hold" by the newly appointed Minister of Learning, Lyle Oberg. This action followed the presentation of a joint brief to the government in May 1999 by the Alberta School Boards' Association, Alberta Teachers' Association, Alberta Home and School Councils' Association, and the College of Alberta School Superintendents. The brief (see "Joint Proposal," 1999) criticized the role of incentives and rewards as a motivator and proposed a different model, fundamentally shifting from an incentive program to seed money for school improvement.

Through a consultation process, Alberta Learning and its education partners jointly developed the Alberta Initiative for School Improvement (AISI), introduced in December 1999 (Alberta Learning, 1999). AISI gives school boards the autonomy to propose research-based improvement strategies such as early reading interventions, smaller classes, and stay-in-school initiatives developed in consultation with their school communities. Indicators of success may be qualitative or quantitative, with 60% of these measures determined locally. The province will support AISI with $66 million in the 2000–2001 school year and $66 million the following school year. Approved projects will be funded on an annual basis beginning in September 2000, with funding to be discontinued in subsequent years of the project if there were not "evidence of success."

Meanwhile, in neighboring British Columbia, the Kamloops/Thompson school district has entered into a pilot performance incentive agreement with the government of British Columbia. ("Kamloops/Thompson Pilots Program," 1999). This agreement provides an increase of 10% over base funding for Aboriginal programs if a complicated set of performance targets are met. These include reducing the gap between aboriginal and nonaboriginal students by 2% annually on a number of key indicators such as attendance and graduation rates. The district has been given considerable local autonomy in achieving the specified targets. The agreement lasts until June 2004, with targets to be assessed annually.

How Effective Are CPI Plans?

In evaluating the effectiveness of this new approach, a number of aspects are being examined. Policymakers are seeking to understand more fully their impact on teachers, on the education climate or culture, and on student achievement.

Teachers' Motivation

Researchers have been curious to learn if school award programs are more effective in motivating educators than earlier individual merit pay schemes. Between 1996 and 1998, a team of researchers probed the impact of two comprehensive school reward plans on teacher motivation. Kelley et al. (1999) examined teacher responses to the programs and whether the responses were predictive of their school's subsequent success. Their findings, based on extensive teacher surveys and interviews in Kentucky and North Carolina's CMS, provide insight into the impact of CPI as reported by the professionals they seek to engage.

Kelley identified three critical factors that drive teacher motivation: expectancy, instrumentality, and valence. Teacher decisions to expend effort are influenced by their beliefs about the likelihood (expectancy) of attaining the required student achievement goals. That is, the greater the belief that working hard will be rewarded, the greater teachers' desire to endeavor to do so. The instrumentality factor refers to teacher beliefs about their own competencies and the presence of enabling conditions to assist them in the attaining student achievement goals. The latter might include such things as principal support, professional training, and sufficient feedback on progress toward the goals. Valence relates to the values, both desirable and undesirable, that teachers attribute to the outcomes of the program. Positively valued outcomes included the actual bonus, public recognition, and pride of accomplishment. Among negative values were increased stress, public criticism, threats to job security, and personal disappointment. Both positive and negative outcomes could be motivators.

The key findings for Kentucky and the CMS district were that teachers reported a high level of commitment and that the vast majority were trying to meet their school's goals of improved student achievement. Many reported they had made changes in instructional practices to better align with program goals. Significantly positive coefficients were obtained for the effect of the bonus on goal commitment in both jurisdictions, suggesting the positive role bonuses can play in increased teacher understanding of and commitment to the goals.

Interview findings from teachers in the two programs shed further light on their perceptions of the bonuses:

- Teachers felt it was appropriate to receive bonuses and that receiving a bonus was deserved.
- The teachers varied in how meaningful the size of the bonus they could receive actually was, especially after deductions for taxes.
- The teachers varied in how much the possibility of earning a bonus motivated them to improve student achievement, or whether an even larger bonus would motivate them more.
- Teachers were skeptical that earned bonuses would actually be paid, due to past experiences with actual reneging on bonus payments or beliefs that the funding for the bonuses would not be continued.
- Teachers varied as to whether they wanted the bonus part of the School Based Performance Awards (SBPA) program to continue.
- The meaning of the bonus varied, with teachers variously viewing it as an appropriate "thank you," a formal recognition, reimbursement for personal expenditures on school-related items, a reward that allowed for the purchase of desired goods, or that it was simply irrelevant.
- Teachers in Kentucky found that having to decide among themselves how to divide up the bonus money among teachers and staff was a divisive process that created tension within and between schools.
- Awards paid as salary bonuses appeared to have more visibility than awards paid as school improvement funds. (Kelley et al., 1999, pp. 18–19)

In both jurisdictions, however, teachers in successful schools indicated that meeting goals would get increasingly difficult over time. They were uncertain they could work hard enough to meet the next cycle's goals. This may suggest a problematic impediment in sustaining teachers' motivation to continue working hard to improve student achievement. Teachers in both jurisdictions had some reservations that the programs were administered fairly. Researchers cautioned that low levels of desirability and motivation where expressed could reflect on either the implementation details of the bonus programs or the concept itself.

Attempts to establish a direct correlation between teacher motivational responses and actual school success in meeting student achievement goals were inconclusive. Evidence suggests that for the CMS teachers, the positive awards associated with the program may contribute to school performance and influence teachers' attitudes. As for Kentucky teachers, only the average goal clarity (understanding and commitment) level was significantly related to school performance. Teachers' individual and group expectancy levels were greater in schools in which teachers perceived stronger assessment data feedback mechanisms, principal support or professional community, lack of goal conflict, and higher levels of perceived fairness of the program. Previous success in the program was an influencing factor as well; these teachers' expectations were higher given their school's past history of success using SBPA programs. These are all important aspects of implementation and design to consider. Kelley et al. (1999) noted,

> We clearly and convincingly found an SBPA program is not just a bonus program; rather it is one element in an interrelated system of rewards, opportunities, and demands that influences teachers' jobs and lives in a multitude of ways, leading them to experience (and form values about) a variety of both extrinsic and intrinsic outcomes. (p. 17)

Educational Results

Some evidence is now available about the effect of CPI plans on the system at large. A direct relation to student achievement levels is much harder to establish, because plans are rarely introduced in isolation and often accompany a range of new policy initiatives, fiscal interventions, and curricular changes.

The Southern Regional Education Board in Atlanta has monitored cooperative teacher incentive programs since 1984. Among their conclusions are:

- Incentive programs that fundamentally alter pay structure based on performance can produce fundamental change in school operations and principal and teacher roles.

- Without a guiding vision and state support, pilot programs designed at the district level have resulted in few fundamental or lasting reforms.
- Teachers who participate in incentive programs are positive about them; those who do not are negative. (Cornett, 1995, pp. 4–9)

In Kentucky and North Carolina, researchers concluded it provided teachers with a focus for their work, increased the energy devoted to instruction, and helped channel teachers' work to the most important goals of the system (Fuhrman, 1999).

Eight years of annual assessment and school-based rewards and sanctions in Texas and North Carolina have produced steadily rising achievement gains. In 1994, barely half of Texas students passed the TAAS math exam. In 1998 that figure had risen to 80%, and the number of Black and Hispanic children who passed the test doubled to 64% and 72%, respectively. The number of schools receiving the Exemplary award rose from 67 in 1994 to 683 in 1998 (Palmaffy, 1998, p. 29). North Carolina students on average score 8 or 9 percentile points higher on math and reading than their counterparts in 1992–1993. This progress is corroborated by student gains well above the national average on the National Assessments of Educational Progress (NAEP), as shown in Figure 1.

Is it coincidental that the most rapid student gains have been made in Texas and North Carolina where CPI plans have been in place for most of the decade? Grissmer's research notes that teachers and administrators in Texas and North Carolina appear to be changing their methods of teaching and managing in ways that produce higher results, though much of the evidence is anecdotal and further data must be gathered to record these

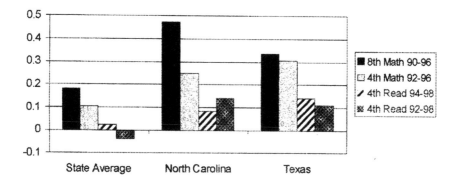

Figure 1. Average gains in scores on the state National Assessments of Educational Progress achievement tests. David Grissmer, Rand, used by permission.

changes precisely (Grissmer & Flannigan, 1998, p. 20). He lists some of these changing practices to investigate further:

> Given specific teaching objectives, teachers are probably increasing the time and attention devoted [to] achieving the learning standards. Teachers have much better and more timely information in each state about each child's areas of good and poor performance, and there is evidence that such information is commonly utilized. There is some evidence that teachers are allocating their time differently, perhaps making better choices where time can be spent most productively. There is also increased evidence in some places of increased use of after-school, weekend and summer time for learning. There is some evidence of tutoring activity. Because schools are the primary focus of rewards and sanctions, there is evidence of increased cooperation within schools. (p. 20)

The benefits of accountability programs in Texas are reported by Phelps (1999) as:

- A greater focus on academic learning.
- A culture of high expectations and enthusiasm for reaching standards.
- Generous and immediate remediation efforts toward poorly performing students.
- Greater interest among teachers in academic strategies and more cooperation with each other.
- Quicker feedback for school faculty on which instructional strategies work best. (p. 5)

Almost a decade into its ambitious reforms, Kentucky is showing achievement gains. The percentage of elementary students scoring at the proficient level rose from 8% in 1993 to 38% in 1997 (Palmaffy, 1998, p. 30). Reading results on the 1998 national assessments (NAEP) show Kentucky's students are raising their achievement faster than most other states. Placing 2 points below the national average in 1992, Kentucky is now 4 points above, despite having higher than average poverty levels and lower adult education levels (Hoff, 1999).

Still, further research must be done to establish a clear relation between and student achievement and CPI plans.

Implementation Considerations

It is obvious from the earlier descriptions that CPI plans are complex instruments. Part of the new "systems thinking," they cannot be viewed in isolation, nor can they be instantaneously achieved. They often require 3 to 5 years to fully implement. The experience to date suggests that CPI plans need certain key conditions to be viable.

Those conditions have been defined as: open and public access to performance information, site-based decision making, a support system to help schools disaggregate and interpret data, persistence over years, and a significant commitment of resources. Perceived fairness is critical to a CPI plan's acceptance, with care taken to ensure a level playing field and that progress for each unit is measured on a value-added basis (Richards, Fishbein, & Massell, 1993). Districts that have successfully implemented CPI programs have sought cooperative input from the field at all phases of design and implementation and offer rewards commensurate with the level of effort required to attain (Kelley, 1997).

Barriers and Obstacles

A number of challenges to the successful implementation of CPI plans have been identified. These include:

Inadequate assessment systems. The Kentucky and CMS research found feedback has the strongest effect on teacher expectancy of success. This was described as the ability to receive and interpret results of past assessments and use this information to refine curriculum and instructional programs (Kelley et al., 1999). Some jurisdictions implementing early plans lacked the clear benchmarks and consistent assessment tools to monitor results over time. In some cases, there was a lack of confidence in the assessment instruments. Providing one striking example, in 1997 Kentucky terminated its contract with the technical management firm handling the assessment program on which school awards were based in the face of increasing evidence that the instruments being used were unreliable. Kentucky has since redesigned its CPI plan to rely more on standardized instruments to measure achievement in the schools.

Lack of capacity. If we wish to encourage schools to use results and reward them for improving student success, the system must be designed in a way that identifies goals *and* enables those responsible to respond. School improvement is a highly complex and collaborative exercise. Many schools may lack the inherent capacity to implement substantial change. They require additional support and training to incorporate a range of data into future performance planning and the flexibility and resources to execute research-based solutions.

Some researchers (see, e.g., Darling-Hammond, 1996) point to a lack of school autonomy inhibiting true site-based management. Educating diverse learners to much higher standards of learning requires more responsive schools than present bureaucracies allow. Earlier accountability systems often failed because they attempted to employ top-down approaches that ignored the high-involvement principles at the site level necessary to impact student learning. Without the power to make significant changes at the school level to improve the learning environment, schools are unable to fully benefit from CPI plans.

Others look beyond governance issues, suggesting that even where flexibility and management structures have been addressed, we have yet to begin the process of changing *instruction* (DeBray, 1999). DeBray noted that many educational reforms of this century have been hindered because the reformers did not know how to share knowledge about changing the core of instructional practice. Research and dissemination then becomes a critical aspect of building capacity, along with teacher training, investing in technology, reducing class sizes, and changing teacher schedules to accommodate planning for improvement and ongoing professional development. Kerchner et al. (1997) envisioned a lengthened school year for teachers to address the gaps in teacher knowledge and skills required for high-performance schools of the future.

The Kentucky data suggest that award schools in which teachers had high levels of expectancy were

> characterized by principal and district support for goals of the program, high-quality professional development linked with the accountability program, meaningful collaboration among teachers, and connections to external professional communities. Non-award schools were characterized by an absence of these conditions and multiple or conflicting goals that competed with the accountability program. (Kelley et al., 1999, p. 21)

Weak performance culture.   Some policy analysts (e.g., Wohlstetter, Van Kirk, Robertson, & Mohrman, 1997) attribute inconclusive results to the length of time it takes to build a performance culture in schools. Wohlstetter et al.(1997) and Schmoker (1996) noted many school personnel have low comfort levels with issues of outcomes measurement and accountability. Too many schools fail to rigorously collect an array data and evaluate change initiatives or examine performance trends over time to plan next steps. It takes time to build the new skills, roles, and attitudes required to internalize the cycle of continuous school improvement. In Canada, a consensus among the education community on the purpose and use of rigorous comparative assessment for school improvement is even less well-developed than in most other industrialized nations.

Teacher skepticism. It has been noted that teacher attitudes toward CPI vary, with those participating more favorable than those not involved. Colorado's Douglas County is the home of one of the best-known and most comprehensive teacher performance pay plans, including a school award component. "Performance pay can work," states the president of the Douglas County Federation of Teachers, Rob Weil, indicating that 99% of his teachers support performance pay instituted in 1994 (Bushweller, 1999).

Alberta teachers condemned the provincial government's incentive plan, according to Alberta Teachers' Association (ATA) spokesperson Larry Booi (see "Teachers Won't Buy," 1999). ATA policy on this issue reflects that of other teacher federations in Canada: "The single salary schedule based upon a preparational scale is the most equitable salary administration policy for use in establishing professional remuneration. The Alberta Teachers' Association opposes the implementation of a system of merit rating for salary purpose" (Alberta Teacher's Association, 1998, p. 1). Teacher federation policy also "actively opposes the use of standardized tests as means of evaluating individual student, individual teacher or *individual school* performance" (Teacher's Federation, 1995, p. 49).

The National Union of Teachers, responding to the British government's incentive scheme commencing in September 2000, called it "rationing," because only one in four schools might be expected to win awards. Concerned was also expressed that funding levels may not be maintained (see "Blair's Carrot," 1999).

Teacher trust is a key factor in incentive plans. In a number of cases, such as Dallas and Kentucky, awards have been reduced due to fiscal cutbacks or to an increasing number of qualifying schools. This can cause educators to doubt that earned awards will be realized in the future. When more Douglas County schools qualified for awards than planned in 1998, however, $27 million in reserves were used to ensure the bonuses were paid. Confidence in the assessment systems and the fairness of the award distribution plan are also significant factors in teacher acceptance that must be addressed.

Policy Lessons Learned

At this point, the research on CPI plans to date suggests school performance award programs "are potentially a useful tool for policymakers and administrators who are interested in focusing teachers, principals and educational systems on improving student performance" (Kelley et al., 1999, p. 30). It also cautions this potential "may be difficult to achieve due to the complexity of designing and implementing them effectively" (p. 30).

We now have working examples producing positive results in a growing number of schools. However, to reach a meaningful threshold of teacher involvement and the maximum impact on student outcomes, CPI plans must be crafted to reach the vast range of schools functioning in the middle. Current programs are weighted toward rewarding high-performance schools and identifying and improving low-performing schools. As such, they may be limiting the results potentially achievable by the vast majority of schools. Once a state identifies a range of schools that remain static, alternative policies should be found to also enhance *their* capacity to progress.

CPI plans have captured teacher attention. Further research is needed into a number of elements to refine them further. What is the ideal balance between fairness and complexity in school evaluations for awards? What is the optimum size of the bonus? To achieve greater teacher involvement, will CPI plans require significantly increased funding? How can states protect the stability of these plans to ensure high levels of teacher confidence? Can the expectation of "continuous progress" be sustained as a long-term goal? What is the role of the sanctions accompanying most plans, and is reducing negative outcomes a desirable feature? What are the best mechanisms for building school capacity for growth?

Conclusion

CPI systems are a part of the new accountability landscape for schools. Carefully designed plans that are perceived to be meaningful, fair, and stable are "associated with improved student achievement when adequate capacity to improve instruction is present" (Fuhrman, 1999, p. 10). In addition, teachers generally find the new systems motivating (p. 7). However, CPI plans are insufficient in themselves to raise student achievement, and continuing research is needed to provide further information about their most effective use.

References

Alberta Education. (1999, March). *Education budget 99: The right balance*. Edmonton, Canada: Author.

Alberta Learning. (1999, December). *Alberta initiative for school improvement*. Retrieved December 12, 1999 from the World Wide Web: http://www.learning.gov.ab.ca/sib/aisi/

Alberta Teachers' Association. (1998). *Merit pay*. Alberta, Canada: Author.

Blair's carrot for high-performing schools. (1999, January 20). London: BBC News.

Bushweller, K. (1999, August). Bonus bucks for teachers. *American School Board Journal, 186*(8), 18–22.

Cornett, L. (1995). Lessons from 10 years of teacher improvement reform. *Educational Leadership, 54*(5), 4–9.

Darling-Hammond, L. (1996). Restructuring schools for high performance. In S. Fuhrman & J. O'Day (Eds.), *Rewards and reform* (p. 146). San Francisco: Jossey-Bass.

DeBray, E. (1999, April). *Incentives in states' educational accountability systems.* Paper presented at the annual meeting of the American Educational Research Association, Montreal, Canada.

Department for Education and Employment. (1999, January). *Meeting the challenge of change* (Section 93). London: Author.

Fuhrman, S. (1999). *The new accountability.* Philadelphia, PA: Consortium for Policy Research in Education, Graduate School of Education, University of Pennsylvania.

Gonzalez, Y. (1997). *The Dallas value-added accountability system.* Dallas, TX: Division of Research and Evaluation Systems, Dallas Public Schools.

Grissmer, D., & Flannigan, A. (1998). *Exploring rapid achievement gains in North Carolina and Texas.* Washington, DC: RAND Corporation.

Hoff, D. (1999, March 10). A glimpse at the states with big NAEP gains. *Education Week, 18*(26), 13.

Joint proposal to replace school performance incentive program with Alberta School Improvement Program. (1999, May). Alberta, Canada: Alberta Home and School Councils' Association, College of Alberta School Superintendents, Alberta School Boards Association, and Alberta Teacher's Association.

Kamloops/Thompson pilots program linking funding for aboriginal education. (1999, November). *Adminfo*, p. 5.

Kelley, C. (1997, Spring). Teacher compensation and organization. *Educational Evaluation and Policy Analysis, 19*(1), 15–28.

Kelley, C., Heneman, H., & Mianowski, A. (1999, April). *School-based performance awards.* Paper presented at the annual meeting of the American Educational Research Association, Montreal, Canada.

Kentucky Department of Education. (1999, May 5). *School reward amounts announced* [News release]. Frankfort: Author.

Kerchner, C., Koppich, J., & Weeres, J. (1997). *United mindworkers: Unions and teaching in the knowledge society.* San Francisco: Jossey-Bass.

Murnane, R., & Levy, F. (1996). Teaching to new standards. In S. Fuhrman & J. O'Day (Eds.), *Rewards and reform* (p. 266). San Francisco: Jossey-Bass.

Palmaffy, T. (1998, March/April). The gold star state. *Policy Review*, pp. 28–35.

Phelps, R. (1999). *Why testing experts hate testing.* Washington, DC: Fordham Foundation.

Richards, C., Fishbein, D., & Massell, D. (1993). Cooperative performance awards in education. In S. Jacobson & R. Berne (Eds.), *Reforming education* (pp. 28–43). Thousand Oaks, CA: Corwin.

Schmoker, M. (1996). *Results the key to continuous school improvement.* Alexandria, VA: Association for Supervision and Curriculum Development.

Schmoker, M. (1997). Setting goals in turbulent times. In A. Hargreaves (Ed.), *Rethinking educational change with heart and mind* (pp. 128–148). Alexandria, VA: Association for Supervision and Curriculum Development.

Teachers Federation. (1995). *BCTF member guide policy handbook.* British Columbia, Canada: Author.

Teachers won't buy into incentive program. (1999, May 24). *Edmonton Journal*, p. 1.

Wohlstetter, P., Van Kirk, A., Robertson, P., & Mohrman, S. (1997). *Organizing for successful site-based management.* Alexandria, VA: Association for Supervision and Curriculum Development.

PEABODY JOURNAL OF EDUCATION, 75(4), 159–199

Payment for Results: Effects of the Kentucky and Maryland Group-Based Performance Award Programs

Carolyn Kelley
Sharon Conley
Steve Kimball

CAROLYN KELLEY *is Associate Professor in the Department of Educational Administration, University of Wisconsin–Madison, and a researcher for the Consortium for Policy Research in Education.*

SHARON CONLEY *is Professor in the Department of Education, University of California–Santa Barbara.*

STEVE KIMBALL *is a doctoral student in the Department of Education, University of Wisconsin–Madison, and a research assistant for the Consortium for Policy Research in Education.*

The research reported in this article was supported by Grant 97001184000 from the Pew Charitable Trusts and the U.S. Department of Education, Office of Educational Research and Improvement, National Institute of Educational Goverance, Finance, Policy-Making and Management, to the Consortium for Policy Research in Education (CPRE) and the Wisconsin Center for Education Research, School of Education, University of Wisconsin–Madison (Grant OERI–R3086A60003). The opinions expressed are those of the authors and do not necessarily reflect the view of the Pew Charitable Trusts, the National Institute on Educational Governance, Finance, Policy-Making and Management, Office of Educational Research and Improvement, U.S. Department of Education, the institutional partners of CPRE, or the Wisconsin Center for Education Research.

We thank Tom Hruz, Jason Hanna, and Sal Castillo for their research assistance.

Requests for reprints should be sent to Carolyn Kelley, Consortium for Policy Research in Education, University of Wisconsin–Madison, 1025 West Johnson Street, Room 653, Madison, WI 53706. E-mail: kelley@education.wisc.edu

A significant shift in educational administration and policy has taken place in the 1990s, from a reliance on inputs and processes to a reliance on outcomes as a measure of organizational effectiveness (Elmore, Abelmann, & Fuhrman, 1996). Standards and assessments have been developed at local, state, and national levels, along with systematic efforts to utilize a panoply of educational resources and incentives for the purpose of improving student achievement toward these standards. Some of the resources and incentives that have been targeted toward improving performance on the standards include teacher education, certification and licensure, evaluation, professional development, and formal rewards and sanctions related to student performance. In this article, we examine the effects of two state-level rewards and sanctions programs operating in the context of larger comprehensive standards-based reforms. The programs reward entire schools for the achievement of student achievement goals and sanction schools for failure to make progress toward goal achievement.

A number of states and districts have adopted these school-based performance award (SBPA) policies to hold teachers, principals, and schools accountable for improvements in student performance. Examples of established state programs include Kentucky, Maryland, North Carolina, and South Carolina; established district programs include Charlotte–Mecklenburg (North Carolina), Dallas (Texas), and Douglas County (Colorado). The Douglas County program is also notable for its strong joint effort between the district and the union in creating the program (Kelley, 1996; Muncey & Conley, 1999). This article examines the ways in which program design and context interact to produce different accountability pressures at the school level. Using both qualitative and survey data, similarities and differences in teacher and principal perceptions about the characteristics and effects of rewards and sanctions programs in Kentucky and Maryland are examined.

A number of research studies have been conducted on SBPA programs. Researchers to date have found that SBPA programs have a variety of effects on teacher attitudes and behaviors. Awards paid as salary bonuses have been found to improve curriculum alignment (Koretz, Barron, Mitchell, & Stecher, 1996) and enhance teacher collaboration, the quality of feedback that teachers receive on student performance, and the alignment of organizational resources to support student achievement (Hall & Caffarella, 1998; Kelley, 1999a; Kelley & Protsik, 1997). Such research suggests that several process or enabling conditions variables are critical to successful outcomes (Hackman & Oldham, 1980; Kelley, 1998); these enabling conditions facilitate the creation of high teacher expectancies, which in turn produce improvements in student achievement (Kelley, Heneman, & Milanowski, 2000). Most teachers indicate that bonuses do not act as a strong direct incentive for behavioral change, but they are a valued reward (Heneman, 1998;

Kelley & Protsik, 1997). They may also act to leverage system-wide alignment to the rewarded goals and thereby leverage the enhancement of intrinsic rewards associated with goal achievement (Kelley et al., 2000). However, programs with a continuous improvement focus also tend to produce high levels of teacher stress (Heneman, 1998; Kelley, 1999a), and teachers in schools that do not meet performance goals are more likely than others to transfer to a different school (Heneman & Milanowski, 1998).

This study attempts to provide additional insights on the effects of program design and context by examining the similarities and differences in teacher and principal perceptions of the effects of two state-level rewards and sanctions programs. By selecting programs that differed in design (e.g., the Kentucky program paid awards to teachers in the form of salary bonuses, whereas the Maryland program paid awards to schools), we hope to learn more about the ways in which program design and program context produce different school-level effects. The next sections provide descriptions of the two programs.

Rewards and Sanctions in Kentucky

Prodded by a State Supreme Court decision stemming from a challenge to the state finance system (*Rose vs. the Council for Better Education*), in 1990 the Kentucky legislature embarked on one of the most ambitious systemic education reform initiatives undertaken in recent years. The Kentucky Education Reform Act (KERA) involved multiple and comprehensive changes to school governance and finance, curriculum, assessment, and accountability. Although the details of each of these changes is beyond the scope of this article, they provide an important backdrop for understanding the effects of the accountability program (for a more detailed description of KERA, see Steffy, 1993).

Following passage of KERA, the Council on School Performance Standards, accountable to the Kentucky Board of Education, set broad academic expectations for schools. There were 57 academic expectations under six main areas: basic skills, core disciplinary concepts, self-sufficiency, group membership, problem solving, and integration of knowledge. These standards were refined and specified under a curriculum framework, content guidelines, and publicly released assessment items (Kentucky Department of Education, 1998).

To promote changes in instruction, the Commonwealth School Improvement Fund (CSIF) was created to help local schools pursue innovative curriculum and teaching strategies. Since the program was initiated, $2.5 million has been annually appropriated to the CSIF, and that amount was recently increased to $3 million. To further facilitate changes in school organization and curriculum linked to the standards, the state targeted funding for professional development. After an initial investment of $1 per pupil

($575,000) was appropriated statewide, the state increased the amount to $25 per pupil ($1,737,500). Of that amount, 35% was allocated to school districts, and the remaining 65% was available for discretionary use by school councils. This practice of bypassing districts to focus resources and policy pressure directly on schools was a hallmark of the Kentucky reforms.

The centerpiece of the accountability program was the Kentucky Instructional Results Information System (KIRIS), an innovative statewide performance-based student testing system. The assessment system was intended not only to track school progress toward the state standards, but also to determine school monetary awards, sanctions, or assistance. KIRIS was intended to primarily be a performance-based assessment, but has undergone numerous revisions since its inception. Specific assessment methods have included open-ended questions, performance events, multiple-choice questions, portfolios, and on-demand writing prompts. During the evolution of the program the multiple-choice questions were removed and then added back to measures of school performance due to public criticism (Koretz et al., 1996). The performance events were also eliminated until validity concerns could be addressed. (They were subsequently removed completely for accountability purposes.)

KIRIS was used to test students in Grades 4, 5, 7, 8, 11, and 12 in seven academic subject areas: reading, writing, mathematics, science, social studies, arts and humanities, and vocational studies/practical living. The KIRIS accountability assessment was mandatory, and assessment items were specified for certain grades (i.e., writing and math portfolios in Grades 5, 8, and 12; Kentucky Department of Education, 1998).

Accountability System

School performance was a composite of the KIRIS cognitive measures and other noncognitive measures. Performance achievement for each school was based on progress over 2 years on the state-established improvement goals from a baseline first set in 1991–1992. The baseline for each school was adjusted every biennium. The goal was for each school to increase its score 10% of the distance between the baseline score and the proficient level (100) over each biennium. In addition, 10% of "novices" had to move to the "apprentice" category or higher to be eligible to achieve reward status.

School Performance Categories

Depending on their performance over each 2-year cycle, schools were designated by one of five categories: *reward, successful, improving, in decline,* or *in crisis.*

For reward schools, the amount of money awarded depended on the number of certified staff at the school at the end of the accountability cycle and the extent to which the school exceeded the target (Heneman & Milanowski, 1998). Approximately $26–27 million was appropriated in the biennial budget for the awards program. (A total of $95 million was appropriated since the program began.) In 1997, 533 schools shared $27.2 million. Certified staff at the school decided collectively how to use the money. In practice, most of the awards were used for salary bonuses for teachers and other staff.

The School Transformation Assistance and Renewal (STAR) program was established for those schools that failed to meet their targets and were declining in performance. Schools that dropped below baseline by less than 5% were in decline and assigned a distinguished educator to diagnose problems relating to curriculum and school organization and act as an advisor with broad powers. The distinguished educators were educators from Kentucky hired through a rigorous selection process and intensively trained by the state to help schools meet the goals of the accountability program. Schools in decline were also required to develop a school improvement plan and were eligible to receive improvement funds. Schools dropping more than 5% below baseline were deemed schools in crisis, and all staff were placed on probation. The in-crisis schools were also required to develop a school improvement plan, received improvement funds, and were assigned a distinguished educator. In these schools, the distinguished educator also had the power to evaluate the school organization and make recommendations regarding staff retention and dismissal or transfer within 6 months of assignment to the school (Kentucky State Department of Education, 1998).

The research reported in this article was based on the KIRIS statewide assessment and performance award program as described earlier. In 1998, public pressure to modify the program led the legislature to vote to replace KIRIS with a new testing and accountability system called the Commonwealth Accountability Testing System (CATS; White, 1998). CATS includes a new assessment and an attenuated rewards and sanctions program, which provides reduced levels of intervention and assistance to sanctioned schools.

Three advisory panels are guiding CATS. These panels include an Education Assessment and Accountability Review Subcommittee, an arm of the legislature; a School Curriculum, Assessment, and Accountability Council, appointed by the Governor from among various State education interest groups; and a Technical Advisory Panel, consisting of at least three national experts in education testing and measurement (Kentucky State Department of Education [KSDE] Web site). CATS includes a customized or commercially available test with norm-referenced elements (CTB/McGraw Hill has been selected as the vendor); multiple choice and open response prompts are aligned to Kentucky's core content (House Bill 53).

According to the Kentucky State Department of Education, the new testing system will be differentiated from KIRIS in the following elements: It will have reliable and valid use for school and student accountability, teachers will be involved in designing the test and scoring the results, nationally normed test results will be used for school accountability, testing times for schools and students will be reduced, progress of individual students will be measured over time, and test results will be reported to schools and districts in a more timely manner (CATS description, KSDE Web site).

The accountability system is also under major reconstruction. The new awards will be determined by the school site council and used for school improvement purposes. After an extended debate, the KSDE decided to continue to allow awards to be used as teacher salary bonuses. In addition, school districts will be required to issue school report cards on student academic programs, nonacademic achievement, the school learning environment, and parent involvement. The report cards will be sent to parents and published in newspapers.

There were also substantial changes to the sanctions part of the accountability system. Rather than having distinguished educators assigned to their school with broad authority over curriculum and personnel matters, the new law will "permit" schools in decline to request educational assistance that is advisory. Parents may also have their children transfer from a school that would have been formerly classified as in crisis to a successful school. (The in-crisis designation has been eliminated, and these schools will now be classified as in decline.) Another new accountability feature allows the KSDE to establish a system of accountability for school districts. Baseline scores for assessment and nonacademic components are to occur in 1998–1999 and 1999–2000, and the first accountability determinations will be made after the 2001–2002 school year.

During the third and final cycle of the "old" accountability system, schools exceeding their baseline will receive an amount determined by the Kentucky Board of Education, and those schools exceeding their thresholds will receive twice that amount. Certified staff will receive the awards unless they vote to use the funding for other purposes.

Maryland School Performance Program (MSPP)

The MSPP is a state-sponsored school-based performance assessment and accountability program based on the 1989 recommendations of the

"Sondheim Commission," a task force appointed by then Governor William Donald Schaefer (Governor's Commission, 1989). The Commission was charged with investigating how the state could track school system performance and back education funding with school accountability (Governor's Commission, 1989). The culmination of the report and subsequent reform activity represent a confluence of government, business, and public pressure to improve education in the state.

Adopted by the State Board of Education and administered by the Maryland State Department of Education (MSDE), the MSPP includes provisions to hold schools accountable for academic improvement, monitor progress toward state standards, recognize school success with monetary awards, and assist or reconstitute schools declining in performance.

Since 1990, the state has added several elements to encourage districts and schools to move toward goals on performance assessments, student attendance and drop-out rates. These initiatives have largely been generated and implemented by the State Board of Education, which, along with the MSDE, wields considerable policy and regulatory power in Maryland (Goertz, Massell, & Chun, 1997). Initially, incentives included public reporting of scores and the threat of reconstitution by the district or state if a school failed to improve. Starting in 1992, a "Challenge Schools" initiative was established to aid struggling schools. In 1996, a monetary bonus was added for those schools showing significant and sustained improvement on the elementary and middle school assessment. A forthcoming high school assessment is under construction and was trial tested in 1999.

Accountability System

Public reporting represented the first form of accountability. Each December, the MSDE releases a report card on state and district progress toward meeting the standards. The report card compiles statewide averages on the performance assessments or tests, attendance rates, and supporting information (enrollment, wealth, mobility, staffing, etc.). In addition, the report breaks down the information on each of the 24 school districts. The school districts are then responsible for reporting to their communities through the newspapers or other media on individual school performance (MSDE, 1997a). School and system performance has gained wide media coverage, as has criticism leveled at the test (Argetsinger & Nakashima, 1998). Nonetheless, test acceptance among the public and educators has grown over time.

A School Performance Index (SPI) was developed by the MSDE to measure school progress on state standards from a baseline 2-year average.

Data generated by the SPI and other performance indicators are intended not only to inform the public, but also to be used by schools for school improvement, for classroom instruction, and to gauge statewide progress toward education standards. Like the Kentucky program, rather than comparing schools and school systems, each school or system's performance is measured against its own growth (MSDE, 1997a). SPI is the weighted average of a school's relative distance from satisfactory standards for attendance rates and student performance on two test batteries. The measurement varies slightly between elementary and middle schools and significantly for high schools, which have had academic performance based primarily on the Maryland Functional Test Program.

The Maryland Functional Tests are basic skills examinations measuring competencies in reading, mathematics, writing, and citizenship and must be passed for high school graduation. The tests are given as early as Grades 7 and 8 and are reported for Grades 9 and 11. Middle school performance is gauged on the functional tests and the Maryland School Performance Assessment Program (MSPAP) scores for eighth grade students.

The driving force behind the state accountability program is the MSPAP, an assessment aligned to state standards that is used as the primary gauge of elementary and middle school performance. As a performance-based test, MSPAP requires students to apply critical thinking skills and integration of knowledge both individually and in groups. Not only is MSPAP intended to monitor school performance, but it was specifically designed to generate focused instructional change (Koretz et al., 1996; Yen & Ferrara, 1997).[1]

School Performance Categories

In addition to the incentives inherent with public reporting, schools may receive awards or sanctions from the state or from the school district.

---

[1]In its eighth year, the MSPAP is a matrix-sampled, criterion-referenced test that requires students in Grades 3, 5, and 8 to apply what they know about reading, writing, language usage, mathematics, science, and social studies. The test involves about 150,000 students in approximately 990 schools (MSDE, 1996). Test administration occurs each May for 9 hr over 5 days. Rather than setting annual goals for each school, the statewide goal is for all schools to have 70% of students at or above satisfactory performance in all MSPAP subject areas by the year 2000. This target date was previously set at 1996 but was extended by the State. To achieve excellence, a school must have 70% of their students at the satisfactory level and have 25% of students reach levels of excellence on each subject area. No school district has met all of the standards; however, more than half of Maryland's schools are at or near the performance goals (MSDE, 1997b).

Schools are ranked according to their own progress and may receive a monetary award, a nonmonetary certificate of recognition, no award, challenge school status, or reconstitution-eligible status.

The "Rewards for Success" program provides monetary awards to recognize elementary and middle schools that have made "substantial and sustained" or statistically significant progress on the SPI over 2 years.[2] According to the State Department of Education, the reward program provides incentives for schools to continue improving and gives public recognition to those that positively impact student learning (MSDE, 1997b). Like the Kentucky program, funds only go to "improving schools" and not necessarily to high-achieving schools where scores may have leveled off. School Improvement Teams are the recipients of awards and have flexibility in using the funding to build on educational success, but they may not use the award for staff salary. The number of eligible schools and the number of students in the award school determine award sizes. In 1998, 83 elementary and middle schools received monetary awards with sizes ranging from $15,740 to $64,605. Since the first award allocation in 1996, a total of $8.25 million has been disbursed as monetary awards.

Schools may also be eligible for performance certificates. These nonmonetary recognition certificates are awarded to schools that show 1 year of significant improvement. Schools that receive a certificate and continue significant improvements as defined by the state the following year are eligible for a monetary award.

On recommendation by the district, the state may issue "challenge" grants to schools that apply and are at risk of being declared reconstitution-eligible. Schools participate on a voluntary basis and work with a review team on plans to meet state standards. During the 1997–1998 school year, there were 48 challenge schools and one school system (Caroline County) participating in the Challenge initiative. Approximately $9 million is appropriated by the state for this effort (Goertz et al., 1997).

Finally, if a school is performing significantly below satisfactory and declining (based on the SPI), it may be deemed "reconstitution-eligible." To be determined reconstitution-eligible, two conditions must be met: (a) the school's average performance must be far below the satisfactory standard, and (b) the school's average performance must be declining from previous performance levels (MSDE, 1997a). By 2000, 96 schools had been listed as reconstitution-eligible, with 83 in Baltimore

---

[2] High schools are not currently eligible for awards because the test used to gauge high school performance, the Maryland Functional Tests, are basic skills exams.

City, 12 in Prince Georges County, and 1 in Anne Arundel County (MSDE, 2000).[3]

Summary of Program Design and Context

Table 1 summarizes some potentially important similarities and differences between the Kentucky and Maryland programs in design and context that may have an impact on the ways in which the accountability program plays out in schools and classrooms.

Both programs set long-term school-level goals for student achievement. The award amounts paid per school were similar; Maryland's average award was toward the high end of awards paid to Kentucky schools. At the time of our study, the Kentucky program applied to elementary, middle, and high schools; the Maryland program applied to only elementary and middle schools, with plans to extend to high schools. The district played a central role in program administration and implementation in Maryland and a much-reduced role in Kentucky. For example, Maryland districts collaborated with the state to identify reconstitution-eligible schools, and the state encouraged the establishment of intervention programs at the district level.

The two programs also differed in design and motivational philosophy. In Kentucky, teachers could decide how their school's money would be spent. In practice, most schools used some or all of the reward funds for salary bonuses. In Maryland, teachers could decide how their school's money would be spent, but the funds had to be spent on school improvement and could not be used for salary bonuses. In addition, the motivational philosophies of the programs differed. The philosophy underlying the Kentucky program was that of incentive: The program was designed so that teachers could know in advance what level of performance would lead to particular consequences. Any school could receive rewards or sanc-

---

[3]State regulations define school reconstitution as changing one or more of a school's administrative personnel, staffing, organization, or instructional programs. The regulations include procedures for identifying schools in need of reconstitution and for allowing local school systems to address specific problems of the identified schools. When the state identifies a school as reconstitution-eligible, the school district must respond by completing a local school reconstitution proposal, which outlines a framework to address those areas of decline. In some cases, districts have changed administrators and staff. If the framework is approved by the state, the district must submit a transition plan with specific deadlines for completion of improvements. If failure persists, the state may take more drastic measures, including contracting with a third party to run the school. However, this final action has not been pursued to date in Maryland (Goertz et al., 1997).

Table 1
Program Design and Context: Comparison of Kentucky and Maryland

	Kentucky	Maryland
Program design		
Goals	20-year target (2010); high goals that require significant modifications to curriculum and instruction.	Target extended to 2000, likely to be re-extended; high goals that require significant modification to curriculum and instruction; unlikely to be attained by 2000.
School levels	All schools.	Currently includes only elementary and middle schools.
District role	State reforms largely bypassed districts.	District given key role in implementing state reforms.
Award	Incentive. Salary bonuses paid to approximately 40% of schools based on improvement.	Reward. School improvement funds paid to approximately 10% of schools based on improvement.
Sanctions	All schools at risk. Levels of sanctions include improvement plan, state-assigned educator to focus school efforts, funds for improvement, and risk of job security.	Only lowest performing schools at risk. Levels of sanctions include probationary status, risk of state takeover.
Program context		
Rationale	Complete recreation of education system overnight. Court ordered due to system failure.	Part of long-term continuous effort by state to maintain leadership in standards-based reform.
State size	Geographically large state; 124 school districts.	Geographically small state; 24 school districts.
Culture	Cultures vary from cosmopolitan to provincial.	Cultures vary but tend to be more cosmopolitan.
Educational culture	Varies from models of professional competence to patronage systems. Strength of ties to professional educational cultures and institutions vary greatly.	Tend toward stronger ties to professional educational cultures and institutions.

tions regardless of performance level. And although the award amount was not specified in advance (it depended on the number of schools eligible to receive awards and the appropriations level), the specific level of performance required could be anticipated. Approximately 40% of schools received awards, and any school could receive sanctions if their performance declined.

In contrast, the motivational philosophy underlying the Maryland program focused more on reward and sanction (consequences for prior behavior). Although the award could be anticipated by improving schools, it was based on statistically significant improvements in performance, potentially a less conceptually clear target than improvement to a specific performance level. The awards were also funded and awarded retrospectively, so that schools could only be sure that they were going to get the funds *after* the performance was measured. Only about 10% of Maryland schools improved performance enough to be eligible to receive awards. The sanctions component was limited to the lowest performing schools, and the number of schools identified depended on appropriations levels. Given the limited availability of funds for sanctions, most schools could be assured that they would never be sanctioned, despite marginal declines in performance.

Program contexts also differed. Both programs operated in the context of large-scale education reform efforts with rigorous standards and authentic state-level criterion-referenced assessments. The Maryland reforms were part of an incremental, long-term strategy to improve student achievement through standards-based reform, beginning in the 1980s. The Kentucky reforms were more recent and sweeping and were motivated by a perceived failure of the education system. Other important context features include state size and culture. Kentucky is a geographically large and culturally diverse state, whereas Maryland is geographically small and somewhat less culturally diverse. These program design and context features provide an important lens for interpreting variations in principal and teacher response to the programs.

Method

The research methods used in this study combine qualitative and quantitative approaches. In each site, the research began with interviews with teachers and principals, district (in Maryland) personnel, and state-level personnel, followed by surveys of principals in both states. Principals and teachers were interviewed in 16 schools in Kentucky in the Fall of 1996 and in 11 schools in Maryland in the Fall of 1997. The samples in both states included schools with various levels of success in the program. High schools were excluded from the Maryland sample because they were not involved in the accountability program at that time.

Researchers spent a half day in each school interviewing the principal and a sample of teachers, particularly those that taught in the accountability subjects and grades. Typical interviews lasted 45 to 60 min. Interviews with teachers were conducted both individually and in small groups, with between 3 and 10 teachers interviewed at each school site. Information was also gathered from state-level personnel in both states and district-level personnel in Maryland to better understand program context, design, and implementation. District-level personnel were not typically interviewed in Kentucky because the reform design largely bypassed districts.

Interview protocols were used to guide the semi-structured interviews and provide consistency across research teams. Typically, two researchers worked together at each school to provide greater flexibility in data collection and to help interpret findings. Overall, four researchers collected data in each state. Immediately following each school visit, researchers recorded initial perceptions on a summary sheet. Findings from the early data collection and analysis efforts helped to inform later data collection, both within and across research sites. Interviews with teachers and principals were taped, and the tapes were transcribed. Transcripts were content-analyzed to identify the major themes of each interview. Coding categories emerged from the data and were developed separately for Kentucky and Maryland.

Findings from the qualitative phase of the research, along with the literature on high-performance organizations, effective schools, and motivation, were used to develop the survey instruments (see Kelley et al., 2000). The survey was administered to 392 principals in Kentucky. The schools were selected from a list of schools provided by the Kentucky Department of Education based on prior accountability status (e.g., reward both cycles, nonreward both cycles) and school level (elementary, middle, and high). There were a total of 15 strata. Within each strata, 40 schools were chosen (or all the schools if there were 40 or fewer schools in the stratum), for a total of 392 schools. In all, 204 useable questionnaires were returned, for a response rate of 52%.

In Maryland, principals were sent questionnaires in the Spring of 1998. A sample size of 500 was allocated equally between middle and elementary schools. A simple random sample of 250 schools was taken within each strata, based on mailing lists provided by the Maryland Department of Education. After the initial mailing, Prince George's County asked that their principals not be contacted. Responses received from this district were deleted from subsequent analyses and destroyed. Eight of the schools on the mailing list did not participate in the program, so they were removed from the sample. Useable responses were received from 252 principals in participating counties, for a response rate of 51%.

Findings From Interviews With Principals and Teachers

The interview data show interesting similarities and differences in implementation and effects across the two programs. The data will be explored with respect to overall program impact, organizational characteristics and strategies used by successful schools (enabling conditions), and barriers to goal achievement.

Overall Program Impact

Consistent with prior research (Koretz et al., 1996), teachers and principals in both Kentucky and Maryland reported that they had made changes in teaching practice to improve student achievement on the state assessment. From the interview data, it was not possible to distinguish whether one state or the other had made more movement in teaching practice, but both showed evidence of attention to state goals and alignment of teaching practice. Teachers in the assessment subjects and grades were more likely than other teachers to report changes to their teaching practice. Teachers and principals in both states also reported that efforts to align teaching practice to state goals had promoted collaboration among teachers as they struggled to align curriculum to the state standards and assessments.

Despite these commonalties, there were also some interesting differences that emerged between the two states. First, there appeared to be much higher penetration of the accountability program in Kentucky than in Maryland. All of the Kentucky teachers we interviewed were very aware of the accountability program and could describe it clearly. In contrast, there was a significant range of familiarity with rewards and sanctions in Maryland. A few Maryland teachers were completely unaware of the reward component of the program, and some were unclear about the specifics of the program. Similarly, some Maryland teachers had limited familiarity with the sanctions component, and many referred to it as a program for Baltimore City (which contained many of the schools identified for sanctions).

Similarly, in Kentucky, teachers equated "accountability" with rewards and sanctions, whereas in Maryland, teachers equated "accountability" with the state student assessment. Teachers in Kentucky were somewhat more likely to attribute the motivation for changes in teaching practice to the accountability program (rewards and sanctions) first and to good teaching practice second, compared to Maryland teachers, who were more likely to attribute their primary motivation to efforts to adopt good teaching practice. A Maryland elementary school teacher explained:

> I think teachers are evaluating their instruction and using the information from the Maryland test as a model for good teaching instruction. Not necessarily just an assessment, [but] they are recognizing that this is a good way to be teaching. (Maryland Elementary School Teacher)

Compare this explanation to that of a Kentucky elementary school teacher:

> And I'll never forget a staff meeting when we had our baseline and we had our next year's scores, and we were in [the successful category] but not quite to [rewards], ... [and] it was proof that the instructional strategies that we had decided that we needed to do in the classrooms worked, because that school ended up being a couple of points, three points above threshold. (Kentucky Elementary School Teacher)

In Kentucky, the teachers experienced a significant amount of stress as a result of the accountability program. Maryland teachers seemed somewhat less stressed. One hypothesis that emerged from the interview data was that the burden of accountability fell heaviest on *teachers* in Kentucky and on *principals* in Maryland. This makes sense if one considers that both rewards and sanctions in Kentucky focused largely on teachers, whereas in Maryland principals were most likely to benefit from awards (because they are largely responsible for the school budget) and the most likely to suffer from (formal and informal) sanctions imposed by districts. Both of the districts we studied in Maryland evaluated principals based on their schools' performance on the state assessment and held annual meetings to identify within-district rankings of schools, celebrating the successes of schools that met their goals. Principals in schools that did not receive high rankings consistently reported that the meetings made them feel uncomfortable and embarrassed. These principals typically chose to downplay school rankings with their teachers.

The pressure and stress on teachers in Kentucky, combined with the burden of accountability and some problems with the scoring of the assessment instrument, led to declines in teacher buy-in to the program over time. By 1998–1999, the state legislature approved significant modifications to the program in Kentucky, including a new state assessment instrument that had a heavier emphasis on multiple choice questions, an extended debate about whether to continue salary bonuses (they were ultimately retained), and a weakened sanctions program. In contrast, teacher buy-in appeared to strengthen in Maryland over time, with teachers indicating that the state had been responsive to early concerns about the assessment and had made modifications that improved the assessment instrument. As a Maryland elementary school teacher explained:

> My impressions have been changing. In the beginning I just was appalled, [the tests] weren't ready when we'd get [them]. The first couple of years it really was not ready to be used. My mind has changed a lot. I think it has become a much better tool. They've refined it a lot. It's starting to be more useable. (Maryland Elementary School Teacher)

Enabling Conditions

Enabling conditions were identified in each of the programs by comparing the strategies used by award schools with those that failed to achieve award status (see also Kelley, 1998). Strikingly similar enabling conditions were present in both Kentucky and Maryland, although in some cases there were differences related to context and program design. Important enabling conditions as described by teachers and principals include data analysis and feedback into the curriculum and instructional program and curriculum alignment that takes place across subjects and grades (despite that fact that in both programs, the assessment was targeted to a few grade levels and did not cover all subject areas). The most successful schools in both Kentucky and Maryland had a tightly knit, collaborative culture with a clear focus on the goals of the accountability program. As one Maryland teacher explained:

> We spend a lot of time going over the test results for both the MSPAP and the CRT's. … And even though [all of the grade levels] don't take the test, basically we do it as a whole staff so that we can say … "these are areas that we are doing well in". … And in those areas that we are low … when the school improvement team gets together [they say], "what things can we do to help improve those areas?" You know, if it's in writing, … maybe we need to be looking at focusing on persuasive writing if that's where we are deficient. What kind of activities can we do … [to] make it … a whole-school-wide effort to make sure that we're giving [students] enough experiences in those areas for them to be successful. (Maryland Elementary School Teacher, Reward School)

Teachers and principals in the most successful schools also had a strong and ongoing professional development program related to the state assessment shaped by needs identified at the school level. Strategies included visiting other schools to learn best practices, focused training in reading and writing, and (in Maryland) supplementing the state's relatively low wages for summer scoring of MSPAP to give teachers an extra incentive to participate in the grading and thereby learn more about the assessment and its scoring. One Kentucky high school showed how sanctions could help to raise the level of teacher connectedness to the professional education community, while providing focused information related to the state educational goals. As a result, the school moved from sanctions to rewards:

> There's probably no way to access [professional development] benefits without a sanction, but we took that [reward] money and invested it in the future of these kids ... and in teacher development and professional development. I think some teachers had no idea that there were National Standards; ... now we know ... what they are and we've participated in the conferences that discussed them. (Kentucky High School Principal)

Principal leadership was also important in both Kentucky and Maryland. Principals in the most successful schools had a clear focus on and commitment to the goals of the accountability program, believed that their staffs could improve student achievement, provided feedback on prior performance, and facilitated professional development and opportunities for collaboration among staff to retool the curriculum and instructional program. The principal in one reward high school in Kentucky described his efforts:

> If you came [to our school] next week, you'd see our poster out here. It shows, this is where we are right now on our goal, we want to go from 38% to 50% proficient or higher in reading. We've never done that in our school before. How am I going to get that accomplished? Teachers are going to have to be led. I have to be a leader of leaders rather than just tell all the teachers what to do. I've got my department chairs collecting the data, putting it together, leading discussion, finding out who in the department is doing a good job, and giving me some strategies that I can record that I can broadcast to the other departments. If I'm going to get change to occur, then it's got to come from them. (Kentucky High School Principal)

Successful schools in both Kentucky and Maryland also implemented a variety of student incentives to promote student effort on the assessment and student attendance during assessment week. The strategies ranged from (a) having principals and teachers give pep talks to students before the assessment to (b) having popular teachers roaming through classrooms during the assessment to (c) highly visible countdowns to the assessment to (d) rewards (such as parties) for students if they attended and appeared to be expending effort during the testing period.

Two factors that were more heavily emphasized in Kentucky than in Maryland were the significant high skill levels of teachers in the highest performing schools and their often unique professional relationships that gave them "insider information." Such professional relationships included working with the KSDE on curriculum and assessment development, participating in KIRIS-related leadership groups sponsored by the state, or working closely with nearby universities. For example, differences emerged in high- and low-performing schools. The higher performing schools tended to view the information from the state as voluminous and helpful, but one low-performing school in Kentucky complained to the research team that the state never provided any information and that they discarded what they did get because it was all marked "DRAFT." High-performing schools had professional savvy or personal contacts that helped them more accurately interpret and utilize state resources.

Barriers to Improvement

Teachers and principals in Kentucky and Maryland identified a number of barriers to improvement in student performance. The barriers include a variety of issues related to the fairness of the assessment, student characteristics and motivation, and resource constraints. Variations in program design and emphasis produced slightly different lists of barriers in Kentucky and Maryland.

Perceptions of barriers shared by the two programs included problems related to comparing performance across cohort groups, large populations of special education and at-risk populations of students (or variations in these student groups across cohorts, which made continuous improvement difficult), high student mobility, and a lack of incentives for students to perform well on the assessment.

> My problem is sometimes we have these genius kids who pull their score up really high and the next year ... we have several Special Ed students being tested, and this test is not real conclusive [for] Special Ed students. So [the scores are] really going to drop, when really it doesn't mean our teaching has gone down. (Kentucky Elementary Teacher, p. 1)

Barriers that were unique to Kentucky included concerns about the validity and reliability of the assessment instrument and the cultural bias of the test, which advantages students from more urban areas:

Instead of making [the question on the assessment about] play[ing] in a playground at your school, [the students] have to figure out what site would be the best place to put a factory in your town and why. ... [But] in the rural areas, you know that we don't have all those things that [students can] identify with on a day-to-day basis. ... Some of the topics and the concepts they give I think are very biased. (Kentucky Elementary Teacher, p. 24)

Barriers that were unique to Maryland included concerns that the assessment was developmentally inappropriate at the third grade level, concerns that the testing burden would reduce student effort on the assessment over time, lack of resources to support changes in teaching practice, and test security policies that prevented teachers from openly discussing the assessment and its implications for teaching practice. Some of these factors appeared to be addressed by the state to some extent over time. For example, in the initial years of the program, the assessments included performance events that had the effect of creating melee in the classroom or were not designed with facilities' limitations in mind. The interviews included rich stories that teachers told us in confidence (because they believed they were not supposed to reveal the contents of the assessment). However, teachers also indicated that the assessment instrument had been improved over time to be more appropriate for young students.

The test security policies still inhibited teachers from collaborating with others on ways to better focus instruction to meet the demands of the assessment. State officials viewed these restrictions as limited, yet teachers often misinterpreted state directives as precluding them from discussing the assessment at the school level at risk of severe penalty.

Interviewer: Did the teachers participate in test development?

Principal: There may have been one or two who may have been part of [it, but] you know all this was done so secretive[ly], especially the test. When I was on that at one time as a teacher, we would work on a task and we had to sign little affidavits that [said] you know you can't whisper this [to anyone] or else we'll take your first child away, ah, things like that. (Maryland Middle School Principal)

Together, this review of program effects, enablers, and barriers provides a snapshot of the impressions of teachers and principals regarding the implementation of the accountability programs in these states. In the next section, we examine findings of surveys of principals in the two states, which provide complementary information about the programs.

Findings From the Principal Survey

The principal survey data show some additional similarities and differences in enablers and barriers across the two programs. The data are explored with regard to primarily program aims, effects, and enabling conditions.

Samples and Measures

All measures were gathered by the survey administered to principals in Kentucky and Maryland. As described previously, for Kentucky, surveys were sent to school principals in the Fall of 1997 (n = 204). For Maryland, surveys were mailed to school principals about 1 year later in the Spring of 1998 (n = 252). Because the programs in the two states were structured differently, a somewhat modified version of the Kentucky principal survey was used in Maryland. Seventy of approximately 90 questions were nearly identical in the two surveys and were modified only slightly to note dissimilar program terms.[4]

Based on previous research on employee (Heneman, 1998) and teacher (Kelley, 1998; Kelley et al., 2000; Kelley & Protsik, 1997) reward programs, several variables related to effective schools, characteristics of effective reward programs, and teacher motivation were identified. These variables included aims of the incentive program (i.e., motivating financial incentives), program effects (i.e., improvement of teaching), and several enabling conditions (e.g., district support and teacher teamwork). Principals rated the extent to which such effects, aims, or enabling conditions were present using one of two scales, ranging from 1 (*strongly disagree*) to 5 (*strongly agree*) or from 1 (*not at all*) to 5 (*to a very great extent*).

We conducted a factor analysis to confirm the expected variable groupings. Seventy items were included in the analysis, which yielded 17 factors with eigenvalues exceeding 1.0. Seven factors were selected for analysis because they appeared particularly relevant to our questions and our previously established constructs (e.g., enabling conditions in school incentive programs). Forty-three items on the survey loaded on the seven factors. Table 2 shows the abbreviated items and factor loadings for these factors. (Full items are shown in Appendix A.)

The items comprising each factor were averaged to form scales that were used in the subsequent analyses. The reliabilities for the scales are presented in Table 3.

---

[4]We located items that were in both surveys and deleted from the data set items that were in one and not the other. The Kentucky survey had more questions than the other survey, although the Maryland survey had some items that were not included on the Kentucky survey.

The following paragraphs describe the variables used in this study. They include: Financial Incentives, Improvement of Teaching, Principal Understanding/Commitment, District Support, Resource Allocation, Principal Skill, and Teacher Teamwork and Learning.

Financial Incentives. Financial Incentives emphasize the financial as opposed to nonfinancial aspects of rewards. (Nonfinancial incentives include seeing students succeed or having chances to do interesting work.) Within the context of SBPA programs, financial incentives deal with the extent to which the monetary bonus is providing motivation to teachers and principals. The eight items included in this scale asked principals whether the possibility of a bonus, among other things, helped motivate teachers to work toward the accountability goals and whether it provided a shared goal that encouraged school staff to work together. Ratings ranged from 1 (*strongly disagree*) to 5 (*strongly agree*).

Improvement of Teaching. The Improvement of Teaching variable taps the extent to which principals believe teachers are focusing their efforts on improving teaching and the teaching process. In eight items, principals were asked to rate the extent to which teaching had improved in their schools. For example, they were asked whether teachers were changing the way that they teach, changing the content of their teaching, and placing more time and effort into teaching. This variable captures an important outcome or effect of SBPA programs, because such programs aim to encourage teachers to focus on and improve their teaching (Kelley, 1999b). Ratings ranged from 1 (*not at all*) to 5 (*to a very great extent*).

Principal Understanding/Commitment. The Principal Understanding/Commitment variable reflects the extent to which principals both understand and are dedicated to the goals of the accountability program. In five items, principals were asked to rate the extent of their knowledge of their school's accountability goals and their commitment to pursuing those goals. Ratings ranged from 1 (*strongly disagree*) to 5 (*strongly agree*).

District Support. District Support deals with the extent to which principals view the district as helpful to the site by, for example, helping it meet its goals and providing it with technical and resource support. Excluded from these items is the notion of pressure from the district. In the factor

Table 2
Rotated Factor Loadings Obtained From Factor Analysis of Items on the Kentucky and Maryland Principals' Survey [a]

Item		1	2	3	4	5	6	7
					Factor			
Qvii6	Tripling reward motivates teachers	.85	.02	.00	.04	-.03	.06	-.01
Qvii4	Possibility bonus helps me motivate	.83	.01	.07	.02	.02	.05	.00
Qvii8	Tripling reward motivates me	.82	.05	-.08	-.01	.03	-.01	.01
Qvii5	Bonus provides shared goal	.81	.01	.11	.05	.06	.02	.03
Qvii7	Bonus motivates me more	.77	.03	-.11	-.06	.05	.03	-.06
Qvii10	Bonus award should continue	.76	-.05	.06	.04	-.12	.09	.03
Qvii3	Fair for teachers to get reward	.71	-.04	.08	.05	-.19	.05	.09
Qiii5	Principal referred to bonus	.60	.02	-.03	.01	.05	.05	.08
Qii5	Teachers worked change teach.	.03	.75	.04	.08	.05	.20	.24
Qii3	Teachers changed way teach	.07	.71	.06	.06	-.07	-.02	.11
Qii1	Teachers spent hours teaching	.00	.64	.04	-.01	.14	.10	.05
Qii4	Teachers prof. dev. Activities	-.04	.63	.08	.18	.22	-.01	.06
Qii2	Teachers changed content	-.09	.56	.07	-.08	.28	.02	-.04
Qii9	Have knowledge help teachers	.16	.53	-.01	.11	.04	.26	.25
Qii6	Teachers focused stud. learning	-.11	.52	.24	.11	.16	.07	.19
Qiii20	Teachers provided time plan	.05	.49	.05	.25	.04	.16	.46
Qi2	Know improve to meet goals	.00	.14	.82	.09	.03	.12	.00
Qi4	Could explain goals to others	-.09	.08	.81	.07	.13	.14	.01
Qi1	Clear understanding goals	.03	-.02	.80	.19	.02	.05	.05
Qi3	Understanding stud. ach. meas.	.04	.00	.77	.16	.04	.19	.04

Item	Description	1	2	3	4	5	6	7
Qt9	Committed to pursuing goals	.01	.22	.50	.14	-.05	.01	.02
Qv2	District staff support efforts	.02	.08	.12	.84	-.04	.11	.12
Qv3	District provided tech. assistance	.02	.04	.21	.79	.16	.09	.12
Qv5	District provided resources	.01	.04	.16	.75	.21	.02	.17
Qv1	District admin. staff committed	.09	.12	.11	.73	-.13	.16	.01
Qv6	District provided you discretion	.02	.16	.16	.67	.03	.06	.08
Qiii11	Budgeted funds reallocated	.00	.15	.01	-.01	.73	.08	.16
Qiii14	School invested new technology	-.01	.03	.05	.12	.72	.06	.23
Qiii12	Tutoring/programs established	-.03	.19	.00	.08	.67	.10	.00
Qiii10	Staff realloc. assign teachers	.00	.21	.13	-.02	.62	.03	-.16
Qiii9	Incentives/rewards for students	.20	.00	.13	.10	.42	.03	.00
Qiii7	New curr. development efforts	-.13	.21	.07	.15	.34	.05	.27
Qiii1	Knowledge help teachers	.05	.07	.14	.09	.12	.79	.08
Qiii12	Skills mobilize school	.14	.07	.18	.14	.08	.74	.15
Qiii1	Helped teachers figure out	.09	.22	.22	.08	.00	.59	.22
Qiii10	Know use assessments	.07	.17	.45	.12	.04	.57	-.01
Qiii2	Worked individually teachers	.09	.30	.19	.10	.05	.48	.20
Qiii36	School mobilized resources	.09	.29	.20	.23	.12	.31	.20
Qiii18	Teachers provided time plan	.04	.10	-.04	.07	.01	.11	.73
Qiii21	Teachers opport. best practices	.12	.20	.10	.15	.21	.10	.67
Qiii19	Prof. dev. programs help teachers	-.01	.24	.11	.14	.30	.11	.56
Qiii17	Teachers encouraged team	.08	.37	-.08	.10	.00	.16	.51
Qiii15	Using results guide teaching	-.03	.31	.12	.18	.28	.02	.34

Note. 1 = Financial Incentives; 2 = Improvement of Teaching; 3 = Principal Understanding; 4 = District Support; 5 = Resource Allocation; 6 = Principal Skill; 7 = Teamwork and Learning.
ªVarimax rotation.

Table 3
Coefficient Alpha Reliabilities for the Scales

Scale	α
Financial Incentives	.90
Improvement of Teaching	.81
Principal Understanding	.86
District Support	.87
Resource Allocation	.76
Principal Skill	.81
Teamwork and Learning	.77

analysis, one item in the same section of the survey dealt with the extent to which the district was placing pressure on the site; its failure to load on this factor suggests that principals are making a distinction between district support and pressure. Ratings on five items ranged from 1 (*not at all*) to 5 (*to a very great extent*).

Resource Allocation.   Resource Allocation deals with principals' perceptions that resources have been reallocated for the purposes of reforming or changing the school to meet the goals of the accountability program. Six items asked principals about the allocation of budgeted funds, new technology, tutoring, incentives for students, staff, and curriculum development efforts to meet the accountability goals. Indeed, tutoring programs require the reallocation of person resources if not money. Furthermore, principals view incentives provided to students and not to teachers and principals (Item xiii9) as one type of resource allocation. Finally, curricular efforts will involve time, if not money devoted to curriculum development (e.g., for development and preparation of new curriculum materials). Ratings by principals ranged from 1 (*not at all*) to 5 (*to a very great extent*).

Principal Skill.   Principal Skill deals with the extent to which principals perceive that they possess the skills necessary to enact the accountability reform or change effort. This ability to carry out the accountability reform is different from our third variable, principal understanding/commitment (described earlier). That is, a principal might understand the reform and be committed to its goals but feel that he or she does not have the knowledge and skills to carry it out. Knowledge and skills appear to deal with leadership that emphasizes "purposes," like building "consensus about school goals and practices" (Leithwood, 1994, p. 510) In a 5-item scale, principals were asked whether they themselves had, for example, the knowledge and skills to help teachers improve their teaching and the knowledge and skills to mobilize their school to achieve its goals. Ratings ranged from 1 (*not at all*) to 5 (*to a very great extent*).

Teacher Teamwork and Learning.   A 5-item scale assessed our final variable, Teacher Teamwork and Learning. This variable deals with principals' perceptions that teachers have the opportunity to work together and that they use that opportunity to collaborate and develop professionally. This variable is similar to the improvement of teaching variable (our second variable) but deals more directly with teachers having opportunities to team and network together to learn new skills and knowledge. Principals were asked whether teachers were given opportunities to learn about best practices of other schools that, for example, could be used to raise accountability program scores. Responses from principals about such aspects of teaming and learning ranged from 1 (*not at all*) to 5 (*to a very great extent*).

As described previously, the aforementioned variables may be grouped into three broad categories: SBPA program effects (e.g., improvement of teaching), aims (e.g., motivating incentives), and enabling conditions (e.g., principal understanding and commitment). Enhanced teacher motivation and efforts to improve one's teaching appear to indicate program effectiveness. Furthermore, existing research, theory, and practice suggest that several enabling conditions foster and support teachers in improving their teaching. Schools must (a) receive support from the school district to meet its accountability program's goals, (b) be led by principals who understand and are committed to the school's goals, (c) reallocate resources to meet the accountability goals, and (d) provide opportunities for teachers to team and network to improve their professional practice (see Kelley, 1998).

Analysis

A variety of statistical analyses were conducted to examine the effects of the two accountability programs, including examining similarities and differences in impact given the different program designs and contexts. In each case, the unit of analysis was the individual principal. The means and standard deviations for the aforementioned seven variables—as well as two variables tapping principal experience—were computed separately for the Maryland and Kentucky samples. Independent sample *t* tests were then run to determine whether the means differed significantly from each other for the two samples. The means, standard deviations, and the significance of mean differences for the variables on the principal survey in the two samples are presented in Table 4. Means, standard deviations, and significance of mean differences for individual survey items are shown in Appendix B.

Maryland principals responding to the survey reported having more years of experience working in the field of educational administration on average than did the Kentucky sample ($M = 12.93$ and 10.54, respectively). However, Kentucky principals had more years of experience at their current schools than did Maryland principals ($M = 5.57$ and 4.71, respectively).

With two exceptions, the mean scores for the remaining variables for both states were between 3 and 4, corresponding, for most items, to between "a moderate" and "great" extent. (These values indicate general agreement with the items associated with the variable. For items measured on the second scale, most means similarly correspond to between *neither agree nor disagree* and *agree*.) Although we are primarily interested in identifying differences in perceptions, it should be noted that there are fairly positive perceptions about most variables for both states.

Regarding the effect of the financial incentive, Maryland principals have significantly higher average perceptions than do Kentucky principals that the monetary bonus or award is motivating to teachers. Indeed, there is a fairly large absolute difference (i.e., three fourths of one point) between the means. Maryland principals are closer to the *neither agree nor disagree* response, whereas Kentucky principals are closer to *disagree* on, for example, the item

Table 4

Means, Standard Deviations, and Significance of Mean Differences on Variables for Maryland and Kentucky

Variable	Maryland[a]		Kentucky[b]		Difference	Significance
	M	SD	M	SD		
Principal Experience						
Years in field	12.93†	6.78	10.54	7.59	2.39	**
Years in school	4.71	3.65	5.57†	4.87	−.85	*
Financial Incentive	3.10†	.84	2.36	.90	.75	**
Improvement of Teaching	3.67	.62	3.82†	.52	−.15	**
Principal Understanding	3.82	.86	4.13†	.69	−.31	**
District Support	3.61	.76	3.69	.83	−.08	ns
Resource Allocation	3.15	.79	3.51†	.71	−.35	**
Principal Skill	3.80†	.60	3.69	.53	.11	*
Teamwork and Learning	3.87	.65	3.80	.64	.08	ns

[a]$n = 252.$ [b]$n = 204.$

*$p < .05.$ **$p < .01.$ †Indicates highest mean in the pair.

"the possibility of a bonus helps me motivate teachers." This finding is somewhat surprising. Because of what we have described as a strong accountability focus and emphasis on awarding individual teachers in Kentucky, principals might be expected to find the bonus to be more motivating. However, to the degree that Kentucky principals see the bonus as having negative as well as positive consequences (e.g., increased teacher stress), they may downplay its value. Furthermore, in Maryland, providing money to schools as opposed to individual staff members may have enhanced the motivational value for the principals, as was suggested previously.

With regard to the improvement of teaching, Kentucky principals were higher in their perceptions that a strong focus on improved teaching and learning exists in their schools. There is a modest absolute difference between the means (.15); this is statistically significant. Again, this difference may be attributable to the design of the programs in the two states. In Kentucky, the reform effort was much more comprehensive than in Maryland. Furthermore, in Kentucky, there was a serious alignment of professional development around teaching and learning (Kelley, 1998). In Kentucky, a combination of outstanding educators provided by the state and financial resources to support poorly performing schools, for example, provided a powerful comprehensive package focusing on teaching and learning (Kelley, 1998). In Maryland, the program's premise was to change assessments as a way of changing teaching, providing a somewhat more narrow approach to improving teaching and learning.

Our examination of the individual items comprising the improvement of teaching variable revealed some additional differences. Kentucky principals were significantly higher than Maryland principals on the item, "Have teachers changed the content of what they teach?" (Qii2). In addition, the absolute point difference between the two states was fairly substantial, just over one half of one point.[5] Indeed, in Kentucky, substantial information and professional development assistance about the content of the test was available to teachers, perhaps encouraging them to change their focus to specific subject areas (Kelley, 1998). The early and timely feedback provided to teachers in Kentucky may have encouraged teachers to alter their focus on content as well.

Kentucky principals were also higher, on average, in principal understanding/commitment than Maryland principals. (The difference was moderate but statistically significant: about one third of one point.) Kentucky principals may have had a greater understanding of and commit-

---

[5]However, Item Qii3, dealing with whether teachers have changed the way they teach (e.g., used different teaching methods), was higher for Maryland (see Appendix B).

ment to the program because of the effort expended to communicate goals in that state (discussed previously). In addition, the specification of a target for school improvement may have made the accountability goals clearer than in Maryland. Interestingly, when examining individual items comprising this scale, the largest absolute difference is for the Item Qi4, "I could explain my school's accountability goals to others if asked" (nearly two thirds of a point difference, with Kentucky higher). The smallest difference is for the Item Qi9, "I am strongly committed to pursuing my school's accountability goals."

Our fourth variable, district support, generated means that were very close to each other for the two states. Both principal samples ranked questions concerning district support (e.g., do district staff support your efforts … ?) as between to a "moderate" and "great" extent. Thus, principals in both states, on average, perceived their districts to be supportive and did not differ from each other in their perceptions. This finding is interesting because in Kentucky, the program design largely bypassed districts (discussed previously). However, in examining individual items, one item concerning the commitment of district administrative staff to the goals of the program was higher for principals in Maryland. This finding is consistent with the program design used in Maryland, whereby the state administers the program through local districts.

The fifth variable, resource allocation, had means that are significantly higher in Kentucky. (The difference is moderate: about one third of one point.) Resource allocation deals with such things as providing tutoring and similar programs in subjects covered by the tests, new technology, and the reassignment of teachers within the school. In Kentucky, several components of KERA directed state resources to schools to be used for these purposes. For example, funds were allocated by the state for technology and tutoring programs. In addition, our qualitative data provided examples of Kentucky principals who reallocated staff to the assessment grade levels in response to the high-stakes accountability program as a short-term strategy to improve scores.

With regard to our sixth variable, principal skill, the difference between the means is slight in absolute terms (.11) but statistically significant, with Maryland higher. Maryland principals may view themselves as more skilled to mobilize the school toward the reform effort because of the more incremental nature of the accountability program in the state (e.g., Maryland Functional Tests predated the SBPA program) and their historically stronger ties to professional education communities in Maryland compared to Kentucky. This finding may also reflect a "hidden result"; principals who are more experienced may also report themselves as being more skilled.

Finally, concerning teamwork, the mean scores were nearly identical for the two states. Average responses on such items as "teachers in related subjects or functions are encouraged to work together as teams" were for the most part between "to a moderate" and "great" extent. This may suggest that both accountability approaches encouraged collaboration among teachers to achieve accountability goals. Furthermore, there was a slight but statistically significant difference in the means for two items comprising this scale: "Teachers in related subjects or functions are encouraged to work together in teams" and "Teachers are provided time to plan together about how to achieve the accountability goals," with Maryland higher.

To examine the relations among the variables, correlation coefficients were calculated. Table 5 presents the zero-order correlation coefficients among the seven variables for the entire sample and the two states separately. All of the correlations are positive, and most are moderate in strength. The highest correlations are between teacher teamwork/learning and improvement of teaching for both Maryland (.60) and Kentucky (.62) principals. A different pattern of correlations for financial incentives is noteworthy. In Maryland, the correlations between principal skill and resource allocation with financial incentives are weak but statistically significant (.24 and .21, respectively), whereas in Kentucky they are not significantly different from zero. Thus, in Maryland, there is a weak positive connection between principal skill and changes in resource allocation to meet the goals of the accountability program and principals' perceptions that the bonus is motivating to teachers.

Finally, to examine the effects of the previous variables on improvement of teaching, this variable was regressed on financial incentives and the five enabling conditions (principal understanding, district support, resources, principal skill, and teacher teamwork and learning). As an ancillary analysis, group expectancy was also regressed on this set of variables.

Table 6 presents the results of the regression analyses examining the predictive effect of this set of variables on improvement of teaching in Maryland and Kentucky. The combined set of variables explain 43% and 41% of the variance in improvement of teaching for Maryland and Kentucky, respectively. For each state, two of the variables are statistically significant: teacher teamwork/learning and principal skill (for Maryland, $b = .399$, $p = .000$ and $b = .324$, $p = .000$; for Kentucky, $b = .380$, $p = .000$ and $b = .157$, $p = .026$, respectively, for the two variables). Teacher teamwork and learning is the strongest predictor of principals' perceptions that teachers are improving their teaching for both groups. (In Kentucky, this variable has over twice the effect of the next strongest predictor.) As in the earlier analyses of the survey data, one limitation is that these findings represent only principals' perceptions. Nonetheless, to the degree that principals re-

Table 5

Correlations for the Variables in the Entire Sample[a] and Maryland[b] and Kentucky[c] Samples

	Variable						
	1	2	3	4	5	6	7
Entire sample							
1 District Support	—						
2 Financial Incentives	.11*	—					
3 Improvement of Teaching	.32**	.02	—				
4 Principal Understanding	.41**	.06	.27**	—			
5 Principal Skill	.42**	.20**	.48**	.50**	—		
6 Resource Allocation	.26**	.06	.40**	.25**	.34**	—	
7 Teacher Teamwork and Learning	.39**	.12*	.59**	.23**	.49**	.47**	—
Maryland							
1 District Support	—						
2 Financial Incentives	.14*	—					
3 Improvement of Teaching	.31**	.11	—				
4 Principal Understanding	.40**	.16	.21**	—			
5 Principal Skill	.41**	.24**	.53**	.51**	—		
6 Resource Allocation	.23**	.21**	.36**	.23**	.36**	—	
7 Teacher Teamwork and Learning	.39**	.06	.60**	.19**	.50**	.44**	—
Kentucky							
1 District Support	—						
2 Financial Incentives	.13*	—					
3 Improvement of Teaching	.33**	.04	—				
4 Principal Understanding	.42**	.15*	.33**	—			
5 Principal Skill	.44**	.11	.45**	.56**	—		
6 Resource Allocation	.29**	.13	.44**	.21**	.39**	—	
7 Teacher Teamwork and Learning	.40**	.15*	.62**	.35**	.47**	.58**	—

[a]$N = 456.$ [b]$n = 252.$ [c]$n = 204.$

$*p < .05.$ $**p < .01.$

flect accurately what is happening in the schools, the findings provide strong evidence that teacher teaming and professional learning is important for teachers to focus on and improve their teaching. Principals who view teachers as planning and working together and networking to meet the goals of the accountability program also view teachers as doing more to improve their teaching.

The finding that principal understanding/commitment was not a significant predictor is somewhat surprising. Our principal understanding measure tapped fairly in-depth knowledge about aspects of the account-

Table 6

Unstandardized Coefficients Obtained From Regression of Improvement of Teaching on Financial Incentives, Principal Understanding, District Support, Resources, Principal Skill, and Teacher Teamwork

	Maryland[a]			Kentucky[b]		
	b	*SE*	*p*	*b*	*SE*	*p*
Financial Incentives	.002	.037	.958	−.039	.032	.213
Principal Understanding/ Commitment	−.040	.042	.345	.040	.051	.427
District Support	.022	.046	.637	.021	.040	.594
Resource Allocation	.050	.043	.248	.069	.049	.163
Principal Skill	.324	.068	.000	.157	.070	.026
Teacher Teamwork and Learning	.399	.058	.000	.380	.059	.000
R^2	.439			.430		
F	31.784		.000	24.612		.000
Adjusted R^2	.425			.412		

[a]$n = 252$. [b]$n = 204$.

ability programs such as "how much each factor of the accountability index needs to improve to reach this cycle's accountability goals" and "how student achievement is measured." Furthermore, our qualitative analysis reported that, in both states, state departments of education worked hard to facilitate principal understanding of the accountability program. Combining the nonsignificant results for principal understanding with the significant findings for principal skill indicates that it is not sufficient for principals to understand or be dedicated to the goals of the accountability program; they must have the skills to enact the reform. (From the qualitative analysis, this was exemplified by the Kentucky high school principal who provided examples of enacting the reform such as facilitating communication and enhancing skills with data analysis.)

The failure of district support to emerge as a significant predictor may be attributed to how it was operationalized in this study. District involvement may have been perceived by principals as pressure from the district, perhaps explaining why the measure was less powerful in the presence of other predictors. Although the factor analysis (previously discussed) excluded one item that dealt with district pressure—and another item dealt with districts providing discretion to principals—other items tapped high district administrator commitment to the program and provision of technical assistance toward achieving the accountability goals.

Ancillary analysis. Group expectancy has been conceptualized as an important outcome of school-based performance programs (Kelley, 1999a). Although group expectancy items were not a focus of this article, it is examined here because of its importance in previous research. Principals were asked, in two items on the survey, to estimate the likelihood (from 0 to 100) that if they and their staffs worked as hard as they could, their schools could (a) avoid being eligible for reconstitution and (b) improve enough to receive a school performance award. A comparison of the means for the two states indicates that Maryland principals rated both types of group expectancy higher on average than did Kentucky principals.[6] That is, principals in Maryland rated their schools as having a higher likelihood than did principals in Kentucky of both avoiding very low performance and exceeding current performance (with sufficient effort). The lower group expectancies for Kentucky are perhaps not surprising, given differences in the goals and design features of the two programs. It may be that a more tangible threat of sanctions in the Kentucky accountability program (Kelley, 1998) heightened principals' concerns about their school's eligibility for sanctions despite their and their staff's best efforts. Similarly, the incremental nature of the Maryland reforms may have raised principal expectancy compared to Kentucky principals, who were forced to implement an entirely new comprehensive educational reform program all at once.

Table 7 presents the results of the regression analysis examining the predictive effects of financial incentives and the five enabling conditions on group expectancy for receiving a reward (a single item). The adjusted r-square for this outcome is .22 for Maryland principals and .16 for Kentucky principals. For principals in both states, financial incentives are a significant positive predictor ($b = 12.649$, $p = .000$, and $b = 7.887$, $p = .000$ for Maryland and Kentucky, respectively). Furthermore, for both states, financial incentives are the strongest predictor. Thus, in principals' views, motivating financial bonuses are strongly associated with the expectation that extra effort will lead to a school award.

For Kentucky principals, principal understanding/commitment is also a significant predictor ($b = 7.258$, $p = .026$). Because the Kentucky program is quite comprehensive and complex, principals may need to understand it in order to judge that effort on the part of school staff will produce a reward. In a less comprehensive approach, a thorough understanding of the program may not be necessary to decide that the goals are attainable. An

---

[6]In addition, for both principal samples, the expectancy for avoiding being eligible for reconstitution was higher than that for exceeding the goals. This likely reflects the relative ease of maintaining current performance and/or avoiding very low performance as opposed to exceeding current performance.

Table 7
Unstandardized Coefficients Obtained From Regression of Reward Expectancy on Financial Incentives, Principal Understanding, District Support, Resources, Principal Skill, and Teacher Teamwork

	Maryland[a]			Kentucky[b]		
	b	SE	p	b	SE	p
Financial Incentives	12.649	1.765	.000	7.887	2.016	.000
Principal Understanding/Commitment	-2.967	2.054	.150	7.258	3.228	.026
District Support	8.623	2.202	.637	4.704	2.539	.594
Resource Allocation	-3.236	2.058	.117	-7.082	3.132	.025
Principal Skill	.831	3.245	.798	1.954	4.446	.661
Teacher Teamwork and Learning	-.005	2.774	.999	2.508	3.735	.503
R^2	.242			.180		
F	12.717		.000	7.160		.000
Adjusted R^2	.223			.155		

[a] $n = 252$. [b] $n = 204$.

intriguing finding is that resource allocation is a negative predictor of group expectancy ($b = -7.082, p = .025$). This is counterintuitive; realigning resources to meet the goals of the accountability program would seemingly create a greater expectation on the part of principals that increased effort would lead to a reward.

Summary

A number of differences emerged between Maryland and Kentucky principals on the quantitative survey. Maryland principals were higher than Kentucky principals on seeing the motivational value of financial incentives and estimating their own skills to enact change to meet the accountability goals. Kentucky principals, by contrast, rated teachers' focus on improving teaching, principals' understanding of and commitment to the goals of the program, and reallocation of resources higher than Maryland principals. No differences were found between the two states for the variables of district support and teamwork. It is interesting that there were no differences on district support because of the administrative model in Maryland emphasizing district involvement. It is also somewhat surprising that there were no differences between the two states on teamwork and learning because professional development was heavily emphasized in Kentucky. Finally,

191

the regression analysis revealed that principals' perceptions that teachers were teaming and learning professionally was most strongly associated with their perceptions that teachers were focusing on and improving their teaching.

Conclusions and Implications

The results reported here reflect the perceptions of principals and (in the qualitative research) teachers. They also reflect the realities of the specific program designs and contexts within which these programs operate. Therefore, we take a cautious approach to generalizing these findings to other states or contexts.

Nevertheless, our results from the principal survey indicate that principals in Kentucky (a state that used a salary bonus with strong sanctions) and Maryland (a state that used a school improvement fund with weaker sanctions) both had positive average perceptions of improvement of teaching, principal understanding, district support, resource allocation, principal skills, and teacher teamwork and learning.

Principal perceptions were statistically significantly *higher* in Kentucky on improvement of teaching, principal understanding, and resource allocation. Principals reported that Kentucky teachers were more likely to have access to focused professional development and to change the content of what they taught, whereas Maryland teachers were more likely to change their teaching methods. This difference may be explained in part by different approaches in the two states to the funding of professional development and to the sharing of information about the contents of the assessment. The Commonwealth of Kentucky played a much more active role in funding and providing professional development and invested a considerable effort to communicate curriculum content guidelines. Maryland left the funding of professional development largely to districts and maintained a tighter hold of information about the assessment.

Maryland principals perceived financial incentives and principal skill more positively than Kentucky principals did. The low ratings of financial incentives in Kentucky is likely attributable to the higher stakes of the accountability program there (rewards to teachers and sanctions to any school whose performance declined, regardless of overall level of performance) and to the timing of the survey, which was administered shortly after the state identified a significant error in the scoring of the assessment. Another explanation from the qualitative data is that Kentucky principals' perceptions of the financial incentive may be related to the creation of higher levels of stress and anxiety among teachers in Kentucky compared to Maryland. Our qualitative data in particular suggest that the Kentucky design places more of the burden of accountability on teachers, whereas the Maryland design places more of the burden on principals.

Principals in both states reported similar positive perceptions of district support, despite the fact that Kentucky districts had a much weaker formal role in administration of the accountability program than they did in Maryland. Principals in both states also reported similarly high positive perceptions of the extent to which teachers were working together in teams to improve student performance on the state assessments. Teacher teaming and learning were important themes that emerged from the qualitative data as well. These findings highlight the contribution that strong, accountable learning communities make to school improvement, as emphasized in previous literature (Darling-Hammond, 1997). They also suggest the importance of organizational learning or "collective capacity development" in school reform (Leithwood, 1994, p. 504). Commonalities in other strategies to improve performance that emerged from the qualitative data include data analysis and feedback (which is part of our teacher teaming variable), school-wide curriculum alignment (part of improvement of teaching), principal leadership (related to resource allocation and principal skill), and goal focus (related to resource allocation and principal understanding).

These data are not conclusive, and implications regarding program design need to be considered in the larger cultural, educational, and reform context. However, one interpretation of these findings is that the salary bonus program with sanctions linked to a comprehensive education reform initiative provided a stronger impact on the improvement of teaching, principal understanding, and resource allocation to support student achievement goals. The greater attention to the accountability goals was not without cost, however; principals also reported negative reactions to the financial incentive. Thus, although Kentucky's program design proved to be more effective in improving teaching, it also created a greater negative reaction from principals and teachers. From the interview data, it was clear that teachers in Kentucky were more aware of the accountability program and felt greater pressure and stress as a result of it. How much accountability is enough to strengthen teacher collaboration while not undermining the personal well-being of teachers? Judging from the reported perceptions of principals, both programs promoted changes in teaching practice, teacher teamwork, and learning, and at least some modest reallocation of resources to support the reform.

Our impression is that given the context in Kentucky at the time of reform implementation, policymakers there made a good decision to utilize the more powerful accountability tools. The need to improve a failing system and encourage the creation of stronger professional cultures in some areas of the state with very weak ties to professional educational communities outweighed the potential negative consequences to morale.

The weaker design of the Maryland program is also consistent with its longer term incremental approach to school improvement. Although the Maryland program did not generate high levels of pressure or stress on teachers, it left greater discretionary control in the hands of principals, who in some cases acted as gatekeepers of teacher knowledge of the accountability program. In Maryland, the assessment appeared to serve as a stronger accountability mechanism for most teachers and schools than the rewards and sanctions.

The cases illustrate how variations in program design and implementation produce variations in program impact. Policymakers need to carefully weigh program design features (e.g., bonuses to teachers or schools, percentage of schools eligible for rewards, whether the program is primarily a reward or an incentive for improved performance) in light of program context (e.g., political support for accountability, perceptions of the urgency of the problem, local capacity to reform, availability of new resources to assist struggling schools, and the overall alignment of educational policies with program goals) in designing effective and appropriate accountability systems to promote improvements in teaching and student learning.

References

Argetsinger, A., & Nakashima, E. (1998). In Md., the "bubble" test has burst. *Washington Post* [On-line]. Retrieved May 11, 1998 from the World Wide Web: http://www.WashingtonPost.com/wp-s...te/1998–05

Darling-Hammond, L. (1997). School reform at the crossroads: Confronting the critical issue of teaching. *Educational Policy, 11,* 151–166.

Elmore, R. F., Abelmann, C., & Fuhrman, S. H. (1996). The new accountability in state education policy. In H. Ladd (Ed.), *Holding schools accountable: Performance-based reform in education* (pp. 65–98). Washington, DC: Brookings Institution.

Goertz, M., Massell, D., & Chun, T. (1997). *Education reform policy: From Congress to the classroom. Maryland case study, 1996–1997.* Philadelphia: Consortium for Policy Research in Education, University of Pennsylvania.

Governor's Commission on School Performance. (1989). *The report of the governor's commission on school performance.* Annapolis, MD: Author.

Hackman, J. R., & Oldham, G. (1980). *Work redesign.* Reading, MA: Addison-Wesley.

Hall, E., & Caffarella, E. (1998). *Third year implementation assessment of the Douglas County, Colorado School District performance pay plan for teachers (1996–1997).* Greely: University of Northern Colorado School of Education.

Heneman, H. G., III. (1998). Assessment of the motivational reactions of teachers to a school-based performance award program. *Journal of Personnel Evaluation in Education, 12*(1), 43–59.

Heneman, H. G., III, & Milanowski, A. T. (1998). *Teachers attitudes about teacher bonuses under school-based performance award programs*. Manuscript submitted for publication.

Kelley, C. (1996). Implementing teacher compensation reform in public schools: Lessons from the field. *Journal of School Business Management, 8*(1), 37–54.

Kelley, C. (1998). The Kentucky school-based performance award program: School-level effects. *Educational Policy, 12*, 305–324.

Kelley, C. (1999a). *The effects of organizational context on teacher expectancy*. Consortium for Policy Research in Education: University of Wisconsin–Madison.

Kelley, C. (1999b). The motivational impact of school-based performance awards. *Journal of Personnel Evaluation in Education, 12*, 309–326.

Kelley, C., Heneman, H. G., III, & Milanowski, A. (2000). *School-based performance award programs, teacher motivation, and school performance: Findings from a study of three programs* [CPRE Research Report]. Madison, WI: Consortium for Policy Research in Education.

Kelley, C., & Protsik, J. (1997). Risk and reward: Perspectives on the implementation of Kentucky's school-based performance award program. *Educational Administration Quarterly, 33*, 474–505.

Kentucky Department of Education. (1998, October). *Kentucky instructional results information system*. Case study presented at CPRE School-based Performance Award conference, Chicago.

Koretz, D. M., Barron, S., Mitchell, K. J., & Stecher, B. M. (1996). *Perceived effects of the Kentucky instructional results information system (KIRIS)*. Washington, DC: RAND, Institute on Education and Training.

Leithwood, K. A. (1994). Leadership for school restructuring. *Educational Administration Quarterly, 30*, 498–518.

Maryland State Department of Education. (1996). *Maryland school "report card" shows solid gains: Schools continue making progress on state tests* [Press Release]. Annapolis: Author.

Maryland State Department of Education. (1997a). *Maryland school performance report, 1997: State and schools systems*. Annapolis: Author.

Maryland State Department of Education. (1997b, January). *School performance recognition awards: Fact sheet 20*. Annapolis: Author.

Maryland State Department of Education. (2000, January). *School reconstitution: State intervention procedures for schools not progressing toward states standards: Fact sheet 5*. Annapolis: Author.

Muncey, D. E., & Conley, S. (1999). Teacher compensation and teacher training: Sketching the terrain. *Journal of Personnel Evaluation in Education, 12*, 365–385.

Steffy, B. E. (1993). *The Kentucky education reform: Lessons for America*. Lancaster, PA: Technomic.

White, K. A. (1998). Kentucky bids KIRIS farewell, ushers in new test. *Education Week* [On-line]. Retrieved April 22, 1998 from the World Wide Web: http://www.edweek.com/htbin

Yen, W. M., & Ferrara, S. (1997). The Maryland school performance assessment program: Performance assessment with psychometric quality suitable for high stakes usage. *Educational and Psychological Measurement, 57*, 60–84.

Appendix A
Full Items Comprising Each Factor

Financial Incentives (Factor 1)

Qvii6   Tripling the size of the reward available would greatly increase the motivation of teachers to meet our school's goals.*

Qvii4   The possibility of a bonus helps me motivate teachers to work toward the accountability goals.*

Qvii8   Tripling the size of the reward available would greatly increase the motivation of teachers to meet our school's goals.*

Qvii5   The bonus provides a shared goal that encourages school staff to work together.*

Qvii7   The possibility of the bonus motivates me to work toward achieving the accountability goals.*

Qvii10 The bonus part of the accountability program should be continued.*

Qvii3   Is it fair for teachers who increase student achievement to receive a bonus?*

Qviii5   To what extent have you as a principal referred to the possibility of getting a bonus in discussing the school's accountability goals with the teachers?

Improvement of Teaching (Factor 2)
To what extent …

Qii5   have teachers worked together to plan and implement changes in what is taught or how teaching is done?

Qii3   have teachers changed the way they teach (e.g., used different teaching methods)?

Qii1   have teachers spent more hours on teaching and teaching-related tasks?

Qii4   have teachers engaged in professional development activities (e.g., in-service or other training) aimed at increasing their ability to help students achieve higher [accountability program] scores?

Qii2   have teachers changed the content of what they teach?

Qii9   does the typical teacher in this school continually strive to keep up with the latest developments in curriculum and instructional practice?

Qii6   have teachers focused their teaching more on those aspects of student learning related to the [accountability program] assessments?

Qii20 are teachers provided time to plan together about how to improve students scores on the [accountability program] tests?

District Support (Factor 3)
To what extent …

Qv2   do district staff support your efforts to achieve your school's accountability goals?

Qv3   has your district provided you with technical assistance toward achieving your school's accountability goals?

Qv5   has your district provided you with the resources you need to achieve your school's accountability goals?

Qv1   are district administrative staff committed to the accountability program?

Qv6   has your district provided you the discretion to do what needs to be done to achieve your school's accountability goals?

Principal Understanding/Commitment (Factor 4)

Qi2   I know how much each factor of the accountability index needs to improve to reach this cycle's accountability goals.*

Qi4   I could explain my school's accountability goals to others if asked.*

Qi1   I have a clear understanding of what my school's accountability goals are.*

Qi3   I have a good understanding of how student achievement is measured by the … tests used in the accountability program.*

Qi9   I am strongly committed to pursuing my school's accountability goals.*

Resource Allocation (Factor 5)

To what extent …

Qii11   have budgeted funds been reallocated to acquire instructional materials that would contribute to better [accountability program] scores?

Qii14   has your school invested in new technology (e.g., computers, Internet) to achieve the accountability goals?

Qii12   have tutoring or similar programs been established in subjects covered by the [accountability program's] tests?

Qii10   has staff been reallocated to assign the better teachers to the [accountability program's] assessment grades?

Qii9   are incentives or rewards provided for students to do well on the tests?

Qii7   are new curriculum development efforts linked to the [accountability program's] assessments?

Principal Skill (Factor 6)

To what extent …

Qii11   do you yourself have the knowledge and skills to help teachers improve their teaching?

Qii12   do you have the skills needed to mobilize your school to achieve its accountability goals?

Qii1   have you as a principal helped teachers figure out what they need to do to help achieve the accountability goals?

Qii10   do you know how to use the results of the [accountability program's] assessments to figure out what needs to be done to meet your school's accountability goals?

Qiii36   has your school mobilized all its resources to meet its accountability goals?

Teacher Teamwork and Learning (Factor 7)

To what extent …

Qii18   are teachers provided time to plan together about how to achieve the accountability goals?

Qii21   are teachers given opportunities to learn about best practices of other schools that can be used to raise [accountability program] scores?

Qii19   are professional development programs focused on helping teachers acquire knowledge and skills needed to improve students scores on the [accountability program's] tests?

Qii17   are teachers in related subjects or functions encouraged to work together in teams?

Qii15   has more emphasis been put on using assessment results to guide teaching efforts?

Note. Most items were measured on a 5-point scale ranging from 1 (*not at all*) to 5 (*to a very great extent*). Starred items (*) were measured on a 5-point scale ranging from 1 (*strongly disagree*) to 5 (*strongly agree*).

Appendix B

Means, Standard Deviations, and Significance of Mean Differences on
Individual Items for Maryland and Kentucky

		Kentucky[a]		Maryland[b]		Difference	Significance
		M	SD	M	SD		
Financial Incentives							
Qvii6	Triple reward motivates teachers	2.33	1.19	2.88†	1.19	.56	**
Qvii4	Reward motivates teachers	2.35	1.08	2.97†	1.08	.63	**
Qvii8	Triple reward motivates me	2.04	1.10	2.75†	1.21	.71	**
Qvii5	Bonus provides shared goal	2.43	1.18	3.22†	1.07	.79	**
Qvii7	Bonus motivates me more	2.05	1.03	2.89†	1.26	.83	**
Qvii10	Bonus award should continue	2.31	1.27	3.46†	1.13	1.16	**
Qvii3	Fair for teachers to get reward	2.85	1.19	3.65†	.98	.80	**
Qiii5	Principal referred to bonus	2.48	1.21	2.99†	1.30	.51	**
Improvement of Teaching							
Qii5	Teachers worked change teaching	3.94	.77	3.91	.82	-.02	ns
Qii3	Teachers changed way teach	3.65	.78	3.86†	.85	.21	**
Qii1	Teachers spent hours teaching	3.84	.83	3.69	.96	-.14	ns
Qii4	Teachers professional development	4.25†	.65	3.90	.80	-.35	**
Qii2	Teachers changed content teach	3.68†	.82	3.12	1.01	-.56	**
Qii9	Teachers keep up developments	3.54	.79	4.03†	.85	.49	**
Qii6	Teachers focused teaching	3.99†	.77	2.98	1.04	-1.00	**
Qii20	Teachers provided time plan	3.62	.86	3.81†	.86	.19	*
Principal Understanding/Commitment							
Qi2	Know how much needs improve	3.92†	1.01	3.59	1.21	-.33	**
Qi4	Could explain goals to others	4.12†	.82	3.48	1.12	-.64	**
Qi1	Clear understanding of goals	4.35†	.82	4.03	1.03	-.32	**
Qi3	Understanding achievement meas.	3.86†	1.00	3.66	1.10	-.20	*
Qi9	Committed to pursuing goals	4.39	.72	4.33	.78	-.06	ns

District Support							
Qv2	District staff supports efforts	3.86	.94	3.92	.94	.06	ns
Qv3	District provided tech. assistance	3.57†	1.02	3.35	1.02	-.21	*
Qv5	District provided resources	3.41†	.98	3.02	.99	-.38	**
Qv1	District admin. staff committed	3.89	.86	4.24†	.85	.35	**
Qv6	District provided you discretion	3.71†	1.05	3.49	1.02	-.22	*
Resource Allocation							
Qiii1	Budgeted funds reallocated	3.43	1.07	3.24	1.17	-.19	ns
Qiii4	School invested new technology	3.75†	1.05	3.21	1.34	-.54	**
Qiii12	Tutoring/programs established	3.57†	1.02	2.92	1.21	-.65	**
Qiii10	Staff realloc. assign teachers	2.96†	1.10	2.25	1.25	-.71	**
Qiii9	Incentives/rewards for students	3.19	1.19	3.22	1.29	.03	ns
Qiii7	New curriculum development	4.12	.76	4.08	.82	-.04	ns
Principal Skill							
Qii11	Knowledge help teachers	3.69	.72	3.95†	.75	.26	**
Qii12	Skills mobilize school	3.74	.74	3.88	.75	.14	ns
Qii1	Helped teachers figure out	3.77	.72	3.95†	.80	.18	*
Qii10	Know use assessments	3.82†	.79	3.65	.89	-.18	*
Qii2	Worked individually teachers	3.39	.77	3.64†	.90	.25	**
Qii36	School mobilized resources	3.73	.76	3.76	.80	.03	ns
Teacher Teamwork and Learning							
Qiii18	Teachers provided time plan	3.57	1.13	3.78†	1.02	.21	*
Qiii21	Teachers opport. best pract.	3.61	.87	3.53	.92	-.08	ns
Qiii19	Prof. development help teachers	4.12	.75	4.01	.82	-.11	ns
Qiii17	Teachers encouraged teams	3.87	.88	4.11†	.86	.24	**
Qiii15	Using results guide teaching	3.82	.74	3.93	.85	.11	ns

Note. Inaccuracy in difference column in some cases is due to rounding.
[a] $n = 204$. [b] $n = 252$.

*$p < .05$. **$p < .01$. † Indicates highest mean in pair.

199

PEABODY JOURNAL OF EDUCATION, 75(4), 200–215

Using Performance Indicators to Hold Schools Accountable: Implicit Assumptions and Inherent Tensions

Rodney T. Ogawa and Ed Collom

As reformers have sought to improve the academic performance of public schools in the United States, they have employed widely varying strategies. Recently, several states have combined two of these strategies to improve the academic performance of schools: performance indicators and accountability.

In this article, we examine the high-stakes use of educational indicators to hold schools accountable for the academic performance of their students. Drawing chiefly on examples from California's Public Schools Accountability Act of 1999 (PSAA), we examine the assumptions on which this strategy is based, revealing a quasi-market rationale. Then, we place the assumptions against the literature on the use of educational indicators to identify issues that might arise with implementation, uncovering fundamental tensions that could undermine the intended consequences of holding schools accountable for attaining specific levels on performance indicators.

RODNEY T. OGAWA is Professor and Associate Dean in the Graduate School of Education, University of California, Riverside.

ED COLLOM is a doctoral student in the Department of Sociology, and a Research Fellow with the California Educational Research Cooperative, University of California, Riverside.

Requests for reprints should be sent to Rodney T. Ogawa, School of Education, University of California, Riverside, CA 92521. E-mail: rodney.ogawa@ucr.edu

To set the stage, we begin by briefly examining the history of educational indicators in the United States and discussing the several uses of indicators that have been proposed by educational reformers.

Background

The backdrop against which the use of performance indicators in educational accountability systems arises has two revealing dimensions. First, the United States has a long history of compiling educational indicators. Second, the use of indicators as accountability standards is more feasible than other high-stakes uses of indicators that have been proposed by educational reformers.

History of Educational Indicators

Although educational indicators recently gained widespread attention as tools of educational reform and improvement, they actually have had a long history in the United States. That history began in 1867 when the U.S. Department of Education was formed to collect and report educational statistics. The recent interest in using educational indicators as policy tools can be traced to the successful use of economic indicators by policy makers to stimulate economic development in the 1960s (Burstein, Oakes, & Guiton, 1992; Shavelson, McDonnell, & Oakes, 1991). Enthusiasm for indicators as policy tools waned when policy makers were unable to use social indicators to craft programs that effectively addressed the nation's social ills in the 1960s and 1970s.

Despite these mixed results, reform-minded policymakers and scholars tout the potential of educational indicators as tools to improve the performance of public education. The recent emergence of educational indicators can be traced to the 1983 publication of *A Nation at Risk* and other reports that cited statistics in documenting the failure of public education (Bryk & Hermanson, 1993; Burstein et al., 1992; Selden, 1994). This led to the creation and distribution of the Secretary of Education's "Wall Chart," which offered state-by-state comparisons on indicators that included SAT scores and per-pupil expenditures (Selden, 1994). Indicators seemed to provide concrete evidence of the ills plaguing education. Soon, however, indicators began to be viewed as being capable of more than simply describing problems; they came to be seen as tools of reform and improvement.

Varied Uses of Indicators and Their Relative Feasibility

Reformers and scholars promote five different but overlapping uses of educational indicators: to describe, to advance policy agendas, to serve as the basis for accountability, to evaluate policies and programs, and to serve as information management systems. These uses of indicators vary in terms of the degree to which they expose schools and districts to high stakes and the feasibility with which they can be implemented. Here, we should note that most discussions of educational indicators focus on indicator systems. *Indicator systems* are sets of indicators that are generally conceptualized as reflecting key aspects of an education system (Selden, 1994) and their interrelationships (Burstein et al., 1992; Jones & Neilsen, 1994; Oakes, 1986; Shavelson, McDonnell, Oakes, Carey, & Picus, 1987).

The stakes involved. The most elementary use of indicators is to describe the condition and performance of a school or system (Burstein et al., 1992; Edmond, 1992; Nuttall, 1994; Oakes, 1986). Over time, indicators can also be used to track trends and changes (Guthrie, 1990; Oakes, 1986). Some analysts argue that indicators should not be used beyond these descriptive purposes, although there is some disagreement about the utility of descriptive data. Shavelson, McDonnell, and Oakes (1989, 1991) contended that indicators cannot replace the political process for setting goals and priorities and thus have only limited capacity for informing policy discussions. Bryk and Hermanson (1993), however, suggested that the ultimate function of indicators is to inform broad and sustained public discourse about the means and ends of education. Description is a relatively low stakes use of educational indicators. Even when indicators are used to inform public discourse, programs, schools, or districts do not face formal sanctions, either positive or negative, depending on their "indicated" performance.

A second and related use of indicators is to advance policy agendas. This can occur on two levels. On one level, indicators are political because they reflect the predispositions of the policy makers who create and use them, marking what is important and what warrants attention (Burstein et al., 1992; Nuttall, 1994). On another level, policy makers can use indicators to promote or defend ideological stances (Ruby, 1994). That is, they can selectively use indicator data to bolster their positions. In either case, although this use of indicators may have high stakes for politicians, it does not directly pose high stakes for schools and districts. Although schools and districts may be affected by the decisions informed by the political use of indicators, they do not face sanctions from this form of indicator data.

The three remaining uses of indicators all can present schools and districts with relatively higher stakes. The first of these is the use of indicators as the basis for holding schools or districts accountable. Indicators can be used to hold systems accountable in a number of ways. The form of accountability that currently is seeing widespread application and presents the highest stakes is "performance monitoring" (Burstein et al., 1992; David, 1987; Nuttall, 1994; Selden, 1994). Here, policy makers establish minimum standards for student outcomes and hold districts, schools, or both accountable for attaining them. This form of accountability forces public schools into a market-like situation as those units that attain the standards are rewarded, whereas those that fail to attain the standards are punished (Richards, 1988).

A second high-stakes use of educational indicators is to provide data for evaluating the effectiveness of policies or programs. Proponents of the evaluative use of indicators argue that it can enhance the rational bases of policy analysis by providing feedback on program effectiveness and efficiency (Nuttall, 1994). Such feedback enables policy makers and administrators to bolster effective programs, adjust marginal ones, and reduce or close those that are found to be ineffective. In this use of indicators, the stakes can be high for programs and their administrators. Programs for which indicator data indicate a lack of effectiveness face the possibility of elimination.

The final way in which educational indicators can be used is to provide data for diagnosing and prescribing treatments for emergent problems (Guthrie, 1990; Oakes, 1986; Shavelson et al., 1989; Smith, 1988). This use of indicators requires the development and operation of sophisticated information management systems (Scheerens, 1991), which continuously monitor outcomes, explain why goals have not been attained (Porter, 1991), and identify interventions that will enhance goal attainment (Shavelson et al., 1989). Some analysts contend that, for information management systems to affect the academic performance of students, they must operate at all levels of an educational system, including the classroom, school, and district. The incumbents of positions at each of these levels may confront high stakes if continued employment and rewards are associated with measured performance. Moreover, information management systems run the potential risk of prescribing wrongful treatments that may have serious consequences.

Discussions of educational indicators typically turn to those uses that have relatively higher stakes associated with them: accountability, and evaluation and information management. This likely results from the desire to use indicators to do more than simply describe the status of schools and districts. Policymakers and scholars alike are motivated to use indicators as tools to enhance the performance of schools. In selecting how to use indicators, a second issue, feasibility of implementation, intrudes.

Feasibility of indicator uses. The feasibility of any use of educational indicators is in part a function of its information demands. The issue of information demand is reflected in a debate over the merits of comprehensive versus parsimonious indicator systems. Some authors explain that only extensive systems can accurately model the complexity of educational systems. Oversimplifications could misinform policy makers and practitioners alike. Others, however, encourage the use of parsimonious systems, arguing that more extensive systems would be unmanageable and overly complex (Blank, 1993; Shavelson et al., 1989). Comprehensive systems, they explain, would be very costly to develop and maintain (Oakes, 1986) and would not be useful to policy makers (Porter, 1991), who require manageably clear and concise information. In short, only parsimonious, not comprehensive, systems would be feasible.

Information demand has two dimensions. One, information varies in "density." That is, more or less information is required. Density is a direct function of the number of indicators that make up a system. Two, information demand is more or less complex. Complexity involves the number of relations between indicators that systems examine. Information density and complexity vary substantially across the three high-stakes uses of indicators, ranging from the high density and complexity of information management systems to the moderately high density and complexity of evaluation systems to the relatively low density and complexity of accountability systems.

Information demand would be greatest for information management systems. The information would be dense because data on a large number of indicators would be required to monitor performance, isolate problems, and prescribe fixes. Information would also be complex because information management systems would have to analyze relations among large numbers of indicators to adequately model the operation of schools and districts. These high-information demands would exact high technical and financial costs and thus greatly limit the feasibility of designing and operating information management systems.

Using educational indicators to evaluate programs and policies would also place relatively high information demands on educational systems. Some authors have warned that indicator systems, which they consider to be best suited to revealing the overall status of educational systems, would lack the rigor of design and depth of data analysis required to provide valid evaluations of policies and programs (Shavelson et al., 1989, 1991). Information would necessarily have to be both dense and complex if it were to produce valid evaluations. Information density would arise from the need to include several indicators in order to weigh the impact of particular policies and programs against numerous conditions in school systems. Information complexity similarly would arise from having to assess the relations between the many indicators. Thus, again, the costs of using educational indicators to evaluate would run relatively high, compromising the feasibility of this use.

This leaves accountability as the last high-stakes use of educational indicators. As it turns out, using indicators as the basis for holding school organizations accountable would place a relatively low information demand on educational systems. In the case of performance monitoring, data would have to be collected on only those outcomes for which school organizations are being held accountable. In some instances, such as the California program that we examine in this article, schools are accountable for just one index, which is composed of student performance on a standardized achievement test and other yet-to-be-determined outcome measures. That's it. Low density, to be sure, and the governing agency does not have to examine the relation between the focal outcome and other characteristics or conditions of schools or districts, resulting in very low complexity.

Given the low information demands of accountability systems, it is a highly feasible use of educational indicators. Therefore, it is not surprising that many states have adopted accountability systems—typically, performance monitoring systems—as a strategy for improving the academic performance of schools (Selden, 1994). It is for this reason that we have chosen to examine performance monitoring systems in this chapter.

Accountability in California

California's PSAA is a new law that is very indicator-oriented. The intent of the law, according to the California Legislature, is to provide for the academic development of every pupil and to remedy the lack of student progress toward achieving a high-quality education (California Department of Education, 1999). The PSAA is based on four components: the state Academic Performance Index (API), the High Achieving/Improving Schools Program (HAISP), the Immediate Intervention/Underperforming Schools Program (IIUSP), and the Governor's Performance Award Program (GPAP).

The API is currently being developed and will be used to measure the performance of schools. Schools will receive annual API growth targets for each school year as determined by the HAISP. Accountability enters the picture as schools who do not meet their growth target are subjected to the IIUSP, whereas those that do meet the target are rewarded with the GPAP. Fiscally, the IIUSP and the GPAP are financed equivalently at $96 million each.

The API will be a composite of various indicators. The PSAA mandates that the Stanford 9 achievement test (the basis of California's Standardized Testing and Reporting program) comprises at least 60% of the API. The index is under development, so the remaining indicators and their relative weight are unclear at this point. However, the following have been listed as potential API candidates: attendance rates for pupils and certificated school personnel, graduation rates for pupils in secondary schools, indicators addressing the state's curriculum content standards, a primary language test, and a high school exit examination.

The HAISP is the basis of the API annual growth targets. The growth target is the amount of improvement that a school is expected to make in its API score by the end of the school year. According to the HAISP, the State Superintendent of Public Instruction (SSPI) will rank all public schools on the API in decile categories by grade level of instruction. These rankings will determine a school's growth target, and the minimum amount is set at 5%. The SSPI will annually publish the rankings on the Internet, and all schools are required to report their ranking in an annual school accountability report card.

The PSAA's IIUSP is the sanction against those schools who do not meet their annual growth targets. Those schools subjected to the IIUSP are required to select and contract with an external evaluator from the SSPI's approved list. The PSAA is billed as a constructive and collaborative process that includes all relevant stakeholders. Therefore, the external evaluator will work closely with the school site and "community team." This coalition is then required to develop an action plan to be submitted to the local governing board for approval. Under the IIUSP, if the annual growth target is not met after implementation of the action plan, there are sanctions. After the first year, the district governing board of the school is required to hold a public hearing documenting their lack of progress. The governing board must then intervene in the school as directed. If the annual growth target is not met after 2 years of implementation of the action plan, there are more dire consequences. The SSPI legally assumes the rights, duties, and powers of the governing board in respect to the individual school. The principal of the school will be "reassigned," and the SSPI is required to take at least one of the following actions (California Department of Education, 1999):

1. Revise attendance options for pupils to allow them to attend any public school in which space is available.
2. Allow parents to apply directly to the SBE for the establishment of a charter school.
3. Assign the management of the school to a college, university, county office of education, or other appropriate educational institution.

4. Reassign other certificated employees of the school.
5. Renegotiate a new collective bargaining agreement at the expiration of the existing agreement.
6. Reorganize the school.
7. Close the school.

Schools that meet their annual growth targets are eligible to participate in the PSAA's GPAP. There are both monetary and nonmonetary awards. The monetary awards are not to exceed $150 per enrolled pupil. The nonmonetary awards may include (but are not limited to): classification as a distinguished school, listing on a published public school honor roll, public commendations by the Governor and the Legislature, waiver of some Education Code requirements, and maximum flexibility in the expenditure of categorical funds. The latter two are clearly the most relevant. A school that is eligible to participate in the GPAP may make a request to the State Board of Education to waive all or any part of any provision of the Education Code. Also, a school demonstrating significant growth in its API will be granted maximum flexibility in its expenditure of any new or existing categorical funds that are not otherwise restricted by state or federal law.

Assumptions Underlying California's PSAA

A close examination of California's PSAA and its components reveals that it is based on a rationalistic conception of school organizations. That is, as we noted earlier, proponents claim that educational accountability systems place schools in a quasi-market environment (Richards, 1988). In markets, firms are oriented toward the attainment of specific goals or the production or provision of quality goods or services (Scott, 1998). Organizations develop or adopt structures and practices that contribute to goal attainment while lowering production costs. Organizations that are successful (i.e., produce high-quality goods or services inexpensively) will thrive. Unsuccessful organizations must adjust or run the risk of going out of business. To enhance success, organizations utilize information from the market and about internal operations to enhance their effectiveness and efficiency. The market does not dictate how organizations should operate but simply sustains success and drives out failure.

Accountability systems create market-like conditions in the following ways. They establish clear performance standards. California's PSAA calls for the development of the API, which will be weighted toward the Stanford 9 standardized achievement test (60%). The other 40% of the index will include other, yet-to-be-specified measures, such as student and certificated staff attendance rates, high school graduation rates, attainment of state curriculum standards, a primary language test, and high school exit examination. In addition, the HAISP will set growth targets for all schools, which will be based in part on their ranking and will be no lower than 5%.

Just as markets favor successful firms over unsuccessful competitors, accountability systems reward high-performing schools and negatively sanction low-performing schools. In California, the GPAP will reward schools that meet annual growth targets with both monetary and nonmonetary incentives. Schools that fail to meet growth targets after 2 years face a range of consequences, the most extreme of which is closure.

Like their market-driven counterparts, schools operating in accountability systems are expected to draw on feedback from the environment and internal operations to improve performance. The PSAA's IIUSP will require each school that does not reach its annual growth target to work with a state-approved external evaluator. The evaluator will provide the underperforming school with data and work closely with the school team to develop an action plan to meet growth targets. Thus, like a market, the accountability system does not dictate how schools should operate. Instead, it leaves local schools to determine how best to attain accountability standards with the support and input of an external evaluator.

California's PSAA, then, provides all of the elements required to place schools in a market-like environment. The performance index and growth targets establish a clear-cut goal for each school. External evaluators provide information to underperforming schools. The state will not dictate what schools should do to improve performance. Instead, teams of stakeholders develop plans to improve school organization and operations and thus enhance outcomes. Finally, successful schools will be rewarded, whereas unsuccessful schools face a series of possible sanctions, including termination.

Compromising Conditions

On its face, California's PSAA, with its multiple components, seems to provide a relatively straightforward strategy for improving school performance. However, the literature on the use of educational indicators as the basis of accountability systems calls into question many of the assumptions on which the PSAA and other educational accountability systems are based. Specifically, existing evidence, although limited, suggests that many of the elements and conditions that enable accountability systems to exert market-like pressure on public schools do not, and perhaps cannot, in most instances exist.

Absence of Goal Consensus and Clarity

As we have noted, the first condition that accountability systems rest on is the clarification of performance goals for schools. The PSAA will present an index that incorporates standardized test scores and other indicators of school performance. This seems simple enough. However, the literature on educational indicators indicates that no one statistic can adequately capture the pulse of education. Unlike the financial sector, there is no "Dow Jones" average for education (Special Study Panel on Education Indicators, 1991). Moreover, several authors raise serious questions about the validity of a small, narrow set of performance indicators (Koretz, 1992). The difficulty begins with the lack of agreement among experts on criteria for determining the health and performance of school organizations (Scheerens, 1991). Accordingly, indicators can only provide the basis for making value judgments, not objective assessments of success or failure. Indicators are also context-dependent, not necessarily having the same salience in schools that serve widely varying communities. Finally, a narrow set of performance indicators cannot reflect the full range of outcomes sought by policy makers and the communities that schools serve. Consequently, improvement plans predicated on data from a small number of indicators might well address only a portion of schools' overall missions.

The lack of consensus, context dependence, and narrowness of the performance indicators on which educational accountability systems are based belie the apparent clarity of goals they provide to schools. As we discuss later in this section, the consequences of the absence of clear goals, coupled with the absence of other necessary conditions for rationality, can distort the responses of schools to accountability standards.

Limited Use of Information

A second condition contributing to the presumed efficacy of educational accountability systems is that schools will use information from performance indicators to enhance their organization and instruction. There are two problems with this assumption. First, there is the issue of the quality of information that indicators can provide about schooling. Scholars caution that indicator systems lack the rigor of design and depth of data and analysis to provide valid evaluations of the effectiveness of programs. An absence of valid information will greatly compromise the ability of educators to develop effective school improvement plans.

Second, research on policy development and school-based management suggests that educators may not use information well. Research suggests that administrators and policy makers do not reliably and effectively use data to make decisions and adopt policies (David, 1988). Instead, they tend to utilize information to bolster their predispositions, often ignoring data that do not support their stance. Similarly, research on school-based management suggests that site councils, even in schools where school-based management is operating well, do not effectively use data. Site councils typically do not carefully analyze or consciously utilize needs assessment data to develop school improvement plans (Malen, Ogawa, & Kranz, 1990).

Moreover, site-level actors are less likely to use indicators to improve instructional practice and programs if they are not involved in building the indicator system (David, 1988; Levesque, Bradby, & Rossi, 1996). As we have noted, according to the PSAA, underperforming schools will be judged on a state-wide performance index and develop action plans based on feedback from external evaluators.

Complexity and Uncertainty of Schooling

The ability of site-level actors to develop effective action plans is compromised by another factor: the inherent complexity and uncertainty of schooling itself. Scholars have long characterized the core technology of schools—teaching and learning—as unclear (Cohen, March, & Olsen, 1972). That is, the causes and effects that comprise schooling and instruction are poorly understood. The literature on educational indicators reinforces this view. Although some authors argue that indicator systems can be used to identify problems and prescribe solutions (Nuttall, 1994; Odden, 1990; Scheerens, 1991; Shavelson et al., 1989), others are much less sanguine. They suggest that such claims are based on an overly simplistic view of schools and ignore the limitations of social and behavioral science research (Bryk & Hermanson, 1993).

The difficulty of providing an adequate representation of schooling and instruction is reflected in the inability of analysts to agree on a conceptual model of schooling, which could serve as the basis of indicator systems. Some authors question the validity of proposed models, criticizing them as overly mechanistic and relying too heavily on a production metaphor (Bramley, 1995; Bryk & Hermanson, 1993).

However, even if a consensus were to develop around a particular model of schooling, analysts disagree on the number of indicators that should be included. Some believe that less information would be most useful, whereas others argue that more is necessary. Some scholars explain that policy makers and educators would be best served by fairly parsimonious models of schooling that would emphasize a small and manageable number of factors (Blank, 1993; Porter, 1991; Shavelson et al., 1989). Others, however, note that overly simplistic models can misinform policy makers and practitioners by overlooking important factors that may contribute to the performance of schools (Special Study Panel on Education Indicators, 1991). Stecher and Koretz (1996) insightfully summarized this dilemma:

> There is a fundamental tension between simplicity and comprehensiveness ... By design, indicators are simple statistics, but they are valued as a way to understand diverse, complex systems. An immediate challenge in developing indicator systems is to balance simplicity with comprehensiveness. A desire for completeness and explanatory power argues for increasing the number of variables. ... However, indicator systems are valuable because they are limited, succinct and parsimonious. ... One cannot achieve both goals ... . (p. 58)

Summary: Missing Conditions

Thus, three key conditions on which the purported effectiveness of educational accountability systems, such as California's PSAA, rest are compromised, at best, and not attainable, at worst (see Table 1). First, the development of an API and establishment of annual growth targets would seem to present schools with clear performance goals. But, this is compromised by the lack of consensus regarding what constitutes the health and appropriate outcomes of educational systems and the context dependence of indicators. This is exacerbated by the tendency of narrow measures of educational outcomes to mislead local policy makers and educators.

Second, the PSAA and other accountability systems count on local educators to use information regarding their schools' performance and operations to develop action plans. But, narrow indexes of performance lack the depth to provide valid assessments of educational outcomes. In addition, local stakeholders tend not to use data to inform decisions regarding policies and programs, particularly if the data are provided by external sources.

Third, California's PSAA expects local stakeholders to develop action plans that will effectively improve school performance. If they fail, the state can—among other remedies—assign the management of the school to another educational institution or reorganize the school itself. However, this assumes that educators, at some level, possess the understanding of schooling and instruction necessary to derive such plans. Despite years of theorizing and research, educational research has yet to provide such a model. Nor can policy makers and practitioners unequivocally identify the "levers" that can be pushed or prodded to improve school performance.

Table 1
Assumptions and Compromises in Accountability

The Ideal: Assumptions of Accountability Systems	*The Actual: Compromises That Accountability Systems Face*
Goals are made clear by the adoption of a single performance index and annual growth targets	• No consensus over indicators that measure health of system • Indicators are context dependent • Indicators are too narrow, misguiding policy information
Information can be used to enhance schools	• Information from indicator systems lacks depth required for valid evaluations • Educators tend to use information only to support predetermined positions • Educators tend to dismiss information from external sources
Local educators can develop effective action plans to improve school performance	• Social science community unable to agree on a conceptual model of schooling • Complexity and uncertainty of schooling limits ability to control the improvement of schools

How Schools Are Likely to Respond

One major assumption about the operation of educational accountability systems does hold: Successful schools will be rewarded; underperforming schools will be sanctioned. California's PSAA includes both. Schools that meet annual growth targets will be eligible to receive monetary and nonmonetary awards from the GPAP. Schools that do not meet their growth targets will, with the assistance of external evaluators, develop action plans to improve their performance. If schools continue to miss their growth targets over a 2-year period, the state will legally assume control over underperforming schools and can exact sanctions that include school closure.

Faced with the possibility of such dire consequences and the compromised ability to use information to develop effective action plans, how are schools likely to react? The literature on educational indicators suggests that schools will respond on two levels.

On the surface it will appear that much has changed. Schools and districts will develop committees, task forces, programs, and new position titles in response to the accountability initiatives. But, most of the activity in schools and classrooms will not be altered. Consequently, the overall operations and performance of schools will not be markedly different. Those schools whose students confront the greatest obstacles to academic success will continue to perform relatively poorly compared to those schools whose students enjoy the advantages of affluence and cultural capital.

At a deeper level, changes will also occur, but not the comprehensive changes foreseen by those who promote accountability as a stimulus for the overall improvement of schools. The literature on educational indicators warns that narrow sets of outcome measures can be "corrupted" (Oakes, 1989). That is, schools can directly manipulate indicators, thereby invalidating them as measures of the overall performance of schools. If a performance index includes a standardized achievement test, as California's PSAA does, the most common way to corrupt the index is to simply "teach to the test." Schools also corrupt standardized achievement test scores by systematically eliminating groups of students who are likely to perform poorly.

The tendency of schools to corrupt performance indicators is directly linked to the faulty assumptions on which accountability systems are built. First, schools are able to corrupt outcome measures because these indicators are typically narrow and reflect only a small subset of the outcomes of schooling. Second, faced with limited data and the absence of a clear and comprehensive model of schooling and instruction, educators are not able to enact reliable school improvement plans. Third, confronted with high stakes, local stakeholders will seek ways to meet performance goals despite the difficulty of improving the overall performance of schools. Under these conditions, corrupting indicators is an available and effective tactic. The problem, of course, is that the organization of schools and overall classroom instruction are not likely to improve; only test scores and other performance goals will be nudged higher.

References

Blank, R. K. (1993). Developing a system of education indicators: Selecting, implementing, and reporting indicators. *Educational Evaluation and Policy Analysis, 11*(2), 65–80.

Bramley, G. (1995). *School performance indicators and school effectiveness: The conceptions and the critiques* (Working Papers in Education). Wolverhampton, England: University of Wolverhampton.

Bryk, A. S., & Hermanson, K. L. (1993). Educational indicator systems: Observations on their structure, interpretation, and use. *Review of Research in Education, 19*, 451–484.

Burstein, L., Oakes, J., & Guiton, G. (1992). Education indicators. In M. C. Alkin (Ed.), *Encyclopedia of educational research* (6th ed., pp. 409–418). New York: Macmillan.

California Department of Education. (1999, November 1). *Public Schools Accountability Act: Performance indicators, accountability procedures, and reform efforts for California Schools* [Online]. Retrieved November 1, 1999 from the World Wide Web: http://www.cde.ca.gov/psaa/

Cohen, M. D., March, J. G., & Olsen, J. P. (1972). A garbage can model of organizational choice. *Administrative Science Quarterly, 17*, 1–25.

David, J. L. (1987). *Improving education with locally developed indicators* (Rep. No. CPRE–RR–004). New Brunswick: State University of New Jersey, Center for Policy Research in Education.

David, J. L. (1988). The use of indicators by school districts: Aid or threat to improvement? *Phi Delta Kappan, 69,* 499–503.

Edmond, D. R. (1992, Winter). The development and use of educational indicator systems. *Education Canada,* pp. 8–13, 19.

Guthrie, J. W. (1990). The evolving political economy of education and the implications for educational evaluation. *Educational Review, 42*(2), 109–131.

Jones, R. M., & Nielsen, J. I. (1994, Summer). Saskatchewan's education indicators program. *Education Canada,* pp. 4–8.

Koretz, D. (1992). *Evaluating and validating indicators of mathematics and science education* (Rep. No. RAND/N–2900–NSF). Santa Monica, CA: RAND Corporation.

Levesque, K., Bradby, D., & Rossi, K. (1996, May). Using data for program improvement: How do we encourage schools to do it?" *Centerfocus, 12,* 1–6.

Malen, B., Ogawa, R. T., & Kranz, J. (1990). What do we know about school-based management? A case study of the literature—A call for research. In W. H. Clune & J. F. Witte (Eds.), *Choice and control in American education* (Vol. 2, pp. 289–342). New York: Falmer.

Nuttall, D. L. (1994). Choosing indicators. In K. A. Riley & D. L. Nuttall (Eds.), *Measuring quality: Education indicators—United Kingdom and international perspectives* (pp. 17–40). Bristol, PA: Falmer.

Oakes, J. (1986). *Educational indicators: A guide for policymakers* (Rep. No. OPE–01). Santa Monica, CA: RAND Corporation, Center for Policy Research in Education.

Oakes, J. (1989). What educational indicators? The case for assessing the school context. *Educational Evaluation and Policy Analysis, 11*(2), 181–199.

Odden, A. (1990, June/July). Educational indicators in the United States: The need for analysis. *Educational Researcher, 19,* 24–29.

Porter, A. (1991). Creating a system of school process indicators. *Educational Evaluation and Policy Analysis, 11*(2), 13–29.

Richards, C. E. (1988). Indicators and three types of educational monitoring systems: Implications for design. *Phi Delta Kappan, 69,* 495–499.

Ruby, A. (1994). Education indicators: Officials, ministers and the demand for information. In K. A. Riley & D. L. Nuttall (Eds.), *Measuring quality: Education indicators—United Kingdom and international perspectives* (pp. 6–16). Bristol, PA: Falmer.

Scheerens, J. (1991). Process indicators of school functioning: A selection based on the research literature on school effectiveness. *Studies in Educational Evaluation, 17,* 371–403.

Scott, W. R. (1998). *Organizations: Rational, natural, and open systems* (4th ed.). Upper Saddle River, NJ: Prentice Hall.

Selden, R. W. (1994). How indicators have been used in the USA. In K. A. Riley & D. L. Nuttall (Eds.), *Measuring quality: Education indicators—United Kingdom and international perspectives* (pp. 41–48). Bristol, PA: Falmer.

Shavelson, R. J., McDonnell, L. M., & Oakes, J. (Eds.). (1989). *Indicators for monitoring mathematics and science education: A sourcebook* (Rep. No. R–3742–NSF/RC). Santa Monica, CA: RAND Corporation.

Shavelson, R. J., McDonnell, L. M., & Oakes, J. (1991, July). What are educational indicators and indicator systems? *ERIC Clearinghouse on Tests, Measurements, and Evaluation,* pp. 1–2.

Shavelson, R., McDonnell, L., Oakes, J., Carey, N., & Picus, L. (1987). *Indicator systems for monitoring mathematics and science education* (Rep. No. R–3570–NSF). Santa Monica, CA: RAND Corporation.

Smith, M. S. (1988). Educational indicators. *Phi Delta Kappan, 69,* 487–491.

Special Study Panel on Education Indicators. (1991). *Education counts: An indicator system to monitor the nation's educational health.* Washington, DC: National Center for Education Statistics.

Stecher, B. M., & Koretz, D. (1996). *Issues in building an indicator system for mathematics and science education* (Rep. No. DRU–467–NSF). Santa Monica, CA: RAND Corporation.